"Evangelicals want heart and minds for Jesus Christ. ... e
university campus to the individual Christian."
Leith Anderson, president, National Association of Evangelicals

"In *The Pietist Vision of Christian Higher Education,* Professor Gehrz makes a significant contribution to the growing literature exploring theological foundations for the life of the mind beyond the Reformed tradition. In this collection of essays, we are invited into a conversation that began among Professor Gehrz and his colleagues at Bethel University as they sought to discover the theological roots of their own institution. The book actually embodies the richness and the distinctiveness of the Pietist tradition's approach to higher education: first, the humility reflected in the careful, exploratory tone of the individual essays; second, the relational element exhibited in the collective wisdom of the entire group; finally, the impact on the heart as well as the mind, as readers are inspired and motivated to pursue a deeper understanding of their own theological roots."
Shirley A. Mullen, president and professor of history, Houghton College

"When Pietism was born as a religious movement in the seventeenth century it was as closely related to the university as it was to the church. Like the original Pietists who insisted that prayer, Bible study and love of neighbor could be wedded to academic rigor, the contributors to this volume share a vision for education that aims at both hearts and minds. These thoughtful essays, representing many different academic disciplines, will hopefully usher Pietism back into evangelical discussions about faith and learning. They surely will inspire readers to think anew about the realities and ideals of Christ-centered higher education in the current age of 'spiritual but not religious' students."
Douglas Jacobsen and Rhonda Hustedt Jacobsen, authors of *No Longer Invisible: Religion in University Education*

"Unfairly blamed for the secularization of American colleges, Pietism has served as a source of renewal and revitalization. Channeling the insights of their German and Scandinavian forebears, Christopher Gehrz and his colleagues articulate a fresh understanding of Christian higher education. Emphasizing the religious virtues of humility and love, they show why Pietism's irenic sensibility is the perfect antidote to today's culture wars."
John A. Schmalzbauer, Blanche Gorman Strong Chair in Protestant Studies, Missouri State University

"Our friends at Bethel University here invite us not only to think about but to feel, imagine, and even desire to actualize a Christian vision of higher education that engages not only heads but also hands and hearts. Herein is a robust call for a Christian university that is concerned about orthodoxy, orthopraxy, and orthopathy, and their interconnections. Evangelical thinking on these matters takes a quantum leap with this volume."
Amos Yong, professor of theology and mission, Fuller Seminary

THE PIETIST VISION
OF CHRISTIAN
HIGHER EDUCATION

FORMING WHOLE AND HOLY PERSONS

EDITED BY

CHRISTOPHER GEHRZ

IVP Academic

An imprint of InterVarsity Press
Downers Grove, Illinois

InterVarsity Press
P.O. Box 1400, Downers Grove, IL 60515-1426
World Wide Web: www.ivpress.com
Email: email@ivpress.com

InterVarsity Press® is the book-publishing division of InterVarsity Christian Fellowship/USA®, a movement of students and faculty active on campus at hundreds of universities, colleges and schools of nursing in the United States of America, and a member movement of the International Fellowship of Evangelical Students. For information about local and regional activities, write Public Relations Dept., InterVarsity Christian Fellowship/USA, 6400 Schroeder Rd., P.O. Box 7895, Madison, WI 53707-7895, or visit the IVCF website at www.intervarsity.org.

Scripture quotations, unless otherwise noted, are from the New Revised Standard Version of the Bible, copyright 1989 by the Division of Christian Education of the National Council of the Churches of Christ in the USA. Used by permission. All rights reserved.

While all stories in this book are true, some names and identifying information in this book have been changed to protect the privacy of the individuals involved.

An earlier version of chapter three appeared as Jenell Williams Paris, "A Pietist Perspective on Love and Learning in Cultural Anthropology," Christian Scholar's Review 35 (Spring 2006): 371-85. Copyright © 2006 by Christian Scholar's Review; reprinted by permission.

Cover design: Cindy Kiple
Interior design: Beth McGill
Images: Bethel University campus: © Bethel University
graduates: © zhudifeng/iStockphoto

ISBN 978-0-8308-4071-7 (print)
ISBN 978-0-8308-9713-1 (digital)

Printed in the United States of America ∞

Library of Congress Cataloging-in-Publication Data

The Pietist vision of Christian higher education : forming whole and holy persons / edited by Christopher Gehrz.
pages cm
Includes index.
ISBN 978-0-8308-4071-7 (pbk. : alk. paper)
1. Christian education—Philosophy. 2. Pietism. 3. Bethel
University. I. Gehrz, Christopher, 1975- editor.
BV1473.P54 2014
268.01—dc23

2014033404

P	24	23	22	21	20	19	18	17	16	15	14	13	12	11	10	9	8	7	6	5	4	3	2	1
Y	36	35	34	33	32	31	30	29	28	27	26	25	24	23	22	21	20	19	18	17	16	15		

For G. W. Carlson and the other

Bethel Pietists on whose shoulders we stand

Contents

CONCLUSION

Preface

Janel M. Curry

◆

I AM A PRODUCT OF the Pietist tradition of the Upper Midwest, as embodied at Bethel University in St. Paul, Minnesota. When I attended Bethel as an undergraduate, both my spiritual and my intellectual life were enriched and shaped by being introduced to a broad range of Christian scholars and Christian intellectual streams of thought. It was the beginning of a journey that demanded both my heart and my head—my whole person. In many ways, my vocational and academic journey, as a geographer and now also as a provost at an evangelical institution of higher education, has involved exploring the balance between the experiential aspects of faith that focus on personal transformation and the intellectual implications that involve precise thinking and the development of theoretical constructs.

After my graduation from Bethel, I spent a term of service with the Mennonite Central Committee, compiling a history of the Houma tribe of Louisiana for its application for federal recognition. This intellectual journey was one that was focused on service, but it led me into deeper theological questions that have continued to shape me over my lifetime about the nature of community, culture and nature. The experience shaped the trajectory of my scholarly life, which has involved research on how communities of faith live in relation to their theological constructs. My personal journey has also embodied this need to grow and understand God's claim on both my heart and my mind.

I went on to spend a great deal of my career among Dutch Calvinists and found their intellectual and theological constructs to represent a way of thinking that was extremely powerful, giving me great insights into the relationship between religious worldviews and the living out of our faith in our communities. Out of that theological understanding I began to explore the variety of Christian religious worldviews and their communal expressions, particularly around the lived relationships among individuals, communities and nature.

But in the end, intellectual constructs and correct doctrine, no matter how accurate and transformational to our thinking, don't transform our hearts or replace our need for a personal relationship with Jesus, a relationship that must be nurtured in order to sustain us in challenging times. So in the midst of benefiting from the rigor of the Reformed tradition, I have been drawn back toward the relational emphasis of my pietistic heritage. More recently I have been drawn to social trinitarian theology. Traditional theological reflection on what it means to be made in the image of God has centered on traits that are possessed by individual humans such as "rational thought." Social trinitarian theology identifies being in the image of God with being created for relationship. This relational emphasis builds an organic and vital faith over one that focuses on order and rationality. And while I have benefited from the Calvinist tradition and its emphasis on the sovereignty of God, I am also drawn to pietistic theological traditions that remind us of God's personal interaction with humanity, bringing God from his distant position to one that recognizes his personal engagement with us, which is necessary for a personal relationship of love to develop.

In the end, I believe I am drawn back to the "posture" of my pietistic heritage as represented at Bethel. This tradition asks us to be intellectually rigorous and theologically conservative yet to live with an openness and warmth grounded in a spirit of humility that puts personal religious experience over debates about theological forms. It is a posture that asks God to radically transform our lives— to first listen rather than critique. The habit of listening leads to greater hospitality and invites dialogue. This posture asks each individual to develop the spiritual discipline of listening to God through the practice of prayer and Scripture reading.

It is this combination of academic rigor, evangelical spirit, deep faith, high regard for Scripture, and the practice of prayer that drew me to Gordon College. It reminded me of the Bethel College I experienced, where an individual's intellectual journey—the journey of the mind—has to be joined with the individual transformation of the heart. And this journey takes place in the context of a community that is on that same journey. The pietistic heritage and Christian higher education: devoted heart, keen mind. It is a lifelong journey. The following essays reflect many perspectives on the Pietist tradition in higher education, out of which my journey began.

Acknowledgments

◆

I'M GRATEFUL TO HAVE had the chance to help bring this book into being, but I know full well that it wouldn't have happened without the support, advice and hard work of many other people. A few of them I can acknowledge here, with apologies to those I've missed.

From the broader *ecclesia*: Jake and Rhonda Jacobsen first sparked my interest in seeking a "usable past" in Pietism for Christian scholarship and higher education. The National Network Board of the Lilly Fellows Program provided two grants that were essential to the development of this book. Jared Burkholder, John Fea, Devin Manzullo-Thomas, Tracy McKenzie and other members of the Conference on Faith and History have helped me understand what it means to be a Christian historian and a scholar for the church. The Evangelical Covenant Church has become again for me what it was in my childhood, a fellowship of "mission friends" such as Mark Pattie, Kurt Peterson, Steve Pitts, Glen Wiberg and the late Jim Hawkinson, all of whom embody the Pietist ethos of which we write in this book.

Then to the people, past and present, of my *ecclesiola*, Bethel University. Jay Barnes and Deb Harless have been ceaseless advocates of our efforts to seek a "usable past" in Pietism, and Deb Sullivan-Trainor and Barrett Fisher are the best deans one could hope to work for. Carrie Peffley was kind enough to offer feedback on the Lilly proposal that led to this book, and two of her colleagues in Bethel's humanities program, Dan Ritchie and Paul Reasoner, were among the many to make suggestions as we thought aloud about aspects of the Pietist vision for higher education. Keith Brooks opened up a substantial portion of the fall 2013 "Not Ready for Prime Time" series of faculty presentations for our contributors to offer previews of their work; Ann Gannon represented the

Bethel Library well in making those presentations come off as well as they did. I couldn't talk them into writing chapters, but Gary Long and Tim Essenburg also gave up two days of lovely June weather to sit inside a classroom for the workshop that launched this project; their questions, concerns and suggestions no doubt have found their way into this book.

I'm lucky to be part of a department that's as collegial as it is committed to teaching and service. I could write paragraphs about each of my fellow Bethel historians, but I especially need to thank three of them: Sam Mulberry, for inviting me to give a talk on innovation that inadvertently provided the organizing theme for this book's conclusion; AnneMarie Kooistra, for her feedback on that conclusion; and Diana Magnuson, who, as the archivist of the Baptist General Conference and Bethel University, makes possible the work I do as a historian of Bethel. Several years apart from each other, my teaching assistants Taylor Ferda and Jacob Manning helped me, respectively, to research the history of the Brethren traditions and to proofread this manuscript.

Then to the contributors who did the real work on this book: thanks for helping launch this conversation and for letting me convince you to take time away from your own important work as teachers and scholars to think, talk and write about Pietism. Special thanks to Jan Curry, Roger Olson, Jenell Paris and David Williams for mentally revisiting your time at Bethel, having long since moved on to bigger and better things elsewhere. (Roger and David also physically revisited Bethel—David twice—to speak to our faculty about the themes in their chapters.) Sara Shady was kind enough to offer comments on the introduction and conclusion. Kent Gerber was tireless in passing along resources to his fellow contributors as he came across them in Bethel's digital library. And Christian Collins Winn has been a wonderful partner on this, our fifth Pietism-related collaboration. (Among other things, Christian suggested that I get in touch with David Congdon, who has been as fine an editor as one could imagine; I'm grateful to him and the rest of the editorial team at IVP for taking a chance on this book.)

Finally, I'm most thankful to Katie, Isaiah and Lena—for putting up with too much of me talking about Pietism and too little of me being a husband and father while I threw myself into this project. I'll be home earlier than usual tonight.

Christopher Gehrz

◆

INTRODUCTION

*To the extent that these institutions seek to structure their work
around a Christian mission at all, [Christian colleges and universities]
inevitably must draw upon their historic Christian identities or
church connections. They really have little other choice
since institutions cannot convert from one tradition
to another as an individual might.*

RICHARD T. HUGHES,
MODELS FOR CHRISTIAN HIGHER EDUCATION

Does Pietism Provide a "Usable Past" for Christian Colleges and Universities?

Christopher Gehrz

◆

Pietism "breathed a badly needed vitality" into European Christianity after the Reformation, according to historian Mark Noll.[1] In North America, argues theologian Roger Olson, "it became *the* main form of Protestantism,"[2] a founding influence on several denominations and contemporary evangelicalism, whose roots Molly Worthen suggests we should trace "all the way back to European Pietists' zeal for private Bible study and personal holiness."[3] And while Noll is far from alone in bemoaning how some offshoots of Pietism tended toward anti-intellectualism, another leading church historian emphasizes that "from its earliest days, Pietism was intimately bound up with education."[4] One of Philipp Jakob Spener's original six "pious wishes" had to do with educational reform, and his call for renewal resonated among university students such as August Hermann Francke. Later, through

---

[1] Mark A. Noll, *The Scandal of the Evangelical Mind* (Grand Rapids: Eerdmans, 1994), pp. 48-49. See also Noll, *The Rise of Evangelicalism: The Age of Edwards, Whitefield and the Wesleys* (Downers Grove, IL: IVP Academic, 2003), pp. 60-65.

[2] Roger E. Olson, *The Story of Christian Theology: Twenty Centuries of Tradition & Reform* (Downers Grove, IL: InterVarsity Press, 1999), p. 491.

[3] Molly Worthen, *Apostles of Reason: The Crisis of Authority in American Evangelicalism* (New York: Oxford University Press, 2014), p. 4.

[4] Diarmaid MacCulloch, *Christianity: The First Three Thousand Years* (New York: Viking, 2009), p. 739.

his leadership of the University of Halle and an array of schools, Francke placed education at the center of his vision of Pietism "changing the world by changing people."[5]

Why, then, is what you're reading the first book devoted to considering how Pietism can sustain its own distinctive approach to Christian higher education? And why are people associated with one small university in the American Midwest the group to start that conversation?

PIETISM AS MOVEMENT AND ETHOS IN AMERICAN RELIGIOUS HISTORY

As a historical *movement* that produced its own institutions, Pietism is largely confined to the seventeenth, eighteenth and perhaps nineteenth centuries and centered primarily in Germany. Defined in these terms, we should not expect to see Pietist churches, colleges or other organizations in the United States in the twenty-first century.

But as Roger Olson has argued, "Pietism was and is a 'spirit' or 'ethos' more than any socially perceptible form."[6] Such an ethos is what Baptist historian Virgil Olson had in mind when he claimed that "pietism" would always arise in reaction against "superficial Christianity whether it be found in rotting formalism, a thinned-out evangelism or a misfired scholasticism, or anything else that has the form of piety and lacks the power thereof."[7]

That spirit has taken a wide variety of forms in the centuries since certain German Protestants were first labeled "Pietists" by their critics. What do these Pietisms have in common? Pietists at all times and in all places seek a more authentic Christianity: not inherited or assumed, coerced or affected, but *lived out* through the transformative experiences of conversion and regeneration. Suspicious of "dead orthodoxy," Pietists subordinate doctrine to Scripture—with an irenic, or peaceable, spirit prevailing in matters where the Bible leaves open a range of interpretations (or where Pietists encounter

---

[5]Quoted in Douglas H. Shantz, *An Introduction to German Pietism: Protestant Renewal at the Dawn of Modern Europe* (Baltimore: John Hopkins University Press, 2013), p. 141. Shantz concludes that, unlike Francke's Reformed contemporaries, "[Francke's] Pietist ethic was directed not so much toward encouraging capitalist activity as to encouraging education and educational activity"; ibid., p. 138.

[6]Olson, *Story of Christian Theology*, p. 474.

[7]Virgil A. Olson, "The Baptist General Conference and Its Pietistic Heritage," *Bethel Seminary Quarterly* 4 (May 1956): 65.

those of other or no religious faith). Clergy and laity alike form a common priesthood actively engaged in worship, education, evangelism and social action, in the firm hope that God intends "better times" for the church and the world.

As an early modern movement and an enduring ethos, Pietism has shaped a wide array of American denominations. Since Radical Pietists from Schwarzenau first immigrated to Pennsylvania in 1719 and founded the German Baptist Brethren (which developed into the present-day Church of the Brethren, Brethren Church and Grace Brethren), Pietists have come to these shores. Throughout the eighteenth and early nineteenth centuries, German Pietism could be found at the origins of denominations like the Brethren in Christ, United Brethren, Mennonite Brethren and what's now the North American Baptist Conference. (They were also present in Lutheran and Reformed churches throughout this time.[8]) A new wave of Pietist immigration took place between 1850 and 1930, as millions of Norwegians and Swedes left a Scandinavia experiencing both economic upheaval and evangelical revival to seek new starts in North America. For example, pietistic Swedish Baptists began settling in the Midwest just before the Civil War and came together (loosely) as the Swedish Baptist General Conference in 1879. (It dropped the ethnic adjective during World War II and began using the "missional name" of Converge Worldwide in 2008.) Other Scandinavian-American Pietists helped found what are now the Evangelical Covenant Church and the Evangelical Free Church, plus a variety of Lutheran synods.

All of these denominations founded institutions of higher learning. Even if we exclude the many schools chiefly associated with Methodism and with non-denominational evangelicalism (both strongly influenced by Pietism, of course) and set aside seminaries, we're left with a long list of American colleges and universities with roots in Pietism (see table 1.1).

Several of these schools have long since abandoned any but the most nominal of Christian identities. But even among those that would describe themselves as "Christian" or "church-related," Pietism is rarely treated as anything but a distant origin, a relic of a past that's not terribly useful in the present.

---

[8]See F. Ernest Stoeffler, ed., *Continental Pietism and Early American Christianity* (Grand Rapids: Eerdmans, 1976).

Table 1.1

Denomination	College/University
Augustana Evangelical Lutheran Church (now Evangelical Lutheran Church in America)	Augustana College (Rock Island, IL) Bethany College (Lindsborg, KS) California Lutheran University (Thousand Oaks, CA) Gustavus Adolphus College (St. Peter, MN) Midland Lutheran College (Fremont, NE)
Baptist General Conference (now Converge Worldwide)	Bethel University (St. Paul, MN)
Brethren Church	Ashland University (Ashland, OH)
Brethren in Christ Church	Messiah College (Mechanicsburg, PA)
Church of the Brethren	Bridgewater College (Bridgewater, VA) Elizabethtown College (Elizabethtown, PA) Juniata College (Huntingdon, PA) Manchester University (North Manchester, IN) McPherson College (McPherson, KS) University of La Verne (La Verne, CA)
Church of the United Brethren in Christ, USA	Huntington University (Huntington, IN)
Evangelical Association (now United Methodist Church)	Albright College (Reading, PA)
Evangelical Covenant Church	North Park University (Chicago, IL)
Evangelical Free Church of America	Trinity International University (Deerfield, IL)
Evangelical Synod of North America (now United Church of Christ)	Elmhurst College (Elmhurst, IL)
Fellowship of Grace Brethren Churches	Grace College (Winona Lake, IN)
Lutheran Free Church (now ELCA)	Augsburg College (Minneapolis, MN)
Missionary Church	Bethel College (Mishiwaka, IN)
Moravian Church in North America	Moravian College (Bethlehem, PA) Salem College (Winston-Salem, NC)
United Brethren in Christ (now UMC)	Lebanon Valley College (Annville, PA) Otterbein University (Westerville, OH) Shenandoah University (Winchester, VA) University of Indianapolis (Indianapolis, IN)
U.S. Mennonite Brethren	Fresno Pacific University (Fresno, CA) Tabor College (Hillsboro, KS)

THE UNUSABLE PAST: PIETISM AND ANTI-INTELLECTUALISM

Historians tend to be uneasy with the notion of a "usable past," a phrase that originated with an essay asking, "If we need another past so badly, is it inconceivable that we might discover one, that we might even *invent* one?"[9] But like nations, families and other groups, learning communities would have little sense of collective identity if they made no attempt to make meaning of their pasts.[10] So historian Richard Hughes writes, of Catholic, Mennonite and other Christian colleges and universities, "to the extent that these institutions seek to structure their work around a Christian mission at all, they inevitably must draw upon their historic Christian identities or church connections. They really have little other choice since institutions cannot convert from one tradition to another as an individual might."[11]

Yet Hughes and coeditor William Adrian did not include a "Pietist Tradition" alongside the Lutheran, Reformed, Wesleyan and other sections of their influential 1999 book, *Models for Christian Higher Education.* And the chapter that has the most to say about Pietism isn't terribly flattering. Equating his institution's "pietist phase" with a fundamentalist strain within the Mennonite Brethren, Fresno Pacific professor Paul Toews celebrates the neo-Anabaptist professors who drafted the "Fresno Pacific College Idea" in the 1960s. They were inspired by Harold Bender's 1943 speech, "The Anabaptist Vision," which "articulated a usable past that could also become a means for defining the present and shaping the future."[12]

Toews's historiography of Fresno Pacific suggests how Pietism has often been overshadowed by other influences, such as Anabaptism and evangelicalism. (Much the same seems to have happened at Messiah College and various schools in the Brethren traditions, such as Elizabethtown, Ashland and Grace.) But the deeper problem is Toews's association of Pietism with a closed-minded fundamentalism.

While those scholars who identify with the ethos of Pietism understandably resent the charge of anti-intellectualism,[13] it's all too easy to find historical ex-

---

[9]Van Wyck Brooks, "On Creating a Usable Past," *The Dial,* April 11, 1918; reprinted in *Van Wyck Brooks: The Early Years,* ed. Claire Sprague, rev. ed. (Boston: Northeastern University Press, 1993), p. 221. Italics mine.

[10]For a balanced examination of the "usable past" by a Christian historian, see John Fea, *Why Study History? Reflecting on the Importance of the Past* (Grand Rapids: Baker Academic, 2013), pp. 25-46.

[11]Richard T. Hughes, "Introduction," in *Models for Christian Higher Education: Strategies for Success in the Twenty-First Century,* ed. Hughes and William B. Adrian (Grand Rapids: Eerdmans, 1997), p. 4.

[12]Paul Toews, "Religious Idealism and Academic Vocation at Fresno Pacific College," in *Models for Christian Higher Education,* p. 229.

[13]For example, see Roger E. Olson, "Pietism: Myths and Realities," in *The Pietist Impulse in Christianity,* ed. Christian T. Collins Winn et al. (Eugene, OR: Pickwick, 2011), pp. 10-12.

amples of Pietist hostility to higher learning. In 1831 and again in 1857 the Annual Meeting of the German Baptist Brethren prohibited college education, which was viewed as an especially prideful way of conforming to the pattern of the world. They heeded the example of one of their Radical Pietist forebears, Gottfried Arnold, who had resigned from the University of Giessen in 1698 because he found that "it was impossible to be a real Christian in such a secular and pagan atmosphere. University education corrupted youths and led to vanity."[14] Likewise, the Methodist ethicist Michael Cartwright finds the early United Brethren strongly pietistic not solely because they prized the "faith of the 'warm' heart formed in a personal relationship with God," but because their "evangelical aspiration . . . to 'raise up' a holy people for the Kingdom of God was not always conjoined with visions of 'higher education.'" Despite their growing need for schools to train clergy, the United Brethren inherited "the intellectual conflictedness of the Pietist religious heritage about how to unite 'head' and 'heart.'"[15]

A similar head-heart tension bedeviled Scandinavian-American immigrants such as the Norwegian Lutherans who founded Augsburg College in 1869. For years that school competed with St. Olaf College, with faculty, students and other supporters of each taking to the immigrant press to cast aspersions on the other. Carl Chrislock sums up the debate in the college's centenary history: "Augsburg spokesmen claimed that their institution fostered true Christian piety, while St. Olaf nurtured a dangerously 'humanistic' view of the world." While everyone respected the academic excellence of St. Olaf, Chrislock concludes that it was hard for the Pietists of Augsburg to shake the idea that their program "tended to substitute piety for scholarship." As late as 1926, a woman applying to teach French found that Augsburg was known, if at all, as "a center of narrow pietism where an outsider could not survive for more than a year."[16]

TOWARD A USABLE PAST

Against this view of Pietism, there have been attempts to retrieve its founders'

---

[14]Quoted in Donald F. Durnbaugh, *The Fruit of the Vine: A History of the Brethren, 1708-1995* (Elgin, IL: Brethren Press, 1997), p. 13.
[15]Michael G. Cartwright, "The Founding of Indiana Central University: Another Chapter in the History of United Brethren Higher Education," *Methodist History* 46 (July 2008): 212, 215, 217.
[16]Carl H. Chrislock, *From Fjord to Freeway: 100 Years, Augsburg College* (Minneapolis: Augsburg College, 1969), pp. 51, 57, 157.

concern for education and demonstrate how a "religion of the heart" can sustain the life of the mind within the modern-day American university. Church of the Brethren leader Donald Miller, for example, credits the influence of Radical Pietism for certain Brethren educational emphases: a commitment to love, joy, truthfulness and other virtues, an openness to new evidence and new interpretations, and an emphasis on preparing students for lives of service.[17] Probably no other denomination has embraced its Pietist heritage as enthusiastically as the Evangelical Covenant Church, whose current president claims that the ECC is "what you get when Pietists join together to do mission."[18] The late Covenant historian Zenos Hawkinson placed his denomination's two most famous educators, North Park founder David Nyvall (president from 1891–1905 and 1912–1923) and Karl A. Olsson (North Park president from 1959–1970), in a line that traced back to A. H. Francke, the original "Pietist schoolman":

> . . . a university graduate profoundly discontented with the state of the church and determined to see it reformed. He was mainline in theological conviction but hungry and thirsty for living faith experienced in the company of others. He tended to place less emphasis on creed than on Bible, less on erudition than on pastoral care, less on the authority than on the responsibility of the pastoral office. The Pietist schoolman was urgent about his responsibility to the children of common people. Francke loved to say that his duty was twofold: God's glory and neighbor's good.[19]

No doubt some of that ethos continues to permeate North Park, but appeals to Pietism are now few and far between in a college that now trumpets its urban location and multicultural community.[20] And Brethren schools like Elizabethtown College, with their emphases on nonviolence and service, make

---

[17]Donald E. Miller, "The Brethren Philosophy of Higher Education," *Brethren Life and Thought* 49 (Summer–Fall 2004): 173-87. Elizabethtown College hosts a center devoted to Anabaptist and Pietist studies, the twin passions of the great Brethren scholar Dale W. Brown, author of the best-known introduction to Pietism in English, *Understanding Pietism*, rev. ed. (Nappanee, IN: Evangel, 1996).

[18]Gary Walter, "Who We Are at Our Best," *The Covenant Companion* (March 2010): 5.

[19]Zenos E. Hawkinson, "The Pietist Schoolman," in *Amicus Dei: Essays on Faith and Friendship*, ed. Philip J. Anderson (Chicago: Covenant Publications, 1988), p. 99.

[20]See how North Park is covered in Samuel Schuman, *Seeing the Light: Religious Colleges in Twenty-First-Century America* (Baltimore: Johns Hopkins University Press, 2010), pp. 132-43.

much more of their Anabaptist than their Radical Pietist roots.[21]

But not far from Chicago, in St. Paul, Minnesota, one of North Park's cousins has frequently returned to Pietism in search of a usable past: Bethel University.

TRAINED MINDS, BURNING HEARTS: BETHEL UNIVERSITY AND PIETISM

Emerging from the same revival as the Covenant Church, Swedish Baptists began to arrive in the United States in the 1850s. In 1871 a sailor turned preacher named John Alexis Edgren founded a Baptist seminary in Chicago, his first (and, until the next year, only) student arriving in the midst of that city's Great Fire. The seminary eventually found a permanent home in St. Paul, Minnesota, merging with a secondary school in 1914 and adding a junior college during the Great Depression. Bethel College began its four-year program in 1947 and became a master's-level university in 2004.

While Edgren's oft-quoted emphases on conversion, biblical knowledge, spiritual and moral formation, and friendly, helpful relationships between teachers and students certainly evoke the pietistic ethos of the Swedish revival, early historians of Bethel and the Baptist General Conference (BGC) tended to emphasize their movement's continuity with other Baptists, or even Anabaptists. But by the 1950s, BGC historians such as Adolf Olson and his son Virgil made clear that it was Pietism that set their Conference and its college and seminary apart from others in the Baptist and evangelical worlds.[22] From 1955 to 1957 alone, Virgil Olson wrote two articles on Pietism for Bethel Seminary's journal; college dean Clifford Larson and history professor Dalphy Fagerstrom gave talks to the faculty on, respectively, education at Francke's University of Halle and "usable elements" in European Pietism; and Covenant Church pres-

---

[21]For example, David Eller notes the dual Anabaptist and Pietist origins of the Church of the Brethren but defines educational ideals for Elizabethtown that are either common to a wide variety of liberal arts colleges (e.g., independent thought, intellectual curiosity, personal integrity, service) or resonate strongly with the Church of the Brethren's development as a "Historic Peace Church" (e.g., peacemaking, nonviolence); David B. Eller, *The Brethren Heritage of Elizabethtown College*, rev. ed. (Elizabethtown, PA: Elizabethtown College, 2003), pp. 19-20.

[22]J. O. Backlund, *Swedish Baptists in America* (Chicago: Conference Press, 1933) and L. J. Ahlstrom, *John Alexis Edgren: Soldier, Educator, Author, Journalist* (Chicago: Conference Press, 1938) are notably disinterested in the history of Pietism. Contrast them with Adolf Olson, *A Centenary History, As Related to the Baptist General Conference of America* (Chicago: Baptist Conference Press, 1952) and Norris A. Magnuson, *Missionsskolan: A History of an Immigrant School: Bethel Theological Seminary, 1871-1981* (St. Paul: Bethel Theological Seminary, 1982).

ident Theodore Anderson visited campus to speak on "Our Pietistic Heritage."

Overseeing all of this was Carl H. Lundquist, Bethel's longest-serving president, who returned to Pietism through his term (1954–1982) to explain Bethel's distinctiveness.[23] Chapters below will discuss Lundquist's educational philosophy in much greater detail, but one example here will suffice. Seeking to explain what distinguished Bethel from other colleges—even those related to churches—in his 1965 report to the BGC, Lundquist stressed four characteristics: conservative theology, evangelistic purpose, irenic spirit and distinctive living. While any two or three, he claimed, could be found at other colleges, that all four came together at Bethel reflected the unique and continuing influence of its origins in the Swedish Pietist revival of the nineteenth century.[24]

George K. Brushaber succeeded Lundquist in 1982, just in time to preside over one of the worst financial crises in the institution's history. Seeking to revive enrollment both by broadening the school's appeal and by reversing declining interest among BGC youth, Brushaber pledged that Bethel would be "just the same as never before."[25]

A vocal minority of long-serving professors complained that, in embracing a more generically evangelical identity, Bethel was losing sight of its Pietist heritage. In 1985 philosopher Stan Anderson provocatively said, "If Bethel College is not distinctly different from other American Christian liberal arts colleges, then maybe Bethel ought not to exist because we may have too many of them." To recover a distinctive identity, he encouraged faculty to "study the past to learn who we are and what we have been. We would find more of value in Conference and Bethel history than most of us think is there; the Conference was not just another American fundamentalist denomination."[26] Ten years later, after enrollment had recovered and new adult programs were beginning, history and political science professor G. W. Carlson still warned that "This [Baptist pietist] heritage is one that ought not to be discarded with great ease.

---

[23]Christopher Gehrz, "Recovering a Pietist Understanding of Christian Higher Education: Carl H. Lundquist and Karl A. Olsson," *Christian Scholar's Review* 40 (Winter 2011): 139-54.

[24]Carl H. Lundquist, 1965 Presidential Report, *1965 Annual—Baptist General Conference* (Chicago: BGC, 1965), pp. 120, 122. This and other BGC Annuals can be found online at the Bethel University Digital Library, http://cdm16120.contentdm.oclc.org/cdm/search/ collection/p16120coll18.

[25]The theme of his report in the *1985 Annual—Baptist General Conference* (Arlington Heights, IL: BGC, 1985), pp. 110-16.

[26]Stanley D. Anderson, "Why Bethel?" *Bethel [College] Faculty Journal* (Spring 1985): 54-56.

The new generic evangelicalism may not be compatible with many of the traditional, pietist, Baptist distinctives."[27]

In recent years Bethel has seen a striking resurgence in appeals to Pietism. (And here I'm very much a participant-observer.) At either end of the summer of 2006, anthropologist Jenell Paris and former theology professor Roger Olson outlined for our faculty how Pietism might shape distinctive approaches to Christian scholarship and higher education. Two years later George Brushaber was succeeded by provost Jay Barnes, who has described himself as an "evangelical with Anabaptist and Pietist leanings" and an "irenic, Pietist evangelical." With substantial support from Barnes and other administrators, Bethel faculty have started to make the school something of a center for a renewed wave of scholarship on Pietism. For example, a 2009 research conference drew American, Canadian and European scholars and spun off a book on *The Pietist Impulse in Christianity* that included chapters by Houghton College president Shirley Mullen (a former Bethel instructor) and then–North Park professors Kurt Peterson and R. J. Snell exploring Pietist views of learning and education.[28] In his preface to that book, Barnes asserted that "Pietism shapes the culture and trajectory of Bethel University," where education has always "been characterized by a devoted heart and a keen mind."[29] The latter phrase echoes some words of Virgil Olson's carved into a plaque that sits in the president's office: "With the trained mind there must be the burning heart."[30]

A PIETIST APPROACH TO CHRISTIAN HIGHER EDUCATION

But *how* has Pietism shaped Bethel's culture such that it is recognizably different from other Christian colleges and universities? At Bethel we often resort to phrases like "a devoted heart and a keen mind," "whole and holy persons" and "the irenic spirit" without knowing how they're rooted in Pietism. Few faculty

---

[27]G. William Carlson, "The Recovery of the Baptist Pietist Tradition: An Investigation of Its Meaning for Education at Bethel in the Twenty-First Century," *Bethel College Faculty Journal* (1994–1995): 26-37.

[28]Shirley A. Mullen, "The 'Strangely Warmed' Mind: John Wesley, Piety, and Higher Education," and Kurt W. Peterson and R. J. Snell, "'Faith Forms the Intellectual Task': The Pietist Option in Christian Higher Education," both in *The Pietist Impulse in Christianity*, ed. Collins Winn et al., pp. 161-71 and pp. 215-30, respectively.

[29]James H. Barnes III, foreword to *The Pietist Impulse in Christianity*, p. xi.

[30]Jay Barnes, "A Trained Mind and a Burning Heart," *Bethel Magazine* (Summer 2013). The quotation is from Virgil A. Olson, "Historical Interpretation of Eighty-Five Years of Bethel Theological Seminary History," *Bethel Seminary Quarterly* 5 (November 1956): 15.

and administrators, and still fewer students, alumni, trustees and staff know the history and theology of the Christian tradition that shapes our community.

To help deepen our understanding of Pietism and higher education, in June 2013 I facilitated "The Pietist Idea of the Christian College," a workshop attended by fourteen current or former members of the Bethel faculty and staff. Having previously read books on Pietism and speeches and articles by several of the Bethel Pietists mentioned above, we spent two days discussing teaching, research, community, outreach and service. Most participants agreed to spend the summer and fall developing some of the ideas discussed into writing projects. With the addition of a few other contributions, the resulting papers became the book you are reading.

We begin with a set of chapters exemplifying how distinctive emphases and practices might be recovered from the history of Pietism and applied to Christian higher education today. **David Williams** encourages evangelical educators seeking to integrate faith and learning to remember that their roots are in Puritanism *and* Pietism; in particular, he finds helpful the German Pietists' organic understanding of "new birth" and the anti-authoritarian impulse within the Pietist conventicle. **Kathy Nevins** revisits Spener's *Pia Desideria* and discovers that his understanding of Christian community reinforces her own approach to teaching, in which students and professor work together to develop as more whole and holy persons. Drawing on the sermons of John Wesley and literature in her field of anthropology, **Jenell Paris** argues that the central intellectual virtue for Pietist scholars is not faith defined by propositions but love of people. **Phyllis Alsdurf** contrasts Carl Lundquist's pietistic vision for Bethel with fellow neo-evangelical leader Carl F. H. Henry's famously unrealized desire for an "evangelical Harvard." Finally, **Roger Olson** revisits his own past to find how a Pietist ethos can inspire institutions of higher learning that both value transformation over information *and* promote sincere questioning and critical thinking.

Next to "anti-intellectual," probably the most familiar negative stereotype attached to Pietists is that they're "world-denying,"[31] so we continue the conversation with a set of chapters investigating how Pietist scholars and students can engage the world beyond the Christian college. **Dale Durie** retrieves the

---

[31]Olson, "Pietism: Myths and Realities," pp. 7-10.

German Pietists' enthusiasm for a "common priesthood" in order to help Christian colleges prepare their students to serve the common good. If they are to help restore civil discourse to a polarized society, **Christian Collins Winn** contends, Christians need to heed Spener's advice and cultivate the virtues of openness, humility, love and hope. **Marion Larson** and **Sara Shady** argue that interfaith education serves several Pietist purposes, making students more spiritually mature and more loving of neighbors, even in matters controversial.

To add some balance to a roster heavy on scholars from the humanities and social sciences, we're happy to include responses from **Richard Peterson** and **Nancy Olen**. Both find that several of the book's recurring themes—the conversional nature of whole-person education, love as a virtue, and preparing students to seek "God's glory and neighbor's good"—permeated their experiences with Bethel's signature programs in physics and nursing, respectively. (Of course, we should also hear from scholars in other professional fields and the fine arts, plus specialists in student development and campus ministries, to cite but a few holes. As I'll reiterate before this introduction concludes, this is just the beginning of the conversation!)

We close with a set of reflections on the practical challenges facing any Christian college seeking to affirm a Pietist identity today. **Ray VanArragon** probes whether Pietists might celebrate one intellectual virtue (open-mindedness) to the detriment of another (concern for truth), and **Joel Ward** asks whether a Pietist university can maintain organizational coherency given Pietists' emphasis on subjective experience. (Both turn to tried-and-true Pietist remedies: prayer, Bible study and conventicles.) **Kent Gerber** urges Pietists to learn from the example of Harold Bender, who successfully promoted his "Anabaptist Vision" partly by curating resources at Goshen College that supported a new wave of Anabaptist scholarship. **Samuel Zalanga** warns that it may be difficult to sustain a Pietist approach to Christian higher education as neoliberal economics reshape American colleges and universities. Finally, I offer a conclusion that suggests how Pietist educators, in the face of a potential "restructuring" of higher education, might simultaneously embrace change and rethink innovation.

Our goal is to present an approach to Christian higher education that is Pietist not just in content but tone. First, if you noticed a heavier use of the "academic I" than is typical for books like this, that's intentional. Karl Olsson once observed that "the first relevant thing that pietism says is that personal time is important," with spiritual autobiographies having been staples of Pietist reading and writing since the days of Johanna Eleonora Petersen and A. H. Francke.[32] So I encouraged our contributors to extend that tradition by sharing their own stories. Second, without resorting to frequent proof-texting, much of what we have to offer serves as extended meditation on scriptural passages (Mt 22:39 and Lk 24:32 have already made appearances; Rev 21:5 looms large at the end of the book) and themes (e.g., new birth, new life, priesthood), remembering that Spener's first proposal for renewing the church in his time was that "thought should be given to a *more extensive use of the Word of God among us.*"[33] Third, we pray that Bethel's much-ballyhooed "irenic spirit" prevails in this collection. Christian Collins Winn is right to insist that "irenic" is not the same thing as "nice," and sometimes we do critique other traditions' approaches to bring into relief what's distinctive about our own. But I hope that we've done so with humility, avoiding needless controversy. In the words of nineteenth-century Swedish revivalist C. O. Rosenius, "We should certainly fear and tremble, if devotion for this same confession [pietism] involved some necessity to be prejudiced against all other confessions, or even to suspect their capability to serve as a means to draw their adherents into the one sheep fold."[34]

When I first began to research Pietist models of higher education, I had the notion that I'd one day write a Pietist version of Arthur Holmes's *Idea of a Christian College.*[35] But it quickly became clear to me that such a work, if it were to reflect the ethos that inspired it, should not come in the form of a sermon but a conversation. If we are casting a "Pietist vision" for higher education, it does not belong to one person but to a community whose members worship, pray, study, serve, rejoice and lament together—people who have a common purpose, even if they're rarely of one mind.

So think of yourself as listening in as members of one learning community—

---

[32]Karl A. Olsson, "Pietism and Its Relevance to the Modern World," *Moravian Theological Seminary Bulletin* (Fall 1965): 40. On the importance to Pietists of autobiographies like Petersen's, see Michelle A. Clifton-Soderstrom, *Angels, Worms, and Bogeys: The Christian Ethic of Pietism* (Eugene, OR: Cascade Books, 2010), pp. 56-60.

[33]Philip Jacob Spener, *Pia Desideria*, trans. Theodore G. Tappert (Philadelphia: Fortress, 1964), p. 87.

[34]From an article published in an 1842 issue of his periodical, *Pietisten*, then recently republished in a present-day journal of the same name: C. O. Rosenius, "Pietism," trans. Mark Safstrom, *Pietisten* 25 (Spring/Summer 2010), available at www.pietisten.org/xxv/1/ pietism.html.

[35]Arthur F. Holmes, *The Idea of a Christian College*, rev. ed. (Grand Rapids: Eerdmans, 1987).

a conventicle or *ecclesiola*, if you will—discuss how Pietism has shaped what they do as teachers, scholars, mentors, curators, colleagues and neighbors to Christians and non-Christians alike. This is not meant to be the final word on Pietism and Christian higher education but the beginning of a conversation that is both specific to one institution and widely resonant with sisters and brothers in Christ serving at an array of other colleges and universities—especially those that might yet recover their own "usable pasts" from Pietism.

PART ONE

TEACHING, SCHOLARSHIP
AND COMMUNITY IN THE
PIETIST UNIVERSITY

Students should unceasingly have it impressed upon them that
holy life is not of less consequence than diligence and study,
indeed that study without piety is worthless.

PHILIPP JAKOB SPENER,
PIA DESIDERIA

The relation between teacher and students should not be that of
superior and subordinate, but one of real friendship and helpfulness,
remembering that One is our Master, and we are all brethren.

JOHN ALEXIS EDGREN,
FOUNDER OF BETHEL UNIVERSITY

1

Pietism and Faith-Learning Integration in the Evangelical University

David C. Williams

◆

WHAT IS THE FUNCTION of the evangelical university? Is it to further scholarship through academic inquiry? Is it for the purposes of spiritual formation? There is, of course, widespread agreement that an evangelical university does and should do both of the aforementioned, but there is no clear consensus on how the two should be related.

Articulating the relationship between these two ends falls under a number of terms like "faith-learning integration," and these issues are pursued primarily at the level of particular academic disciplines—for example, "How does studying physics relate to faith?" But how one understands the relationship between the notions of faith and reason dictates how those in evangelical institutions of higher learning allocate resources, determine what has value and what is honorable, and decide how the Christian life is articulated, understood and lived. Investigate any decision of significance made at evangelical universities in depth and you will discover a position (consciously held or not) on the relationship between faith and reason. No question is more important for determining the function of an evangelical university, yet very little consensus exists regarding the answer.

To some extent, this is because evangelicalism has, like Augustine, a kind of dual parentage that creates specific kinds of tension. The events that shaped evangelicalism to the greatest degree—the Great Awakenings that occurred in Britain and the American colonies during the 1730s and 1740s— embody the tension between the Pietist and the Puritan/Reformed influences. The towering figures of these events were John Wesley and Jonathan Edwards; both were influenced by Pietism as well as Puritan/Reformed theology. The Pietist roots carried a strong emphasis on the experiential, while the Puritan/Reformed strain tended to prefer a "strong interest in correct doctrine and orthodoxy from Protestant Scholasticism. The post-Reformation thinkers embedded within Puritanism lent to evangelicalism a commitment to doctrinal correctness with a strongly Reformed flavor."[1] Roger Olson calls this tension an "unstable compound" because the streams of Pietism and Puritanism combine two extremely strong impulses that at times are in conflict.[2]

I will address two specific problems that arise because of the tension between the Reformed and Pietist positions. The first problem is that the Reformed side of the equation has produced an extremely articulate and influential way of approaching the issue of faith integration, but universities with roots in Pietism have been less interested in matching the precision of the Reformed tradition's answer to Tertullian's question "What has Athens to do with Jerusalem?" This is not to say that many of these pietistic institutions have not flourished in the world of higher education and scholarship, but arguably a student or faculty member at an institution like Bethel will be less able to specify a relationship between the life of the mind and the life of the Spirit, than, say, their counterparts at Dordt or Calvin.

Working from John Calvin's position on how Christianity should engage culture, Reformed thinkers and universities have produced powerful arguments for "transforming culture" (as Richard Niebuhr plots their position on his "Christ and Culture" categories[3]) that provide a mandate for how faith considerations are related to academic inquiry.[4] Figures such as Alvin Plantinga and Nicholas Wolterstorff have altered the landscape of contemporary academic philosophy and the role that Christians play in its practice.

---

[1]Roger E. Olson, *Reformed and Always Reforming: The Postconservative Approach to Evangelical Theology* (Grand Rapids: Baker Academic, 2007), p. 48.
[2]Ibid.
[3]H. Richard Niebuhr, *Christ and Culture* (New York: Harper & Row, 1951).
[4]Alvin Plantinga, "Advice to Christian Philosophers," *Faith and Philosophy* 1 (October 1984): 253-71.

Plantinga's "Reformed Epistemology" and his critiques of naturalism are ones with which all philosophers must contend.

Reformed universities, then, have a clear "usable past" within the history of evangelicalism that allows for the communication of a very specific approach to faith-learning to their administration, faculty, staff and students. Because there is a historical relationship between scholarship and faith that can be used to answer the questions regarding why one would have to study *x* at a Christian university, the Reformed tradition can offer accessible reasons for answering these types of questions. Why has it been so difficult, though, for evangelical universities that do not come out of the Reformed tradition to explain how the life of the mind relates to the life of faith?

The second problem manifested by the tension between the Reformed and Pietist impulses affects all evangelical universities to a degree. Every evangelical university is concerned with both the academic as well as the spiritual life of students and aims to cultivate the "whole person." The experiential impulse to create community and foster rich forms of spirituality is, however, most often the task of Student Affairs (residence life, student development, campus ministries), concerning itself with leadership, community and spiritual life. The academic disciplines, on the other hand, tend to the minds of students. Or so it is assumed. In worst-case scenarios, the academicians can feel that the increased professionalization of the Student Affairs arena creates a cottage industry that dilutes the aims of the university and marginalizes academic pursuits. Student Affairs can view academics as failing to deal with the "whole person," treating students as minds simply and neglecting the most important aspects of their development. A university can have brilliant academic and Student Affairs programs, but it is quite rare for there to be much communication between these aspects of the university. Why?

The attempt to address the "whole person" in evangelical universities will inevitably embody the "unstable compound" of evangelicalism: the experiential energies of Pietism become housed in Student Affairs, while the Reformed energies shape the culture of the academicians. Evangelical universities, then, do appeal to the "whole person" but do so in a highly bifurcated fashion, with students compartmentalizing their university experience accordingly. If there is no overall structural narrative that shapes the relationship between academics and Student Affairs, then those who participate in the life of the university will fail to have a narrative that specifies the function of the university.

Asserting that one must maintain "balance" between one's spiritual life and one's academic development is at least a start, but simply encouraging the development of good multitasking allows the student or faculty member to successfully avoid discovering the *relationship* between a living, vibrant faith and academic inquiry. The question here is not one of time management or simply balancing competing tensions but the function of the evangelical university.

I argue that two aspects of Pietism's usable past are useful in addressing the two problems outlined above. I will show that Pietism's emphasis on new birth (*Wiedergeburt*) can provide the basis for thinking about a distinctively pietistic conception of faith-learning integration, and that the conventicle model so essential to Pietism provides a way of overcoming the bifurcation between Student Affairs and academics.

SALIENT FEATURES OF PIETISM'S USABLE PAST

If we are enquiring into the function of the evangelical university, then the first question we need to ask is whether or not historical Pietism is relevant for the history of evangelicalism. Evangelical universities wishing to utilize a usable evangelical past have only been able to see as far as Edwards and Wesley, but the scholarship of the late W. R. Ward has opened up the seventeenth century to evangelical institutions that are rooted in the traditions that come out of that period.[5] In a tribute entitled "Rewriting the History of Evangelicalism," Mark Noll and Bruce Hindmarsh assert that

> Ward changed the historiography of early evangelicalism. He turned the globe back a quarter turn toward Europe and turned the calendar back a century toward the post-Reformation era. Single-handedly, his herculean scholarship reconstituted 18th-century Anglo-American evangelical history in terms of 17th-century Central European history. This is one of the great contributions in all of modern historical scholarship.[6]

---

[5]Douglas H. Shantz, *An Introduction to German Pietism: Protestant Renewal at the Dawn of Modern Europe* (Baltimore: Johns Hopkins University Press, 2013), pp. 279-80.

[6]Mark Noll and Bruce Hindmarsh, "Rewriting the History of Evangelicalism: W. R. Ward, 1925-2010," *Books and Culture* 17 (March–April 2011): 8.

If Ward's recovery of Pietism in evangelical history is as significant as Noll and Hindmarsh claim, then it surely warrants a look at how this history might contribute to the issue of faith integration in contemporary evangelical universities. For example, Bethel University comes out of Swedish Baptist Pietism, in which figures such as Johann Arndt, Philipp Jakob Spener and August Hermann Francke are treated as formative, yet these figures lack the evangelical *bona fides* of Edwards and Wesley. Ward's account of early evangelicalism shows conclusively that Pietism's heritage is central to the development of evangelicalism.

If it is the case, though, that we have only been using a portion of evangelical history to think about the function of the evangelical university, then Ward's scholarship seems to open up new possibilities for thinking about the Christian life relative to the life of the mind. The following section will consider some aspects of the Pietist heritage that may be useful in thinking through the question of how faith relates to learning in evangelical universities that resonate with the Pietist side of the tension yet have failed to consider the importance of their own historical roots for how they understand what it means to be a Christian university.

Wiedergeburt: *Pietism on the relationship between humans and nature.* One way of contrasting a pietistic orientation to faith-learning integration with the Reformed model is to analyze the relationship between human beings and the created order.[7] There is a longstanding debate in Christian theology about realism, or the belief in the extramental existence of universals (e.g., moral and scientific principles). This was Thomas Aquinas's view, and it maintains that universals are instantiated in the created order and available through the use of reason. Universals like species and genera were real things found through the investigation of nature. The idea that one could discover truth through the investigation of nature opposed Augustine's view that universals are known through illumination. Martin Luther, however, goes beyond even Augustine and accepts a view regarding nature that was influenced by nominalism. Nominalism is the view that universals are not real and that nothing exists but individual bodies that perform purely individual actions. That Luther was highly

---

[7]The intent here is not to present the Reformed model of faith integration as antithetical to a pietistic orientation. I see the two models as simply emphasizing different aspects of Protestant theology. Ideally, each orientation would learn from and augment the other, rather than compete.

influenced by nominalism is well known, but the implications for Reformed theology are less well considered.[8]

What we have, then, are two main approaches to faith and reason offering two differing conceptions of nature and how human beings interact with the created order. The Aristotelian-influenced Thomism—rejected by Reformers like Luther—maintains that God's revelation can be partially discovered in the created order through the use of reason alone. This view is called essentialism, as it maintains that scientific forms or essences inhere within the individual things of God's creation. Natural law ethics, or the view that essences are normative for human conduct, is grounded in this view. On the other hand, we have an entirely desacralized view of nature in the nominalism of Luther. Luther's attempt to equate Scholastic essentialism with idolatry, and John Calvin's extension of this line of thought, have important implications for Protestant theology and ethics, as Charles Taylor points out:

> But Protestants and particularly Calvinism classed it [essentialism] with idolatry and waged unconditional war on it. It is probable that the unremitting struggle to desacralize the world in the name of an undivided devotion to God waged by Calvin and his followers helped destroy the sense that the creation was a locus of meanings in relation to which man had to define himself.[9]

The Catholic and Reformed positions on faith-learning integration articulate, then, two very different conceptions of how Christians relate to the natural world. The scholastically influenced essentialism of Catholicism depicts the human intellect discovering, through the investigation of nature, normative aspects of God's intentions for humans, while the Reformed position shifts the emphasis from the investigation of nature as a locus of theological meaning to the intellect and Scripture alone.[10] Many new faculty members at evangelical institutions could learn a great deal from Aquinas on faith and reason but will most likely be inclined to turn to evangelical sources such as

---

[8]Michael Allen Gillespie comments, "Like the nominalists, [Luther] rejected the belief in the real existence of universals that characterized scholastic realism" (*The Theological Origins of Modernity* [Chicago: University of Chicago Press, 2008], p. 113).

[9]Charles Taylor, *Sources of the Self* (Cambridge, MA: Harvard University Press, 1992), p. 215.

[10]For a dialogue between two articulate representatives of the two traditions, see Mark A. Noll and James Turner, *The Future of Christian Learning: An Evangelical and Catholic Dialogue*, ed. Thomas Albert Howard (Grand Rapids: Brazos Press, 2008).

Mark Noll's *Scandal of the Evangelical Mind.*[11] They will discover, though, that Noll's view is a robust part of the evangelical heritage, but his suggestion that the Puritans, and in particular Edwards, function as the model of faith-learning integration is connected directly to desacralization.

Pietism offers a third way between the desacralization of Reformed nominalism and Catholic essentialism. A helpful way of describing the opposition between Reformed scholasticism and Pietism is to note the differing emphases regarding justification and *Wiedergeburt* ("new birth").[12] Reformed scholasticism offers a juridical worldview wherein justification is the central concern (as it was for Luther), articulated in the Roman legal language of the Middle Ages. Pietism, however, "embodied the final departure of the medieval world and its threefold sense of God's presence in the world—in providence, in the natural order, and in the social orders of ritual and worship. In its place, Pietism created new kinds of religious community in a setting of pluralism and individualism."[13]

The closed world under God had been atomized. Humans did not find themselves any longer in a God-given order but had to construct order on their own. Therefore, theocentric theology, which the Reformation could still do in terms of Roman legal language, had to be replaced by anthropocentric theology, for which the Pietists, borrowing from mysticism, developed an organismic language around the concern for human piety.[14]

Understanding nature in this new way allowed Pietism to overlay and, to an extent, replace the juridical language of the early Reformation and Protestant orthodoxy and see it in terms of birth and development of the new human. "The vitalism that characterized the whole alchemical tradition," observed Ward, "was a clear attraction to men like Arndt and the Pietists of a later generation who were seeking to recover religious vitality."[15]

This search for a new kind of vitality is arguably a search for a new way of conceptualizing nature and the Christian's relationship to it. It is the search for

---

[11]Mark A. Noll, *The Scandal of the Evangelical Mind* (Grand Rapids: Eerdmans, 1994).

[12]On *Wiedergeburt* within Pietism, see W. R. Ward, *Early Evangelicalism: A Global Intellectual History, 1670-1789* (Cambridge: Cambridge University Press, 2010), p. 71; Egon W. Gerdes, "Theological Tenets of Pietism," *The Covenant Quarterly* 34 (February/May 1976): 27-30; and M. W. Kohl, "*Wiedergeburt* as the Central Theme in Pietism," *The Covenant Quarterly* 32 (November 1974): 13-35.

[13]Shantz, *Introduction to German Pietism*, p. 281.

[14]Gerdes, "Theological Tenets of Pietism," p. 27.

[15]Ward, *Early Evangelicalism*, p. 11.

a new language to describe the Christian life. The search converges upon the central theological tenet of Pietism: the notion of *Wiedergeburt*, or "new birth." It is easy to take for granted, from the perspective of contemporary evangelicalism, notions such as rebirth and the emphasis on inner vitality, but the radical nature of this new organicism and the theology that accompanied it cannot be overstated. Philipp Spener, in one of Pietism's central texts, *Pia Desideria*, "seems to follow a medical model of diagnosis, prognosis and therapy. He often refers to the illness afflicting the body of Christ and the urgency of finding an effective medicine so that it might be restored."[16] These medical metaphors are to be found throughout Pietism and constitute a conceptual departure from the juridical notions employed by Luther and Calvin.[17]

It would be a mistake to see a great deal of consensus on the meaning of *Wiedergeburt* because figures like Arndt, Spener and Francke do not agree completely on its definition, yet it is the concept that binds together a Pietist orientation toward the Christian life. It allows Pietism to avoid a conception of the created order as desacralized yet not invest in it the essentialist notions found in Catholicism. *Wiedergeburt* provides Pietism with a new kind of language to describe the vitality of the Christian life.

Wiedergeburt can be used as the basis for thinking through faith-integration issues from a distinctively pietistic perspective. If it is the case, as W. R. Ward contends, that evangelicalism's roots lie in German Pietism, then bringing to the fore features of Pietism like the notion of *Wiedergeburt* can contribute to the evangelical discussion on the relationship between faith and reason.

The conventicle: Politics and the Socratic. If *Wiedergeburt*, with its attending notions regarding human beings and nature, is Pietism's central notion, then conventicle gatherings are the means of achieving the ends of Pietism. As with *Wiedergeburt*, the role of conventicles in the history of Pietism is well documented. Here are two features of the conventicle that can be brought to bear on the consideration of faith-learning questions.

First, conventicle gatherings in Pietism reveal a particular kind of politics. The term *politics* is being used here in the broadest possible sense; it

---

[16]Shantz, *Introduction to German Pietism*, pp. 87-88.
[17]See Christoffer H. Grundmann, "Pietism, Revivalism, and Medical Missions: The Concern for the Corporeality of Salvation in A. H. Francke, P. Parker, and G. Dowkontt," in *The Pietist Impulse in Christianity*, ed. Christian T. Collins Winn et al. (Eugene, OR: Pickwick, 2011), pp. 296-306.

would be helpful to remember that our use of the term *politics* is derived from the Greek word *polis*. How we "are together" is the sense of *politics* here. So while Pietism fails to fit neatly in Niebuhr's Christ and culture categories,[18] that does not mean it does not have a politics in the sense indicated above. One reason for seeing Pietism as ill-defined politically (as opposed, say, to the Reformed "transforming" view) could be the rejection of systematization at its heart, but another is that the conventicle becomes the pietistic way of negotiating one of the fundamental problems of Protestantism: how can unity in multiplicity be achieved? Although conventicles were not viewed in the same light by all Pietists in all historical periods,[19] what conventicles achieve are not alternative churches but gatherings that supplement larger organization that lose their vitality once they take on greater systematization.

In this sense there is a strong Pietist impulse to look upon any large organization (which of necessity requires greater systematization to sustain itself) with skepticism and see any highly systematized entity with suspicion. The process of rebirth is an organic one, and systematization can be the bane of vitality. Every type of evangelical organization utilizes conventicles, and they exist in too many forms to count. The "small group" of evangelical churches and universities is ubiquitous but is based upon a notion of polity that functions to deal with the problem of multiplicity and unity.

Second, Pietism has important connections to Socratic thought and the Socratic spirit of critique. That Socrates is the thinker to whom many Pietists gravitate is not surprising. Socrates thought that philosophizing should be done in small groups and would most likely have eschewed the later systematization given to his thought by Plato. Socrates saw philosophy as intensely personal and ultimately aimed at personal as well as civic transformation. He started no Academy or Lyceum and never wrote anything down. So it is no great surprise that Nicolaus von Zinzendorf launched a weekly periodical writing under the pseudonym "The German Socrates" that sought to critique the church and engage a new generation of philosophers.[20] It is through Pietism

---

[18]Christopher Gehrz, "Missional Pietists: Lessons from Dale W. Brown and Carl H. Lundquist," *The Covenant Quarterly* 70 (August/November 2012): 41.

[19]Jonathan Strom, "The Problem of Conventicles in Early German Pietism," *The Covenant Quarterly* 61 (November 2004): 3-16.

[20]Christopher B. Barnett, "Socrates the Pietist? Tracing the Socratic in Zinzendorf, Hamann, and

that Socrates was transmitted to Søren Kierkegaard, arguably making it the tradition that formed his thinking on this central figure of his thought.[21]

The relationship between conventicle and the Socratic could be put in terms of an example of Socrates's relationship to Athens. Socrates spent his life critiquing Athenians and Athens itself yet willingly submitted to the authority of Athenian law at the cost of his life. He said famously that he was a "gadfly on a sluggish but noble horse."[22] The conventicle functions as a gadfly on the noble but sluggish horse of the Reformation. Just as Socrates never broke faith with Athenian law, many conventicles did not wish to break from established Protestant groups but wanted to have, like Socrates, the right to renew themselves and engage in a critique of the larger operation.

EMPLOYING PIETISM'S USABLE PAST

If Ward is correct, then it is the case that pietistic notions such as *Wiedergeburt* and the conventicle inform the practice and history of evangelicalism. Yet they have not been intentionally considered for how the contemporary evangelical university articulates the relationship between faith and reason. In the next section I first consider *Wiedergeburt* as the basis for thinking about the faith-integration issues from a pietistic perspective and then argue that the conventicle model could be employed to overcome the bifurcation between Student Affairs and academics.

Implications: **Wiedergeburt.** A starting point for thinking about a pietistic orientation to faith-learning integration is the structure of one of Pietism's central texts, Spener's *Pia Desideria.* As mentioned previously, Spener employs a medical model of diagnosis, prognosis and therapy to convey his theology, with the three, points out Douglas Shantz, displaying the Christian virtues of love, hope and faith.[23] In part one of *Pia Desideria,* Spener provides an analysis of the hierarchical worldview impeding the distinctively Christian expression of love. The second part looks to a brighter Christian future modeled on the early church, while the third section "offers means for restoring *true and living*

Kierkegaard," in *Kierkegaard's Late Writings*, ed. Niels Jørgen Cappelørn, Hermann Deuser and K. Brian Söderquist (Berlin: Walter de Gruyter, 2011), p. 310.

[21]Christopher B. Barnett, *Kierkegaard, Pietism and Holiness* (Burlington, VT: Ashgate Press, 2011).

[22]Plato, *Apology*, 30e-31a.

[23]Shantz, *Introduction to German Pietism*, p. 88.

faith by devoted reading and study of God's word."[24] Spener's own pedagogy, then, utilizes a medical model rooted in the organicist concept of *Wiedergeburt*. I would like to explore two notions that arise from Spener's medical model that connect with a pietistic orientation to faith-learning integration.

First, conversion: successful medical treatment will entail a change from one state to another; one is converted from a diseased state to health. Conversion is not simply a juridical notion but an organic one: "new birth." The consideration of ideas in a classroom, then, will not consist simply in the analysis of worldviews but be convertative.

By *convertative* I mean that when one's whole person is involved, one experiences a kind of movement analogous to the movement from sickness to health. The life of the mind becomes more than a mere analysis of propositions. The inquirer needs to see something they did not before and feel the change that has been wrought by having considered the world in a different way. Pietism's central theological notion maintains that an encounter with the transcendent will leave one altered in all senses of what it means to be a person, and this experiential emphasis is carried into the realm of academic inquiry.

The idea that education is a matter of conversion is likewise central in Plato; his *Phaedrus* is an attempt to show that the ability to distinguish truth from falsity must be predicated on a conversion to the love of learning.[25] But this conversion can only occur when student and teacher are in relationship. Here is how Plato describes such a teacher:

> On meeting someone he will be able to discern what he is like and make clear to himself that the person actually standing in front of him is of just this particular sort of character . . . that he must now apply speeches of such-and-such a kind in this particular way in order to secure conviction about such-and-such an issue. When he has learned all this . . . then, and only then, will he have finally mastered the art well and completely.[26]

Conversion to the love of learning occurs best when the teacher knows "the person actually standing in front of him." That education is enhanced by personal relationship runs deep in the pietistic ethos of education.

---

[24]Ibid. Italics original.

[25]Alexander Nehamas, *Virtues of Authenticity: Essays on Plato and Socrates* (Princeton, NJ: Princeton University Press, 1999), pp. 340-50.

[26]Plato, *Phaedrus,* trans. Alexander Nehamas and Paul Woodruff (Indianapolis: Hackett, 1995), 271e.

A second feature of Spener's medical model pertains to the distinction between instrumental and intrinsic goods. An example of the former would be weightlifting: one lifts weights in order to increase one's vertical leap in basketball. An example of the latter would be joy as a good for its own sake. Charles Taylor has argued that the adoption of a nominalist framework gives rise to instrumental forms of reasoning, making goods like education valuable only for the results they produce. Under nominalism it "is no longer a matter of admiring a normative order, in which God has revealed himself through signs and symbols. We rather have to inhabit it as agents of instrumental reason, working the system effectively in order to bring about God's purposes."[27] Spener's medical model puts forth the argument that some goods are instrumentally as well as intrinsically good: medicine is intended to bring about health, and health is both instrumentally valuable (it allows you to do many things) and, like joy, intrinsically good as well (one can simply appreciate being healthy).

A pietistic orientation toward faith-learning integration raises the possibility of scholarship being intrinsically as well as instrumentally good. Perhaps the goal of rational inquiry is to get beyond the need to ask the question "What is it good for?" and internalize the vitality of academic inquiry. Just as the Christian life can be understood as "faith working through love" (Gal 5:6) and be carried out for no other reason than the joy within it, so scholarship can be understood as intrinsically vital: a mind that is challenged should warm the heart. We are not inclined to ask, "What is the Christian life good for?" as it is vital in itself. Scholarship can be viewed in the same way: it may or may not provide instrumental utility, but the experience of probing the universe and the joy brought about by such an endeavor is one that is good in itself, as well as for the transformative benefits derived for the sake of the kingdom.

Let's consider how these two ideas, education as convertative and instrumentally as well as intrinsically good, might occur relative to a typical question often raised in evangelical universities regarding why one has to consider seriously a certain idea or work that is not explicitly Christian. If a student asks why they have to read, say, Homer, a number of responses are possible. Reading Homer may or may not equip you instrumentally to read the poetry of Scripture

---

[27]Charles Taylor, *A Secular Age* (Cambridge, MA: Harvard University Press, 2007), p. 98.

more insightfully (though it probably will). The *Iliad* and the *Odyssey* may or may not give you deeper, propositionally valid insights into the nature of human beings and how their Creator made them as a natural kind (though they probably will). But a pietistic answer could be that it is the experience of reading these works in a communal setting called the university and feeling their beauty, terror and power that will convert you into a lover of knowledge.

The instructor could very well leave the semester's course in which our hypothetical student was enrolled having provided the most convincing instrumental reasons relative to the Christian faith for reading Homer. She may have used all of her pedagogical acumen regarding the *Iliad* and *Odyssey* to produce a rich and deep understanding of Greek epic poetry in all her students. Everyone could have aced the final and shown a mastery of Homer beyond their years. But if no one answered the altar call to experience Homer, to feel Homer as she feels Homer, to be moved by the meeting of Achilles and Priam as she is moved, then the semester has fallen short of what it might have been. The pietistic professorial impulse is to care as much for the arguments and rigor of the discipline as any other practitioner of the academic arts, but what she may care most about is having her students experience those arguments and that rigor because of what they have done *to her whole person*. The content of the arguments have been instrumentally valuable, but it was the *convertative and intrinsically good activity* of reading Homer that affected her heart. And it is *this* that drives her to research, teach and serve.

Implications: The conventicle. The conventicle was and is a way for Christians interested in furthering the aims of the Reformation to engage in the means of continual reform. The Pietist belief that initial reform ultimately crystallizes into scholastic orthodoxy is the impetus for conventicles: a less formal space where individuals can maintain their connection to the larger body of Protestantism yet critique it and preserve a vitality so easily lost in the larger operation. On evangelical campuses one sees students utilizing the conventicle form primarily for the purposes of residence life and spiritual formation, but what about academics? Could the conventicle have an academic use? Could this concept be used to further our understanding of the relationship between the two sides of the evangelical university that seem to work at loggerheads? Two points seem relevant here.

First, one cannot escape the overuse of the term *community* on an evangelical campus. But again, it is primarily used in the context of Student Affairs. In my experience, one rarely hears the call for "authenticity" with respect to students' academic lives (unless related to issues of academic integrity) in the same way that the term is used in residence life contexts. One does not hear students clamoring for true community that has scholarship at its base. Why? Why are the deep evangelical energies that drive students to seek authentic community (on display in any church that identifies even remotely with evangelicalism) rarely connected to the formation of academic community? The raison d'être of a university is academic inquiry, yet making academics and scholarship the basis for authentic community is often overlooked.

What would it mean to create vital forms of community both outside the classroom as well as in it? John Alexis Edgren, the founder of what is now Bethel University, encouraged friendship between faculty and students in part to cut through the formalism associated with universities.[28] But today this call is often seen as simply one more demand made by the administration on an already over-burdened faculty. From Socrates down through the Epicureans and Stoics, every ancient Greek learning community prefigured Edgren's idea that true scholarship occurs best under conditions of friendship. Academicians need to reclaim the notion of community, not as "extracurricular" but as embedded deeply within the practice of teaching, learning and research. The conventicle form, so integral to evangelicalism's usable past, is one means of forming academic community.

Second, the conventicle form is highly Socratic. Not a system builder like his student Plato, Socrates spent most of his time questioning those who boasted of their ability to define key concepts such as piety and justice. The academic side of evangelical universities needs to reconnect with an important part of evangelical history, namely, the Socratic impulse to critique. The conventicle form can be used to structure this Socratic impulse.

This is clearly seen in historian Dalphy Fagerstrom's 1956 address to his Bethel colleagues. Seeking "usable elements" in European Pietism, Fagerstrom identified four characteristics most directly relevant to education at Bethel: concern for "the spirit rather than the forms of Christianity," and so personal experience over dogma; the expectation that Christian belief would bring about a changed life; an individualism that caused Pietists to stress the role of

---

[28]Norris A. Magnuson, *Missionsskolan*, p. 11.

the laity; and "an inherent simplicity" of belief and demeanor. From these characteristics he then derived two basic themes distinctive of education at Bethel College. First, while Conference Baptists had preserved orthodox Protestantism, there was a basic anti-authoritarian streak that emphasized "the Christian commitment of the individual and . . . the working out of the consequences of that commitment in the maturing total personality of the student . . . rather than an imposition of a detailed blueprint of belief and conduct upon the skins of our students."[29]

Among other implications stemming from this anti-authoritarianism, Fagerstrom praised Bethel's embrace of academic freedom and the liberal arts. He assumed "that a faculty of committed Christians can teach fairly and effectively in the liberal arts, and . . . that this can be done coordinately with the Christian instructor's effort to relate the arts to the Christian faith." He then argued that the same impulses in Pietism that produced a high view of spiritual and political freedom also yielded

> a more subtle kind of democratic contribution . . . namely, criticism of the socio-cultural environment. The pietist example for this lies in their criticism of an institutionalized Christianity that was closely tied in with the social and political structure. It also lies in their insistence that the Christian life means a new way of walking in contrast to the world.[30]

The features noted above, the emphasis on new birth and the conventicle movement, offer new ways of discussing energies that already exist within evangelical institutions of higher learning. It is not the case that a desire for authentic community, or a worldview that aims at the vital core of any experience, needs to be dredged up from eighteenth-century Halle. These impulses exist within evangelical universities, but it requires a historical analysis to see them for what they are. This is not a call for a return to an ideal past or a search for a true historical Pietism. There is no such thing.

CONCLUSION

For the past eight years I have been a philosophy professor at Azusa Pacific

---

[29]Dalphy I. Fagerstrom, "Thoughts on the Pietist Heritage and the College," address to Bethel College Faculty, March 21, 1956, Carl H. Lundquist Papers, box 31, The History Center: Archives of the Baptist General Conference and Bethel University.
[30]Ibid.

University, teaching full time in an off-campus humanities program located just outside Yosemite National Park that incorporates academics with wilderness experience. I have spent over 150 days in the backcountry of the Sierra climbing, skiing and backpacking with my students. I get to know them well, and (for better or worse) they know me. It is often assumed that what drove me to this rather odd career in academia is that I enjoy those pursuits that require mountains. This is, of course, part of the story, but the deeper motivation is rooted in the Pietist ethos that I received from Bethel. I am a graduate of Bethel and spent the first eight years of my teaching career there. I was exposed to the idea that learning should affect one's whole being, that it should involve the heart as well as the mind and that scholarship done in the context of personal relationships can be very powerful.

As a student and professor at Bethel I was continually forced to answer Jesus' most important question: "But who do you say that I am?" (Mk 8:29).[31] On one hand, the question extends to the furthest reaches of the cosmos. Answering it qua university requires using all the academic arts because, as John's Gospel tells us from the outset, Christ is *logos* (Jn 1:1): the logic, the explanation, the ratio that structures all of reality. If we are to say who Jesus is, then we must roll up our sleeves and head into our labs, libraries and studios. On the other hand, the question is entirely intimate and requires an emotional response that can only occur in relationship with Christ and his people. He is the ultimate basis for faith-learning integration, modeling for us as the Great Physician a vision of health that ranges from to the theoretical reaches of science to the unique aspects of the person actually in front of him. The evangelical university must embrace both the personal and the theoretical in order to faithfully answer Jesus' question.

To embrace this sort of range is no small task. I have argued that the lack of a clear pietistic orientation regarding faith-learning integration and the bifurcation of academics and Student Affairs impedes the ability of an evangelical university to achieve its function. Administrators must think structurally and avoid bifurcating those energies central to the evangelical tradition in order to produce whole learning communities. Student Affairs must realize that its

---

[31]This question echoes the first question from God to humanity: "Where are you?" (Gen 3:9). See Martin Buber, *The Way of Man: According to the Teaching of Hasidism* (New York: Citadel, 2000), pp. 9-14.

unique and indispensable talents for fostering community and spiritual development occur not in a summer camp or a church but in a university. Faculty must embrace Jesus' charge to "be wise as serpents and innocent as doves" (Mt 10:16). And students, the sine qua non of the whole operation, must strive to become whole and holy persons, realizing that true scholarship is embracing the full range of Jesus' question, "But who do you say that I am?"[32]

---

[32]This paper is dedicated to Stanley Anderson, Don Postema, Paul Reasoner and Melville Stewart for the gift of philosophy.

2

Calling for Pietist Community

Pia Desideria in the Classroom

Katherine J. Nevins

*The nature of community reminds us that we are not alone. We are likely
to achieve more together than we could in isolation. We acknowledge
only one true Master, and as we strive together to bring all of life
under His lordship, we respect each other as partners and friends
in learning. Thus, learning becomes an act of worship, and
community worship becomes part of learning. As members
of this community, we join to spur each other
on toward Christian maturity.*

"COLLEGE OF ARTS & SCIENCES PHILOSOPHY OF HIGHER EDUCATION,"
2013–2014 CATALOG, BETHEL UNIVERSITY

◆

I N RECENT YEARS, community building has become an important and effective pedagogical tool for working with millennial college students, who are relational learners.[1] In a classroom community, students develop a sense of belonging and a responsibility to the whole. They willingly engage with others

---

[1]Neil Howe and William Strauss, *Millennials Go to College: Strategies for a New Generation on Campus*, 2nd ed. (Great Falls, VA: Lifecourse Associates, 2007), pp. 127-29.

to learn from different perspectives, collaboratively building knowledge, and understanding and sharpening higher-order thinking skills. As partners, students and instructor together weigh evidence, share insights and seek synthesis. Outcomes include richer, more nuanced understandings and more sophisticated evaluations of issues and ideas.

While building community in the classroom has been shown to promote knowledge acquisition and the development of higher-order thinking skills,[2] community is even more critical to the Pietist mission of nurturing Christian character: *the development of more whole and holy persons.* Nurturing all aspects of student maturity and identity—including social, moral, ethical and spiritual, as well as intellectual, development—can and indeed should occur in the classroom. What Pietists advocated, and contemporary research and practice supports,[3] is that cultivating Christian maturity is best done in community. In community, students (and faculty) are able to encounter the challenges necessary for growth and to receive the supports needed to meet those challenges.[4] The classroom becomes what Oldenburg called a "third place,"[5] where one is known, feels safe and can engage with others in ways that expand one's understanding of self, others, the world and God[6]—that is, the pietistic pursuit of wholeness and holiness.

For the German Pietists, the community of the conventicle served as the crucible and catalyst for nurturing development.[7] Their early writings offer twenty-first-century educators wise counsel for creating communities that cultivate more "whole and holy" lives. *Pia Desideria,* by Phillip Jakob Spener, a German Lutheran pastor and a founder of Pietism, is one such significant

---

[2]See, for example, David W. Johnson and Roger T. Johnson, *Learning Together and Alone: Cooperative, Competitive and Individualistic Learning,* 5th ed. (Boston: Allyn & Bacon, 1999).

[3]For example: Nancy J. Evans et al., *Student Development in College: Theory, Research and Practice* (San Francisco: Jossey-Bass, 1998); Patricia King and Karen Kitchener, *Developing Reflective Judgment: Understanding and Promoting Intellectual Growth and Critical Thinking in Adolescents and Adults* (San Francisco: Jossey-Bass, 1994).

[4]The adage "challenge and support" as critical to facilitating college student development was first introduced by Nevitt Sanford in *The American College: A Psychological and Social Interpretation of the Higher Learning* (New York: John Wiley & Sons, 1962), p. 259, and refined in Sanford, *Self and Society: Social Change and Individual Development* (New York: Atherton Press, 1966), p. 46.

[5]Ray Oldenburg, *Celebrating the Third Place: Inspiring Stories About the "Great Good Places" at the Heart of Our Communities* (New York: Marlowe & Company, 2000).

[6]Parker Palmer, *To Know as We Are Known: Education as a Spiritual Journey* (New York: Harper Collins, 1993), p. 54.

[7]On conventicles as the basic form of Pietist community, see pp. 42-44 above.

source. His essay was a clarion call to renew educational and ecclesial communities—so as to renew persons, the church and the world.[8] From these pages come sage advice and principles to guide the creation of pietistic learning communities. Three of these themes will be explored here: the common priesthood (or "priesthood of all believers"); Jesus' command to love God *and* neighbors; and the virtues of humility and openness to correction, both central to Pietism's irenic spirit. The chapter will conclude with some examples from my experience illustrating ways these principles can guide the infusion of *Pia Desideria* in the classroom.

SPENER'S "PIOUS WISHES" FOR COMMUNITY

Community was always at the heart of the university, formed in the early Middle Ages by students and professors who lived and studied together.[9] Yet by the time Spener wrote *Pia Desideria* in 1675, the concept of community among professors and students was much eroded and marked by decidedly unpietistic behavior. Even within the various faculties were bitter rivalries and stiff competition for prestige. Acerbic disputes were common and debates often entered into merely for the purpose of humiliating one another.

Yet, faculty did tend to share a common attitude toward students. Whereas once professors had relied on student fees for their livelihoods,[10] now positions were achieved through political or ecclesiastical appointment and provided essentially government-paid faculty salaries. Teachers no longer "served" students and often viewed them with disdain. Some students indeed may have deserved such assessments, for Spener acknowledges that universities had become "places of worldliness, and indeed of the devils of ambition, tippling, carousing, and brawling."[11] It was not uncommon for university towns to have special student jails for these "tippling, carousing and brawling" students who would frequently and repeatedly be rounded up for their unseemly and unholy behavior.

It is this ethos that Spener calls to task in the fifth of the six proposals that make up the closing section of *Pia Desideria*. For him the purpose of the university, led by pious faculty, is the glory of God. To that end, the "fervent

---

[8]These themes are developed further in the conclusion to this book; see pp. 229-33.
[9]Charles Homer Haskins, *The Rise of Universities* (Ithaca, NY: Cornell University Press, 1957), p. 5.
[10]Ibid., p. 9.
[11]Philip Jacob Spener, *Pia Desideria*, trans. Theodore G. Tappert (Philadelphia: Fortress, 1964), p. 103.

practice of holiness and Christian virtues [need to] be better planted, nurtured, and inculcated in the hearts of students."[12] Spener reminds his readers that "growing in learning" without growing in moral behavior is for naught, and that faculty ought to serve as mentors and role models, challenging and encouraging students to grow in wisdom and in stature.

Spener's work doesn't end with a general call for change but with suggestions for reforming the culture of education. His recommendations focus on the role of the faculty and their relationship with students and on the manner by which knowledge is pursued. Undergirding these proposals is a sincere wish to see faculty and students embracing what have come to be considered the pietistic concepts of the *common priesthood, loving God and neighbor* in attitude and practice, and the *irenic spirit* characterized by humility of character and openness to correction. All are aspects to be easily recognized in contemporary conceptualizations of Pietist colleges seeking to be Christian learning communities developing whole and holy persons.

The common priesthood. The common priesthood is a central theme in Pietism.[13] Spener alludes to this principle in *Pia Desideria*, asserting that divine wisdom is not the exclusive privilege of the scholarly, nor is the indwelling of the Holy Spirit limited to ecclesiastical authorities.[14] Students have been vested with raw abilities to understand, to engage and to have insight, even divine insight. Their viewpoints can have validity and deserve consideration.

Spener believed that wisdom and understanding of Scripture comes from the collective, from shared reflection and revelation, not through one individual who imposes his or her perspective on everyone. Spener admonishes faculty to

> exercise no other authority over the consciences given into his[15] care than, as one who is more experienced, to point out, on the basis of the sole authority of the

---

[12]Ibid., quoting John Schmidt, p. 105.

[13]See Dale Durie's chapter below for a fuller explanation of the Pietist understanding of the common priesthood, especially pp. 113-19.

[14]Spener, *Pia Desideria*, p. 92.

[15]While Spener was speaking to a faculty that was all male in 1675, his words ought to be taken as inclusive, especially in the twenty-first century. The Pietist concept of the common priesthood embraced both genders. For example, Johann Jakob Schütz, the lawyer who initially approached Spener in 1670 about setting up a conventicle, asserted that "We are all one, and call one another brother or sister, for there is neither male nor female but we are all one in Christ Jesus"; quoted in Douglas H. Shantz, *An Introduction to German Pietism: Protestant Renewal at the Dawn of Modern Europe* (Baltimore: Johns Hopkins University Press, 2013), p. 79.

Word of God, what his opinion is in any given case may be; and as the students become more and more experienced, the professor should be able to confer with them as colleagues.[16]

Elsewhere, Spener suggests that professors encourage each student to speak to their understanding of a topic and how they see this topic applying to themselves and others. The professor is to reinforce good observations and, in a "friendly fashion," redirect those students who stray from the "end in view."[17] These comments reflect both a respect for students as partners in learning and a recognition that the Holy Spirit can give the gift of insight and revelation when she will, to whom she will.[18] The principle of the common priesthood also implies that learning is no longer a linear, unidirectional process (teacher to student) but circular and multidirectional. What is advocated is a relational learning structure infused with the love of God and love of neighbor that moves among several planes: teachers to students, students to students, students to teachers, "iron sharpening iron," learning together.

Loving God, loving neighbors. Contrary to the prevailing attitude of the times, Spener called for a transformation of the relationship between faculty and student. Faculty are called to know and love their students as Christ called us to love our neighbor out of love and gratitude to God.[19] Faculty *and* students are to encourage one another as godly people.[20] This love and respect for one another as followers of Christ is to emanate from the heart and be evident in one's conduct with the other. Students, and faculty, are not some foreign "object." Not static, empty vessels to be manipulated or ignored or defamed, *all* are divinely created beings, loved by God and precious to him. *All* are valued and valuable participants of the learning endeavor, *all* full members of the learning community, to be loved as "neighbors."

While placing student and faculty on the same plane in relation to God

---

[16]Spener, *Pia Desideria*, p. 114.

[17]Ibid., p. 113.

[18]If not Spener, his more radical followers experimented with the "divine feminine." Nicolaus von Zinzendorf, for example, preached that the Holy Spirit was the "mother" within the Trinity; Aaron Spencer Fogleman, *Jesus Is Female: Moravians and Radical Religion in Early America* (Philadelphia: University of Pennsylvania Press, 2007), pp. 75-76.

[19]Spener, *Pia Desideria*, pp. 90, 96.

[20]By contrast, the anti-Pietist Lutheran theologian Johann Carpzov said—at a student's funeral, of all places—that "our mission as professors is to make students more learned and not more pious"; quoted by Dale W. Brown, *Understanding Pietism*, rev. ed. (Nappanee, IN: Evangel, 1996), p. 13.

and calling both to love one another as neighbor, Spener acknowledges a special status for faculty in the lives of students. Spener is adamant that professors are to be role models, living lives of Christian piety that marry holy living with "diligence and study."[21] Furthermore, they are called to provide wise counsel to students, to "pay attention to the life as well as the studies of the students entrusted to them, and from time to time speak to those who need to be spoken to."[22] In this role of guide or mentor, Spener specifically suggests that the professor (1) advise students as to what "studies might be useful and necessary to each student according to his intellectual gifts, . . . professional goals, and the like"; (2) give "concrete suggestions" to students on how to improve their spiritual life, their self-knowledge, their "growth in goodness"; and (3) counsel them how to refine their ability to live in a world full of temptation and carnal desire.[23] Thus, the work of the teacher is not confined specifically to the classroom or to the content and skills of a particular discipline. Faculty, as mentors, are preparing the student for life beyond the institution through facilitating growth in knowledge, faith, character and competent life skills.

Humility and openness to correction. Humility and openness to correction are vital to the creation of community and are also characteristics refined in community. Humility is a major hallmark of the godly professor and student, in Spener's view, and a critical element of the Pietist concept of the irenic, or peaceable, spirit. Spener calls on professors particularly to "conduct themselves as men who have died unto the world, [and] in everything . . . [to] seek not their own glory, gain, or pleasure, but rather the glory of their God."[24] Humility for Spener takes on both intrapersonal qualities—such as a realistic appraisal of one's imperfections and gifts, and interpersonal qualities—such as unpretentiousness, graciousness and modesty.[25] Of particular importance is respect

---

[21]Spener, *Pia Desideria*, p. 104. This attitude was not limited to Spener among Pietist educators. Dale Brown notes that, for A. H. Francke, "The example of the teacher was considered very important. In Francke's schools students and teachers lived together, a radical innovation for his place and time"; Brown, *Understanding Pietism*, p. 102.

[22]Spener, *Pia Desideria*, p. 107.

[23]Ibid., pp. 108, 112, 113.

[24]Ibid., p. 104.

[25]For a more recent discussion and research on this theme, see Don E. Davis et al., "Relational Humility: Conceptualizing and Measuring Humility as a Personality Judgment," *Journal of Personality Assessment* 93 (May/June 2011): 225-34.

for others and honoring them for their virtues and accomplishments, all without envy or ridicule.[26]

To Spener, arrogance is the mark of a "worldly spirit," not of a true Christian, and defiles a learning community.[27] He protests what he refers to as the "strife of disputation," taking issue with the then- (and even now) current practices of caustic debates, seeing them as motivated by vindictiveness and ambition rather than entered into for the purposes of investigation, edification, enlightenment and illuminating truth.[28] He quotes Martin Luther: "Truth is lost not by teaching but by disputing, for disputations bring with them this evil, that men's souls are, as it were, profaned, and when they are occupied with quarrels they neglect what is most important."[29] While Spener does not condemn all debating, he does caution that disputation wrongly derived can sully souls by making one's ego and the dispute itself the focus rather than the more important motives of loving and serving God; it can detract from the sincere search for truth and can serve as a poor witness "to the erring."[30]

Coupled with Christian humility in Spener's vision of community is a willingness to be open to correction. Spener is adamant that humble persons examine their own shortcomings and make themselves accountable to others for their behavior. Such realistic self-appraisal is critical in acknowledging how one falls short of the glory of God and is in need of grace, always striving to become better witnesses of Christ in one's words and deeds.[31]

The strength of the community is increased when members willingly admit error to others who have one's best interests at heart and are open to suggestions that are given in the loving spirit of improvement. Using himself as an example, Spener personally offers "to be fraternally corrected by others," writing, "I am willing to yield to anybody, no matter how simple minded, who

---

[26]Spener even suggests that only those who live a godly life should be promoted, and that a person "of meager talent and academic achievement" is to be preferred over "a vain and worldly fool with double doctor's degrees who is very clever but has not been taught by God"; Spener, *Pia Desideria*, p. 108.

[27]Ibid., p. 45.

[28]Ibid., p. 50.

[29]Ibid., p. 100.

[30]Ibid., p. 102. Spener also quotes Paul's warning to Timothy to beware of those who have "a morbid craving for controversy, and for disputes about words, which produce envy, dissension, slander, base suspicion, and wrangling among men who are depraved in mind and bereft of the truth, imagining that godliness is a means of gain (1 Tim 6:3-5)."

[31]Spener, *Pia Desideria*, p. 45.

will show me something better and more advantageous for the discharge of my pastoral duties and whatever else has to do with edification, and I shall thank him for teaching me better."[32]

While Spener speaks most often about this privilege of accountability and encouragement in relation to the church, he also applies this concept to students and teachers, particularly as students mature and professors are able to engage with "them as colleagues."[33] In the ideal Pietist classroom, then, both teachers *and* students take seriously their responsibility to give and receive constructive feedback to and from one another so the classroom community can yield a better learning experience, honoring to God. Students are called to "pay attention," to participate in making the course a better educational experience for all, to give feedback and suggestions to professors for this purpose and to support teachers in all their efforts. Likewise, teachers are to facilitate an environment and educational encounters that increase student knowledge, proficiencies and character to prepare them for the standards, expectations and challenges of their calling beyond the classroom.

To create and sustain a transformative learning community, all are accountable, and each has a vital role. Embedded in these roles is the responsibility to seek from one another, and to give one another, encouragement and "correction." Honest, constructive feedback given in love to assist one another in the "pursuit of perfection" is to be welcomed. And, in those times when either student or teacher succumbs to more base motives, and teachers, especially, find themselves degraded for their work, they, as the more mature members of the community, are called to acknowledge the criticisms, separate the wheat from the chaff, retain the grain and release the rest to the winds.

Spener's *Pia Desideria* reminded its readers what should be the distinctives that characterize the Pietist institution. Both the ultimate goal—that is, the glory of God through the preparation of students for their holy calling—and *how this work is carried out*—in humility, mutual honor and respect, and accountability and encouragement in community—serve as measures of the Pietist ideal. Though written for late seventeenth-century contemporaries, Spener's observations and recommendations are relevant today for those

---

[32]Ibid., pp. 45, 86.
[33]Ibid., p. 114.

seeking to create community in our twenty-first-century classrooms in order to contribute to the development of "whole and holy" persons.

"PIOUS WISHES" IN THE TWENTY-FIRST-CENTURY CLASSROOM

The idea of community in higher education is not unprecedented, having been advocated by such respected authors as Parker Palmer and Ernest Boyer.[34] However, what may be the unique contribution of Spener and other early Pietists is their vision of a collaborative, egalitarian learning community whose purpose is the development and edification of the whole person, all to bring glory to God.[35] How then can this vision become a reality? How can Spener's principles be embodied in the twenty-first-century academy? In this section each principle will be examined from a "practice" perspective, sharing ways I have sought to bring Spener's "pious wishes" to life.

The common priesthood in the classroom. The concept of the common priesthood encourages the creation of a classroom where all are needed and welcomed to participate, full members of the learning endeavor. Illustrating the importance of collective participation is not always easy. However, one model that has guided my efforts to create an environment that promotes collaboration is the Cheyenne medicine wheel.

I was first introduced to this Native American sacred symbol in *Seven Arrows* by Hyemeyohsts Storm.[36] Storm's explanation of the medicine wheel illuminates the existence and importance of diversity, the importance of honoring individual talents and experiences in order to highlight the limits of any one person's perspective, and the need to be and work in harmony with others. Storm describes how people are born to a particular "place" on the wheel that represents their unique talents and gifts. These gifts, combined with one's place in the circle, define one's "way of seeing." The People (Cheyenne) are called to a life "journey," to travel the circle and learn the lessons of and respect for other ways of "seeing." In that journey one is called to truly experience, to engage

---

[34]Palmer, *To Know as We Are Known*; Ernest Boyer, *Campus Life: In Search of Community* (Princeton, NJ: Carnegie Foundation for the Advancement of Teaching, 1990). Though neither self-identified as Pietists, their religious traditions shared in embracing principles that resonate with Spener's "pious wishes." Boyer was a favorite son of Messiah College, which inherited the hybrid Anabaptist, Pietist and Wesleyan identity of the Brethren in Christ; Palmer's religious tradition was Quaker.

[35]Michelle A. Clifton-Soderstrom, *Angels, Worms, and Bogeys: The Christian Ethic of Pietism* (Eugene, OR: Cascade, 2010), p. 38.

[36]Hyemeyohsts Storm, *Seven Arrows* (New York: Harper & Row, 1972), pp. 4-11.

fully, gaining skills and enlarging one's perspective through relationships with the world. All of life then is a journey to be in relationship to all who make up the medicine wheel.

This model, with its lessons of perspective and growth, has been useful in the classroom. I often start the semester with the following exercise:

Students arrange themselves in a single circle around a pedestal placed in the center of the room. A covered object is sitting on this pedestal. The rules are simple. Students may not move from their seats to view the object from another vantage point. They are, upon the unveiling of the object, to answer in writing three questions, which I give to them one at a time: (1) "What do you see?" (2) "What is 'it'?" and (3) "What does it mean?" I then ask different people to read what they wrote for the first question. Quickly it becomes obvious that the object does not present itself in exactly the same way to each person. Not only is the external representation different depending on where one sits in the circle, but the way the person views the object differs. The second and third questions foster important dialogue as well, for the total object is unfamiliar to everyone, and one's view of the object is incomplete, requiring interaction with those who have come to "experience" the object from a different perspective. Because the object has the shape of a cross from at least one vantage point, a familiar symbol to all in the circle, I ask, "What if you weren't Christian? What difference would that make to the meaning you ascribe to this object?" The question is often jarring, as students are reminded that their worldview is not universal.

The medicine wheel exercise provides an experience that validates different ways of seeing and emphasizes the inevitable limitations of one's personal viewpoint. Everyone, as Paul admonishes, "see[s] through a glass darkly" (1 Cor 13:12 KJV). The lesson is that in order to know something more accurately, more clearly, more "truly" and to grow in wisdom, one must engage with others, listening and learning what others "see" and finding ways to *synthesize* the collective understandings of a topic or issue or problem.[37] The beauty of the model is that what is in the center of the circle can be an object, a concept, an abstraction, a dilemma, a question or issue with no easy answer. The focus of the class shifts, and the "other" is a needed "neighbor" who brings gifts and

---

[37]Katherine J. Nevins, "Growing in Wisdom: Connecting the Dots," convocation address, Bethel College, September 4, 1991.

talents and experiences to bear on this dilemma, problem or project. Instead of a focus on "winning the right to say one is right," students and teachers become colleagues collaboratively focusing on insight and illumination.[38] Through collaboration in community, Spener's concept of the priesthood of believers comes to life.

Loving and mentoring students as "neighbors." Like one's faith, community in the classroom is fostered through right attitude and right practice. It begins with the faculty member—who has the responsibility and calling to be the author and initiator of an environment noted for engaging the student as a valued part of the whole—being invitational and supportive *and* challenging students to grow.[39]

Viewing students as minions whose whole existence should be dedicated to my course makes regarding students as neighbors whom I am called to love rather difficult. If I am to love my students as "neighbors," if I am to view them as brothers and sisters in Christ, then I need to be cognizant of their life perspectives and care about their livelihood. I need to be a willing mirror and mentor. I am a mirror as I provide feedback to them about their behavior, and at the same time I am giving a message that they are noticed and cared for, that their conduct matters. When meeting with students to have these potentially difficult conversations, my stance is one of respect, curiosity and interest in their welfare. I begin with a description or an observation, not an interpretation, of a behavior. For example: "I have noticed that you have not been in class for the last several sessions. I am concerned about you." Sometimes I need to ask, "What is getting in the way of your being able to [insert what the behavior is at issue]?" My ultimate goal here is that this student be able to access and engage in the course and community and be nurtured toward wholeness.[40] Whatever the circumstances, I must view them as problems to solve with the student and not engage in a war of wills. I am to bring clarity to the situation

---

[38]In collaboration, the focus is on analysis and synthesis *before* evaluation. In competition, synthesis is rarely entertained and students move quickly to a form of evaluation, analyzing to disparage others' points of view and defend one's own, the very thing about disputation that Spener found abhorrent.

[39]Parker Palmer notes that "the community is a discipline of mutual encouragement and mutual testing, keeping me both hopeful and honest about the love that seeks me, the love I seek to be"; *To Know as We Are Known*, p. 18.

[40]However, sometimes this goal is not the student's goal. If so, then it behooves us both to recognize this and work with the situation.

as a mirror and encourage students to find a mature resolution as mentor. Sometimes these confrontational experiences are transformative.

Once, in the days before Turnitin.com, I received a paper I suspected was plagiarized. After identifying the "mother articles" and doing the requisite comparisons, it was clear this student had excerpted numerous sentences verbatim. I needed to meet with her. Frankly, I was not in a charitable frame of mind, since plagiarism seemed like an affront to me personally, demanding hypervigilance and extra time on my part. To compound the problem, I had thought she was a good student. Hence I was both irritated and disappointed. Yet, at some level I was able to recognize this student as someone loved by God. I tempered my accusations and simply presented her with the evidence I had collected. Then, with God-given guidance, instead of moving directly into doling out the consequences, I shared with her my assessment of her as a good student and my confusion as to why she felt it had been necessary to present others' work as her own.

Her response was both telling and wrenching. Her own words, she confessed in tears, were simply not good enough. Further conversation revealed a person who had not been encouraged to find her voice and to share her insights and intelligence with others. She was a woman who was insecure with, even frightened of, her intellectual gifts. While there still was accountability for the plagiarism, this revelation transformed both our views of the situation and our relationship. It became my privilege to be the encourager and mentor she needed to help her develop confidence in herself and her abilities. In the end, she didn't need to co-opt others' words: she found her own.

Community in the classroom begins with me. Do I have *agapē* love for my students as neighbors? Do I engage in the "examined life," choosing my words and conduct with some care so as to be a role model exemplifying Christian character? And do I challenge and encourage class members to do the same in their interactions with one another and with me? If so, then the fabric of a pietistic community is being woven, and all will sense the connections that convey the ethic of care and love for neighbor.

Fostering humility and openness to correction. Fostering humility and openness to correction are perhaps the most critical of Spener's aspects of Pietism to apply to the classroom. However, Paul provides a clue as to how one might address humility in the classroom when he reminds us "not to think of yourself more highly than you ought to think, but to think with sober judgment" (Rom 12:3). Developing a realistic appraisal of oneself is an important skill that can be mentored. As indicated earlier, when debate, discussion or disputation is done in the spirit of conquest, then the remembered outcome will be less likely a clearer understanding of the issue and more about the emotional responses to being shouted down or to being the victorious shouter. As Paul Young, author of *The Shack*, reminded us recently, there are those who find it "easier to be right than to love."[41] Yet another Paul reminds us to strive for the greater gifts, and love is the greatest of these (1 Cor 12:30; 13:13).

I urge my students to enter into debate or discussion for the loving purpose of greater illumination. Assignments and questions for class consideration are carefully written in ways that emphasize thoughtful answers rather than "the right" answer, which shifts the nature of the learning process from defense of a position to investigation and discovery. For example, instead of asking, "Who is right, those who view mental illness as biologically caused or spiritually caused?" the question could be rephrased as, "What kinds of evidence, values and worldviews lead one to conclude mental illness is biologically or spiritually caused? How might one reconcile these different explanations?"

Then there is the ongoing, in-the-moment engagement and reinforcement of student behavior. When there is certainty, particularly that which borders on arrogance, I will question that person's source of knowledge in a Socratic manner. I might ask the student to indicate what degree of certainty she claims in holding a particular position. I frequently ask such students to suspend their position for a bit and take an alternative position. In contrast, when there is insecurity, I will reinforce the sources of knowledge this person can access. While as faculty I am primarily the facilitator of these behaviors, students can also provide these methods of engagement and can be reinforced for their open communication. All of this facilitates a classroom community that students feel has become a "third place," where challenges and openness to correction are more welcome.

In the classroom, being open to correction is expected of students, but not all students—and not all faculty—willingly ask for and graciously receive criticism. Perhaps the difficulty lies, as with some students, in one's developmental

---

[41]William Paul Young, chapel talk, Bethel University, November 18, 2013, available at https://itunes.apple.com/us/podcast/william-paul-young-11-18-2013/id699156802?i=221739717&mt=2.

stage[42] or mistrust of the feedback source. Sometimes the fear stems from one's perceived need to be perfect. Another possibility could be past experience when one received mean-spirited criticism. For multiple reasons, some, perhaps many, students and professors fear project and course evaluations. How does one overcome these attitudes? Again, it begins with me. The fundamental purpose of feedback is the improvement of learning, whether it be in skill or knowledge or character. Therefore I must monitor my attitude and behavior so that the feedback I provide is offered for that purpose and is constructive and respectful. Students will sense sincerity of purpose when feedback is given to help them be better persons.

Then there is the feedback students give faculty. I am also called to be open to correction. Still, after thirty-five years of teaching, I still have tremors when I see the white "confidential" envelopes in my mailbox following the end of the semester. How then can I approach evaluation irenically?

First I remind myself that I am still a teacher in process and can learn something from every student who takes the role of evaluator seriously. In fact, just like students receiving information from me on their projects, I need feedback in order to know when and how I missed or hit the mark. I may think requiring students to do all their major projects in the last three weeks of class is a good thing since we will have covered all the content by then; however, I need to learn that students are overwhelmed then and deep learning doesn't happen when the course is so structured. Thus I open the envelope with a question: "What can I learn from this feedback that will help me improve this course and my teaching?" This question presets my radar to look for what is constructive and to scan over what is not.

In addition to my own obligation to provide useful feedback and be open to correction, I want students to take both giving and receiving feedback seriously. Students often need coaching on what good feedback is as well as a reminder that providing fair, honest and useful responses on evaluations is important to developing community. To that end, when possible, I ask students to evaluate projects as part of the requirements of that assignment. I ask them what they

---

[42]For example, students in William Perry's multiplicity stage are likely to be critical of instructor evaluations of their work. See Cornfeld and Knefelkamp's "Analysis of the Learner Characteristics of Students Implied by the Perry Scheme," Table I.1, in William G. Perry Jr., *Forms of Ethical and Intellectual Development in the College Years: A Scheme* (San Francisco: Jossey-Bass, 1999), pp. xxxi-xxxii.

learned, what worked, what didn't and what remedies they might suggest for the future. When appropriate, I will assign peer feedback projects, which I evaluate, providing "feedback on the feedback" students give one another. I also frequently ask for feedback on the content being absorbed and the instructional methods being used.[43] The class then brainstorms what *we* could do to improve learning and the classroom ethos. These activities reflect the assumption of mutual accountability for a good learning experience—one that promotes insight and personal growth.

Conclusion

When Spener wrote *Pia Desideria*, his "pious wish" for Christian education was to see academic rigor in the formation of head, heart and spirit.[44] His work provides the twenty-first-century classroom with pietistic principles for intentionally building Christian character through practicing Christian community in the classroom. It is a mutually reinforcing relationship. As the principles of Pietism shape the classroom, the classroom shapes the person; as the person develops and matures, so the person reinforces and contributes to the pietistic community. The more we love and respect one another as neighbors, the more our actions emanate from belief in the common priesthood; the more we enter into the work of learning with humility and openness to correction, the stronger will be our learning communities. The stronger our communities, the greater will be our growth in intellect, character and faith: we become more "whole and holy" to bring glory to God.

---

[43]For a treasury of ideas on how to get useful student feedback, see Thomas A. Angelo and K. Patricia Cross, *Classroom Assessment Techniques: A Handbook for College Teachers*, 2nd ed. (San Francisco: Josey-Bass Publishers, 1993). "Clicker" technology can also be used to access student attitudes about instruction.

[44]Clifton-Soderstrom, *Angels, Worms, and Bogeys*, p. 85.

3

Love and Learning

A Model for Pietist Scholarship in the Disciplines[1]

Jenell Paris

◆

RODNEY SAWATSKY, former president of Messiah College, urges Christian scholars to consider not only faith and learning but also faith, hope and love as three dimensions of a full Christian approach to scholarship.[2] He and the other contributors to *Scholarship and Christian Faith: Enlarging the Conversation* promote an irenic approach to exploring intersections of scholarship and Christian identity. This is, in his words, a "broadening of the conversation" beyond the dominant faith-integration approach that focuses on Christian philosophy and presuppositional analysis of the disciplines.[3]

Guided by my tradition, the Pietist impulse within evangelicalism, I explore love as a lens for understanding what Christians do, and could do, with their scholarship, using cultural anthropology as a case study. First, I argue that the

---

[1]An earlier version of this chapter appeared as Jenell Williams Paris, "A Pietist Perspective on Love and Learning in Cultural Anthropology," *Christian Scholar's Review* 35 (Spring 2006): 371-85. Copyright © 2006 by Christian Scholar's Review; reprinted by permission.

[2]Rodney Sawatsky, "Prologue: The Virtue of Scholarly Hope," in *Scholarship and Christian Faith: Enlarging the Conversation*, ed. Douglas Jacobsen and Rhonda Hustedt Jacobsen (New York: Oxford University Press, 2004), pp. 3-14.

[3]Scholars have explored faith-learning integration from numerous Christian traditions. See, for example, Richard T. Hughes and William B. Adrian, eds., *Models for Christian Higher Education: Strategies for Survival and Success in the Twenty-First Century* (Grand Rapids: Eerdmans, 1997). For a recent survey of the literature on faith-learning integration (including approaches that emphasize practice and formation), see Stephen Moroney, "Where Faith and Learning Intersect: Re-Mapping the Contemporary Terrain," *Christian Scholar's Review* 43 (Winter 2014): 139-55.

integrationist model is not very helpful for making sense of the work of Christian anthropologists, because of its emphasis on philosophy and its prioritizing of faith as the element of Christianity that is to be integrated. Second, I show how a Pietist perspective that focuses on love better illuminates the work of some Christian scholars, including anthropologists who contribute in the areas of basic research, mission and applied anthropology. This analysis carries broader implications, as I encourage a decentering of the integrationist approach in favor of a broader conversation that includes numerous Christian traditions and diverse ways of understanding what Christian identity may mean for the scholarly vocation.

SHORTCOMINGS OF THE INTEGRATIONIST MODEL

The dominant integrationist (or Kuyperian) model of Christian scholarship emphasizes articulating the presuppositions of a Christian worldview and those of a discipline and then comparing and contrasting these control beliefs. This approach is associated most closely with the Christian Reformed tradition, though its influence extends across Christian higher education.[4] An ultimate aim of this approach is to seek and speak Christian truth in all arenas, from the philosophy of a discipline to its teaching and public application. It involves "the effort to think like a Christian—to think within a specifically Christian framework—across the whole spectrum of modern learning."[5] This worldview approach encourages a systematic approach to faith integration, usually relying on a biblical metanarrative framework (creation-fall-redemption-consummation or something similar). Its advocates also emphasize the value of teaching, especially inculcating a Christian worldview and a strong sense of vocation in students. In scholarly analyses, however, integrationist approaches focus more on theoretical concerns than on method or application.

When viewed from this perspective, Christians in anthropology seem to be slow to consider the implications of their faith on their science. Eloise Hiebert

---

[4]General examples include Arthur Holmes, *Contours of a Worldview* (Grand Rapids: Eerdmans, 1983); Cornelius Plantinga, *Engaging God's World: A Christian Vision of Faith, Learning, and Living* (Grand Rapids: Eerdmans, 2002); Albert Wolters, *Creation Regained* (Grand Rapids: Eerdmans, 1985). From sociology, see, for example, David Fraser and Tony Campolo, *Sociology Through the Eyes of Faith* (San Francisco: HarperSanFrancisco, 1992); Russell Heddendorf, *Hidden Threads: Social Thought for Christians* (Dallas: Probe Books, 1990).

[5]Mark Noll, *The Scandal of the Evangelical Mind* (Grand Rapids: Eerdmans, 1994), p. 7.

Meneses, anthropologist at Eastern University, summarizes that "while social sciences such as sociology, psychology and economics have wrestled much with faith-science integration, anthropology has not."[6] Some use the integrationist approach, but discussions are detached from the discipline's power centers, focused instead in Christian college and seminary classrooms, Christian networks and Christian publications.[7] Such analyses usually show fundamental differences and hostilities between the faith and the discipline, allowing little room for cooperation or creative synergy at the level of philosophy.

Meager institutional support may help explain why, in comparison with other disciplines, integrationist efforts in anthropology are rare and poorly sustained over time. Faith-integration approaches in many disciplines have strong grounding in and support from Christian colleges and universities. There is, unfortunately, a dearth of anthropology programs, classes and faculty in Christian higher education, which limits scholars' ability to advance integrative thinking in this discipline. Secular universities and Christian seminaries are two other institutional sites in which Christian anthropologists may work, but here also they are marginal and few in number. In a 2014 survey of 120 institutions affiliated with the Council for Christian Colleges and Universities, Jacob Manning found only one institution with a four-field, freestanding anthropology department (Biola University).[8] Eight others have departments that include anthropology alongside sociology, history or intercultural studies. This represents just 7 percent of CCCU institutions. Accordingly, just nine institutions offer a BA in anthropology, the nine institutions with anthropology departments.

An earlier survey by the author showed just thirty-five scholars holding a PhD in anthropology teaching at Christian colleges and universities.[9] Colleges offering a single anthropology course may staff it with a sociologist, historian, missiologist or social worker. Anthropology is more often valued at the institutional level for its contribution to general education, missions and intercultural

---

[6]Eloise Hiebert Meneses, "No Other Foundation: Establishing a Christian Anthropology," *Christian Scholar's Review* 29 (Spring 2000): 535.

[7]Biola University, for example, sponsored a Network of Christian Anthropologists conference in 2000 that explored anthropological theory in Christian perspective. Similarly, in 2003 Wheaton College sponsored a symposium on Christian perspectives on postmodern theory in anthropology.

[8]Manning surveyed the websites of CCCU colleges in spring 2014.

[9]This figure is approximate, because some faculty do not list credentials online.

studies. The 2014 survey showed fifty-six of the 120 institutions offer bachelor's degrees in intercultural or global studies, and anthropology courses are included here. The most common approach to including anthropology is a single course at the introductory level that contributes to general education, with that course also contributing to an interdisciplinary major in intercultural or global studies.

Two recent articles regarding the relationship between Christianity and anthropology reveal limitations of the integrationist approach. Meneses offers her vision of a Christian anthropology and concludes that anthropology and Christianity share little harmony at the level of worldview.[10] She describes secular anthropology as holding an ultimate commitment to humanity as god. Anthropology's penultimate commitments, and those of modern social science more generally, include naturalism (nature constitutes all that exists), evolution (human history has no meaningful telos) and humanism (an optimistic and elevated view of human nature and activity). In contrast, a Christian worldview is ultimately oriented toward God, not humanity. As such, it is holistic (the spiritual aspect of human life is not reducible to the natural) and trinitarian (humans and human history have meaning and purpose as part of a larger narrative). She concludes that there cannot be harmony or synthesis between these two incompatible paradigms. "If one framework is chosen, then the other can be incorporated at a subordinate level, but only by 'chopping it up' and accepting or rejecting portions piecemeal."[11] From this perspective, then, one's commitment to anthropology must be subjugated to one's commitment to Christ.

Meneses's argument seems to show little appreciation for anthropology, describing it as hostile to Christian ideas about the nature of humanity and the world, yet she has worked in the field for years as teacher, scholar and missionary. Her life commitments show that anthropology is well suited for understanding missionary work and development and for teaching responsibility and stewardship to first-world citizens, and that hostile disciplinary presuppositions need not hinder active Christian scholarship. Unfortunately, these rich areas of integration are nearly invisible in Meneses's article because of the integrationist emphasis on philosophy over practice.[12]

---

[10]Meneses, "No Other Foundation," pp. 531-49.

[11]Ibid., p. 531.

[12]See, for example, Paul Hiebert and Eloise Hiebert Meneses, *Incarnational Ministry: Planting Churches in Band, Tribal, Peasant, and Urban Societies* (Grand Rapids: Baker Books, 1995).

Anthropologist Robert Priest, professor of mission and intercultural studies and director of the doctoral program in intercultural studies at Trinity Evangelical Divinity School, analyzes the origins and meanings of the missionary position metaphor, including its use as a tool for exclusion of Christians in the discipline.[13] Anthropologists commonly reference Bronislaw Malinowski, an early ethnographer, as having documented the sexual regulation of indigenous people by missionaries. Priest shows instead that Alfred Kinsey, American biologist and sex researcher, misappropriated Malinowski's ethnography and that the "missionary position" is an ethnographic myth, never appearing in Malinowski's writings.

The missionary position is, instead, a core symbol in modernist and postmodernist discourse. In modern discourse, it distinguishes anthropologists as forward-looking and modern and missionaries as conservative, ethnocentric and premodern. In postmodern discourse, it synthesizes postmodernist objections to modernism. While anthropology has become increasingly open to diverse subject positions (identity of the speaker), the evangelical subject position continues to be maligned, in large part because such discriminations help define the field. Priest argues, in fact, that early anthropologists developed ideas about human nature as a modern replacement for Christian views of humankind, particularly the notion of original sin.[14] In his view, modernist and postmodernist anthropological theories do not merely ignore Christian narratives but instead incorporate Christian narratives and symbols "in ways which dismantle, subvert, and desanctify Christian metanarratives and justify uses of power that silence and exclude Christian voices."[15]

Thirteen anthropologists provided commentary following Priest's article, articulating common views of Christians held among many anthropologists. Michèle Dominy argued that missionaries deserve disrespect because they are "engaged in an unending, unrelenting effort to foist their hegemonic projection onto the non-Western pagan 'Other.'"[16] Neville Hoad suggested that because

---

[13]Robert J. Priest, "Missionary Positions: Christian, Modernist, Postmodernist," *Current Anthropology* 42 (February 2001): 29-68.

[14]Robert J. Priest, "Cultural Anthropology, Sin, and the Missionary," in *God and Culture: Essays in Honor of Carl F. H. Henry*, ed. D. A. Carson and John D. Woodbridge (Grand Rapids: Eerdmans, 1993), pp. 85-105.

[15]Priest, "Missionary Positions," p. 45.

[16]Michèle D. Dominy, comment on Priest, "Missionary Positions," p. 50.

of missionaries' ethnocentrism and exploitation of cultures, anthropologists have "an ethical and political obligation" to "have a little fun at the expense of the missionary position."[17] Several commentators argued that Christians in the academy are simply embarrassing, the "sibling similar in many ways but blunt and tactless."[18]

In addition to these expressions of anthropological ethnocentrism, commentators raised two points that advance my argument about the limitations of faith integration. While Tanya Luhrmann resists prejudice and discrimination against religion and religious people in the academy, she notes that there is also some logic behind it.

> Having a religious conviction is not like being of a different race, gender or sexual orientation, because faith—at least, devout Christian faith—entails a belief commitment about the fundamental nature of reality. . . . Religious faith . . . tends to assert that there is a different kind of world, that it cannot be the case that both the atheist and the believer are correct in their understanding of their world.[19]

Similarly, James Clifford argues that while religious views may be heard in the academy, they must conform to institutionalized protocols for professionalism. Thus religious people cannot make claims about a different sort of reality based upon revelatory knowledge inaccessible to the unconverted. Clifford argues that Priest "does not (yet) offer an academic defense of religious content, an explicit Christian analysis rather than a discussion of the Christian academic predicament."[20]

Indeed, Priest produces knowledge and makes his argument in academically acceptable ways but says the Christian subject position "gave me a perspective which helped me to see certain realities that were not as likely to be seen from another position but quite capable of being considered and evaluated once they were pointed out."[21] Meneses, on the other hand, makes her argument with explicitly Christian presuppositions. The revelatory knowledge she cites about the nature of humanity and the purpose of history cannot be accessed or critiqued with anthropological epistemologies and methodologies, and as theo-

---

[17]Neville Hoad, comment on Priest, "Missionary Positions," p. 53.
[18]Jonathan Benthall, comment on Priest, "Missionary Positions," p. 46.
[19]Tanya Luhrmann, comment on Priest, "Missionary Positions," p. 55.
[20]James Clifford, comment on Priest, "Missionary Positions," p. 48.
[21]Priest, "Missionary Positions," p. 44.

retical underpinnings are not shared with non-Christian scholars. Priest's argument, then, is shared broadly in a flagship journal but does not rely upon or promote a Christian worldview. Meneses's work is thoroughly Christian in its perspective and as such is distributed mostly among Christian scholars.

These examples show that the integrationist project is limited in severe ways in some disciplines, including cultural anthropology. Both Meneses and Priest describe some of the basic ideological hostilities and personal prejudices that exist between Christianity and anthropology (or between Christian anthropologists and secular anthropologists). Discussions of atheism, naturalism, evolution and humanism take place regularly among Christian anthropologists and have for over a century, honing the faith and the intellect of Christian scholars and anthropology students. Publications, conferences and the Network of Christian Anthropologists have all been valuable for developing Christian thought and for building faith-sustaining relationships among scholars who work in a field so influenced by atheism and anti-Christian bias. Priest concludes, and I agree, that while Christian anthropologists are dependent upon the discipline, we must also "self-consciously stand in tension with many of the assumptions, paradigms and values of the discipline."[22]

The discipline itself, however, is untouched by these discussions, and the integrationist project has not been fruitful as an avenue for redemptive change within the discipline. Scholars in other disciplines may consider such pragmatism to be irrelevant or even crass, but it matters greatly to Christian anthropologists. Because of the harmony between anthropology and mission, and because many Christian anthropologists come from activist faith traditions, the redemptive potential of one's career investments are considered important. Christian anthropologists simply have not prioritized the development of theoretical work for a hostile or disinterested audience when arenas for transformative cultural engagement, such as mission, have seemed more open to Christian efforts.

Finally, many faith-integration efforts are more about the integration of Christian philosophy than the integration of faith itself. Scholars work with Christian philosophies, doctrines of creation, fall and redemption, and other doctrines relevant to specific disciplines or issues. While such doctrines are

---

[22]Priest, "Cultural Anthropology, Sin, and the Missionary," p. 105.

broadly accepted across Christian traditions and are useful for some purposes, they are, nonetheless, systematic derivatives from the scriptural narrative and historical experience of God's people. They are also thoughts potentially detached from practice. In this way, the practice of faith—that is, living a life yielded to God—is not even a prerequisite for faith-integration scholarship. A concern for praxis is often noted in prefaces or epilogues of faith-integration writings but not included as substantive analysis. A non-Christian committed to understanding Christian philosophy could potentially analyze a subject with use of Christian doctrine, or a Christian committed to systematic theology or philosophy could do "faith integration," with little personal piety or faith. The faith-integration approach is surely valuable for addressing the secularizing socialization of graduate education, for developing particular areas of systematic philosophy or theology and for pedagogy in Christian colleges, universities and seminaries. It does normally, but does not necessarily, engage the life of faith, however, and it too frequently limits the sphere of inquiry to matters of theory and philosophy. While redemption of disciplinary philosophy may be possible, it is not probable within anthropology, and is perhaps part of the reason why there are so few Kuyperian or Christian Reformed anthropologists. It seems to me that Christians in this field have found urgent and open areas for Christian witness and have developed those areas rather than pursuing the relatively closed venue of disciplinary philosophy and theory.

A Pietist Perspective on Love and Learning

Rather than transforming or critiquing the discipline by analyzing its presuppositions, Christians have more often approached anthropology with a generous sense of commonality and agreement, developing anthropological insights for application in church, mission, society and the discipline.[23] This is not apparent by reading faith-integration publications, because their focus on presuppositions highlights antagonisms between the faith and the discipline, and because they emphasize theoretical work over application.

In practice, however, many Christian anthropologists have developed ca-

---

[23]I do not attempt a comprehensive history of Christians in anthropology in this article. For such history, see a special issue of *Missiology* titled *Missionaries, Anthropologists, and Human Rights* (April 1996), and Darrell L. Whiteman, "Anthropology and Mission: The Incarnational Connection," *International Journal of Frontier Missions* 20 (Winter 2003): 35-44.

reers that transcend traditional bifurcations between theory and practice: missionaries-turned-scholars, missionaries-and-scholars, professors of missiology, mission trainers and applied anthropologists. Indeed, an emerging movement in the discipline as a whole encourages an engaged anthropology that would move beyond the traditional prizing of basic research over application. Engaged anthropology makes social change and advocacy part of the scientific process.

Other Christians have focused their non-mission-related scholarship on disenfranchised social groups or urgent social issues. This scholarship has contributed to the work of mission, to evangelical theology and church practice, to social change and to anthropology as a whole, particularly in cultural and linguistic anthropology. Love for sharing the gospel and love for the disenfranchised have been important motivators for Christian anthropologists since the inception of the discipline.

A Pietist perspective focuses more on the generous, clever and impactful areas of overlap between Christianity and the disciplines and less on philosophical antagonisms. While rigorous in methodology and theory, Pietist approaches tend to be less systematic in terms of analyzing the intersections between Christian "control beliefs" and disciplinary presuppositions.

I refer to Pietism in its broadest sense, as a noninstitutional religious energy present across Christian traditions, one of which is the Wesleyan/Holiness tradition, the one I worship in and have emphasized in this treatment of Pietism. Like its formal origins in late-seventeenth- and eighteenth-century Germany, the Pietist impulse may be broadly characterized as heart focused, in contrast to head-focused approaches to religion that are excessively dogmatic, formalized and lacking individual feeling and participation with God. In numerous denominations and traditions, the Pietist impulse has promoted an individual relationship with God, moral living, participation in small group Bible study and accountability, outreach to the poor and mission. *Pia Desideria* (1675) is commonly referred to as a first statement of Pietism, in which German religious reformer Philipp Jakob Spener wrote that, among other things, Christianity should be a life practice more than a matter of knowledge, that ministers should preach understandable, practical sermons, and that all Christians should live moral lives and practice restraint and charity in their disagreements with unbelievers and with other Christians.

When viewed in Pietist perspective, love offers an interesting focal point for scholarly integration. For Pietists, faith is heartfelt, experiential and not heavily doctrinal. While doctrine is not unimportant, Pietists do not treat it with the reverence or precision of other traditions. John Wesley, a Pietist, relied on Hebrews 11 in describing faith as "'the evidence' and conviction 'of things not seen.'"[24] It is a gift of God that is known and confirmed in the heart. Faith involves trusting in God with conviction, despite not having seen all of the things in which we believe. In a Pietist view, faith is a way of life, not an ideology or a set of control beliefs.

In this view, faith is quite difficult to integrate with scientific rationalism. In extending the mention of Hebrews 11, the people commended by faith in that chapter are those who made choices with incomplete knowledge, who walked into uncertain futures and who did not make full sense of things within their lifetimes. The Scientific Revolution promoted ways of knowing that were more empirical and experimental and less revelatory and intuitive. In general, the scientific approach encourages control, predictability, measurement and systematization. If faith involves believing without seeing, science is about seeing before believing. If faith is about living in trust without certain knowledge of the future, science is about predictability: explaining the present and predicting or controlling the future. If faith is about trust, science is about skepticism, privileging rational and sensory information.

In relating faith, love and reason, Wesley said, "Let reason do all that reason can: employ it as far as it will go. But, at the same time, acknowledge it as utterly incapable of giving either faith, or hope, or love; and consequently, of producing either real virtue or substantial happiness."[25] For Wesley and other intellectual Pietists, reason (scientific rationalism may be considered a subset of reason) is useful to a point, for understanding the world God made and in understanding some parts of religion. It is a limited good, however, because of its detachment from virtue.

Love is thus more amenable for Pietists working to integrate scholarship with the Christian life because it is more visible and tangible than faith and

---

[24]John Wesley, "The Case of Reason Impartially Considered" (sermon, 1781), Wesley Center Online, http://wesley.nnu.edu/john-wesley/the-sermons-of-john-wesley-1872-edition/sermon-70-the-case-of-reason-impartially-considered.
[25]Ibid.

because it merges knowledge and practice. Love is faith in action, a demonstrated care for God, self and neighbor. In Wesley's words again, love is "a calm, generous, disinterested benevolence to every child of man," "an earnest, steady good-will to our fellow-creatures."[26] Theologian Mildred Bangs Wynkoop explicates this Wesleyan emphasis in saying that Wesley's major contribution to the church "was not new dogma but a real, spiritual vitality infused into traditional, mainline Christianity. This vitality is love, and love is by its very nature dynamic."[27]

Next, I will describe how the practice of love influences the work of Christian anthropologists in three areas: basic research, mission and applied anthropology. In each of these spheres, many Christian anthropologists develop dual audiences, Christian and secular, for the dissemination of scholarly products.

BASIC RESEARCH AS LOVE

Many Christian scholars contribute to their disciplines with basic research that is on religious subject matter, or about oppressed or marginal people. This work may be viewed as truth telling, valuable in and of itself.[28] It may also be used to edify the church or the research subject's community. Anthropologist Judith Shapiro argues that missionary linguists have contributed excellent basic research to the discipline "because they had the motivation to stay for very long periods of time in 'the field,' far longer than most academic anthropologists and linguists. Because they shared with their successful academic colleagues the intelligence and patience to grapple with a deeply unfamiliar language."[29] Kenneth Pike was such a Christian anthropologist, contributing to understandings of tone languages, the field of English as a Second Language and tagmemics, and innovating the concepts "emic" and "etic." Pike disseminated his academic and devotional insights to multiple audiences including the academy, the church, missionary trainers and missionaries.[30]

---

[26]Ibid.

[27]Mildred Bangs Wynkoop, *A Theology of Love: The Dynamic of Wesleyanism* (Kansas City, MO: Beacon Hill, 1972), p. 22.

[28]George Marsden, *The Outrageous Idea of Christian Scholarship* (New York: Oxford University Press, 1997), especially chap. 3.

[29]Judith Shapiro, comment on Priest, "Missionary Positions," p. 57.

[30]Among his prolific publications are Kenneth Pike, *Linguistic Concepts: An Introduction to Tagmemics* (Lincoln: University of Nebraska Press, 1982); idem, "Christianity and Culture 1: Conscience and Culture," *Journal of the American Scientific Affiliation* 31 (March 1979): 8-12; idem, *With Heart and*

Much basic research in anthropology involves marginal populations, including the global poor, indigenous cultures, women and other "Others." Many anthropologists, Christian and not, are motivated by love and a desire for social justice as they choose areas for study. Humanism as a common denominator offers rich areas for collaboration between Christians and non-Christians in the field, making philosophical antagonisms less important in arenas of engagement. While some Christians study populations with mission application in mind, others study religious subject matter unrelated to mission, and others subjects that are neither religious nor related to mission. My work is similar in covering both religious and nonreligious subjects: race and ghetto formation, urban queerspace and corporate marketing strategies.[31]

In basic research, processes for producing knowledge are usually entirely secular in methodology and theory. Methodology for fieldwork has established codes of humanistic ethics that are entirely compatible with Christian ethics—in my view, they are a subset of a more inclusive and rigorous Christian ethic.[32] Anthropological theory is less compatible with Christianity, and Christian scholars live with tensions as they develop theoretical niches with secular colleagues. Though couched within larger frameworks of relativism, secular humanism and evolution, however, secular anthropological theory can provide useful understandings of culture and cultural processes.

In a rare counterexample, Eloise Hiebert Meneses and John Stapleford created an explicitly Christian theory to analyze three cultural types (egalitarian tribal, feudal peasant and democratic capitalist) for ways in which each one manifests wealth, justice, love, spirituality and humility.[33] This also makes a valuable contribution to Christian understandings of anthropological theory and to teaching in Christian contexts, but as with other explicitly and/or exclusively Christian points of view in anthropology it is unlikely to influence mainstream theory in the field.

Understanding the integrative aspects of basic research depends upon

Mind: A Personal Synthesis of Scholarship and Devotion (Grand Rapids: Eerdmans, 1962).

[31]For example, Jenell Williams Paris, "'We've Seen This Coming': Resident Activists Shaping Neighborhood Redevelopment in Washington, D.C.," *Transforming Anthropology* 10 (January 2001): 28-38; Paris and Rory E. Anderson, "Faith-Based Queer Space in Washington, D.C.: The Metropolitan Community Church-D.C. and Mount Vernon Square," *Gender, Place & Culture* 8, no. 2 (2001): 149-68.

[32]See the American Anthropological Association, "Statement on Ethics: Principles of Professional Responsibility," approved November 2012, http://ethics.aaanet.org/category/statement.

[33]Eloise Hiebert Meneses and John E. Stapleford, "Defeating the Baals: Balanced Christian Living in Different Cultural Systems," *Christian Scholar's Review* 30 (Fall 2000): 83-106.

knowing the motivation and the full body of work of the scholar. Pike, for example, researched language partly to understand language and partly to better communicate the gospel crossculturally. Some Christian scholars are motivated by love and care to research particular subjects. Others, however, do basic research with no application or dual audience and no explicitly Christian motivation. In basic research, the intensity or integrity of Christian integration is not necessarily apparent in the subject matter or in academic publications. The scholar's motivations may be known by considering her or his broader agenda, which may include communicating with multiple audiences and exerting influence in areas including the academy, the church and society.

MISSION AS LOVE

Christian scholars may also find arenas of application for their scholarship within the church. Synchronicity between anthropology and mission was envisioned by missionaries since the inception of anthropology. In the nineteenth century, missionaries contributed firsthand knowledge of cultures to early "armchair" anthropologists, before the twentieth-century emphasis on firsthand fieldwork. Missionaries served as data gatherers for European and American scholars who used the data to theorize about how societies evolved. Even today, missionaries and anthropologists still frequently help each other with access to populations, language and other elements of fieldwork.[34]

Some early missionary anthropologists strove to reformulate mission strategy in ways that critically engaged colonial contexts. Many of these missionary anthropologists agreed with their secular colleagues' critiques of mission as colonial appendage. Some saw the tendency of some modern Christian groups toward anti-intellectualism and excessive subjectivity in mission, as evangelism and relief work were done without appropriate crosscultural skills and knowledge. They turned to anthropology for insights and concepts that would help the missionary endeavor. Early missionary anthropologists sought to reformulate mission strategy to develop indigenous churches rather than colonial ones.[35]

---

[34]Whiteman, "Anthropology and Mission," pp. 36-42.

[35]See, for example, Louis Luzbetak, *The Church and Cultures: An Applied Anthropology for the Religious Worker* (Techny, IL: Divine Word Publications, 1963); Donald McGavran, *The Clash Between Christianity and Cultures* (Washington: Canon Press, 1974); Eugene Nida, *Customs and Cultures: Anthropology for Christian Missions* (New York: Harper & Row, 1954); and Alan Tippett, ed., *God, Man,*

A second generation of missionary anthropologists continued this emphasis, developing theories of contextualization. They used secular anthropology concepts such as functional equivalents, cultural cues and contextualization, and developed the field of ethnotheology. Their goal was to improve mission practice, especially in contextualizing the gospel and church planting. Sherwood Lingenfelter, anthropologist and provost of Fuller Theological Seminary, for example, offers missionaries models for analyzing social order so that church planting may be done in culturally relevant ways that incorporate existing cultural patterns.[36]

Paul Hiebert is another example, devoting his career to both anthropology and missiology. He worked as a missionary in India and later in higher education as a professor and dean. He contributed to mission in his own work as a missionary in teaching and in writing books such as *Anthropological Insights for Missionaries.*[37]

Anthropology as a tool for mission has been institutionalized in Christian colleges, universities and seminaries. Anthropology programs that prepare students for mission began at Wheaton College, Bethel University and Hartford College in the mid-twentieth century and now exist both as mission preparation and as the study of anthropology itself at some Christian colleges and universities. *Practical Anthropology,* a journal focused on the applications of anthropology for Christian theology and practice, mostly in the area of mission, was founded in 1953. The journal became *Missiology* in 1973 and continues on today as the journal of the American Society of Missiology.[38]

Applied Anthropology as Love

A third arena in which Christian scholars express love is through the ap-

---

and Church Growth (Grand Rapids: Eerdmans, 1973).

[36]Sherwood Lingenfelter, *Transforming Culture: A Challenge for Christian Mission* (Grand Rapids: Baker Book House, 1992). For other examples, see Stephen A. Grunlan and Marvin K. Mayers, eds., *Cultural Anthropology: A Christian Perspective* (Grand Rapids: Zondervan, 1979); and Charles Kraft, *Christianity in Culture: A Study in Dynamic Biblical Theologizing in Cross-Cultural Perspective* (Maryknoll, NY: Orbis Books, 1979).

[37]Paul Hiebert, *Anthropological Insights for Missionaries* (Grand Rapids: Baker Book House, 1999); *Cultural Anthropology* (Grand Rapids: Baker Book House, 1973). See also Hiebert, *Missiological Implications of Epistemological Shifts: Affirming Truth in a Modern/Postmodern World* (Harrisburg, PA: Trinity Press International, 1999).

[38]Collections of articles from *Practical Anthropology* may be found in William Smalley, ed., *Readings in Missionary Anthropology* (Tarrytown, NY: Practical Anthropology, 1967); and Smalley, ed., *Readings in Missionary Anthropology II* (South Pasadena, CA: William Carey Library, 1978).

plied arms of their disciplines. In applied anthropology, Christians have applied theoretical insights, method and research findings in both church and society.[39]

In the church, anthropologists have contributed to theology, church life and teaching Christian adults in colleges and seminaries. In terms of theology, anthropologists have encouraged theologians and laypeople to consider culture when developing theology. Charles Kraft, for example, worked as a missionary, trainer of missionaries and linguist. He applied anthropological insight to evangelical theology, presaging postmodern evangelical theology today. Concerned that Western evangelical theology was too heavily philosophical and too oriented around academic concerns, Kraft felt that an anthropological perspective and method could help theologians understand and better address people's questions in their communities instead of esoteric issues of interest mostly only to themselves. He argued for the inclusion of nonphilosophers and nonacademicians in the making of theology and for a theology that focuses on people (their understandings of God and their relationship with God in various cultures) as much as it focuses on God. He also urged a relativism that situates all theological understandings in cultural contexts, with God alone existing outside culture. Thus Kraft wrote that "theologizing has been and is most appropriately done with specific reference to the concerns and needs of the audience addressed, rather than as a quest for a single set of once-for-all formulations of truth."[40] He called this quest "ethnotheology," the need to understand the relationship between God and humans with both theological and cultural understanding.[41]

Many anthropologists make similar contributions today, and I offer just a few examples. Harold Recinos, at the Perkins School of Theology, wrote two books encouraging pastors and church members to use basic anthro-

---

[39]Though some of the work referenced here would now be labeled "engaged anthropology," most was conceived of at the time as "applied," so I continue use of that term.

[40]Charles H. Kraft, "Can Anthropological Insight Assist Evangelical Theology?" *Christian Scholar's Review* 7, nos. 2–3 (1977): 165-203. For another example of the pastoral application of anthropology, see Robert J. Priest, "Cultural Factors in Victorious Living," *Free and Fulfilled: Victorious Christian Living in the Twenty-First Century*, ed. Robertson McQuilkin (Nashville: Thomas Nelson, 1997), pp. 128-42.

[41]Charles H. Kraft, "Toward a Christian Ethnotheology," in *God, Man and Church Growth*, ed. A. R. Tippett (Grand Rapids: Eerdmans, 1973), pp. 109-26.

pology methods to do neighborhood and area surveys before starting outreach programs, and he uses theories of globalization to encourage contex-
tualized urban ministry in the United States.[42] Both Miriam Adeney,
anthropologist at Seattle Pacific University, and Laura Montgomery help
churches critically analyze and formulate short-term mission programs,
considering the paternalistic and neocolonial aspects of too many mission
encounters with the global poor.[43] Adeney encourages Christians to take
social inequality seriously by writing and speaking about Christian concern
for the oppressed in broader venues such as in her post as board member
for *Christianity Today*.[44]

Many Christian anthropologists contribute to the church by teaching in
Christian colleges, universities and seminaries. Many also teach and consult in
churches on subjects of race and ethnicity, mission, and social inequality.

CONCLUSION

From a Pietist perspective of the faith-hope-love triad from 1 Corinthians,
faith may be particularly difficult to integrate with scholarship. Jesus, for
example, discusses faith with metaphors from nature. The birds and lilies
express faith in the way they live without worry for the future. Though
doctrinal, systematic readings of Scripture seem to be privileged among
Christian scholars, Scripture may also be read as a narrative of people
living lives of faith. In this view, faith is more a way of life and less an
ideology or a set of control beliefs. Thus what is generally referred to as
"integration of faith and learning" may be more precisely called "integration of theology and learning" or "integration of Christian philosophy
and learning." Systematized discussions of the world, religious practice or
religious doctrine are important, but they are derivative from faith itself,
which is more often described biblically in narrative or figurative terms.
Living a life of faith is, in Pietist perspective, no different for a scientist

---

[42]Harold Recinos, *Hear the Cry! A Latino Pastor Challenges the Church* (Louisville, KY: Westminster
John Knox, 1989); Recinos, *Jesus Weeps: Global Encounters on Our Doorstep* (Nashville: Abing-
don, 1992).

[43]Laura Montgomery, "Short-Term Medical Missions: Enhancing or Eroding Health," *Missiology: An
International Review* 21 (July 1993): 333-41.

[44]Miriam Adeney, *Daughters of Islam* (Downers Grove, IL: InterVarsity Press, 2002); Adeney, *God's
Foreign Policy* (Grand Rapids: Eerdmans, 1984); and Adeney, *A Time for Risking: Priorities for Women*
(Portland, OR: Multnomah Press, 1987).

than a nonscientist in that it involves trusting God in the uncertainty of human existence.

Love may provide a more powerful and concrete way of understanding ways in which some Christians live out the academic vocation. For example, Paul describes love in 1 Corinthians 13 as profoundly other centered: patient, kind, not boastful or arrogant or rude. It rejoices in the truth and bears with other people for the long haul. Jesus, and the prophets before him, emphasized the importance of care for the vulnerable and love for God, neighbor and the self. Love, then, carries important implications for how Christian scholars engage in scholarly dialogue, their pedagogy and their attitude toward subject matter. It highlights applications and teaching, aspects of the scholarly vocation that are too often devalued in the academy and at times neglected in faith-integration treatments. It offers a framework for engaged scholarship, moving beyond conventional divisions between theory and application, and concomitant privileging of theory.

On the other hand, a Pietist perspective on love and learning has potential pitfalls. Though there have been many intellectual Pietists, and there is a strong, institutionalized, intellectual movement in the Wesleyan/Holiness tradition, Pietism is sometimes mediocre in its intellectual life, at times even anti-intellectual.[45] An undue emphasis on experience and feeling over rationality and intellectual struggle has, at times, resulted in theological imprecision and social outreach efforts that fail for lack of forethought and/or assessment. Michael Emerson and Christian Smith, both Christian sociologists, critique this impulse with respect to evangelical (not specifically Pietist) efforts toward racial reconciliation. They argue that the activist impulse combined with an anti-intellectual tradition often dooms well-intentioned efforts to failure.[46]

Pietism offers a valuable perspective, however, for Christians seeking integrity and wholeness in their scholarly lives. This Pietist view of anthropology reveals that anthropologists have been integrating their Christian identity with their work in important ways since the discipline's inception, but the dominant

---

[45]Noll, *The Scandal of the Evangelical Mind*, pp. 47-49; John E. and Susie C. Stanley, "What Can the Wesleyan/Holiness Tradition Contribute to Christian Higher Education?" in *Models for Christian Higher Education*, pp. 313-26.

[46]Michael O. Emerson and Christian Smith, *Divided by Faith: Evangelical Religion and the Problem of Race in America* (New York: Oxford University Press, 2000).

faith-integration paradigm renders these efforts nearly invisible. Critical use of numerous faith traditions and broader use of spiritual concepts (love, hope, faith, trust, sin and others) may expand and enrich our efforts to be faithful Christian scholars.[47]

---

[47]This paper was first presented at the Faith in the Academy conference at Messiah College in September 2004. It has benefited from feedback from conference participants, as well as from C. Jeanne Serrao, Susie Stanley, Jynell Brist, Neil Lettinga and two anonymous reviewers.

4

The Quest for an Evangelical University

The Educational Visions of Carl F. H. Henry and Carl H. Lundquist

Phyllis E. Alsdurf

◆

To RECONCILE CONFLICTING DEFINITIONS of Pietism and better understand its somewhat indistinct boundaries, Peter James Yoder has offered prototype theory as a useful lens through which to view the self-conceptions of early Pietists. Emerging from the work of George Lakoff in the 1980s, this theory "recognizes the human tendency to have central, prototypical figures in a given category" even as it allows for fluid category boundaries and degrees of category membership. "As individuals or groups construct categories, they show a propensity to see some category members as better representatives of the grouping than others."[1]

Examining the educational vision of Carl H. Lundquist, one of Pietism's more recent "central, prototypical figures" and arguably one of its better representatives, offers a means of recovering a usable past to inform a contemporary definition of a pietistic approach to Christian higher education. Such an examination of Lundquist's contribution both to Pietism and the wider evangelical

---

[1]Peter James Yoder, "Rendered 'Odious' as Pietists: Anton Wilhelm Böhme's Conception of Pietism and the Possibilities of Prototype Theory," in *The Pietist Impulse in Christianity*, ed. Christian T. Collins Winn et al. (Eugene, OR: Pickwick, 2011), p. 24.

community will be further illuminated when viewed in comparison and contrast to the educational vision of another evangelical prototype: Carl F. H. Henry.

Scan any text on evangelicalism and you'll quickly come upon the name of Carl Henry. Regarded as the intellectual architect of the neo-evangelicalism that emerged after World War II, Henry is widely hailed for crafting and promulgating the theological infrastructure of the movement through his many books and his role as founding editor of *Christianity Today* (*CT*) magazine.

But search that same literature for the name of his contemporary Carl Lundquist and you'll probably come up empty-handed. Randall Balmer's *Encyclopedia of Evangelicalism* (2004), for example, includes a two-column entry for Henry but no reference to Lundquist. The humble and self-effacing Lundquist no doubt would have been filled with glee that his never became a household name within evangelical circles. George K. Brushaber, who succeeded him as president of Bethel College and Seminary in 1982, recalled Lundquist as a humble man who "never aspired to be the leader of the evangelical world," yet noted that he had "huge intellectual capacity" and a curiosity that allowed him to be comfortable with people from other faith traditions. "It was a mark of his generous and irenic spirit," Brushaber concluded.[2]

Though he cast a much smaller shadow than Henry, it could be argued that Lundquist's contributions were no less important. As Bethel's president for almost thirty years, a founder of what is now the Council of Christian Colleges & Universities, and a leader in organizations such as the National Association of Evangelicals and his own Evangelical Order of the Burning Heart, Lundquist was lauded among evangelicals for his irenicism and piety. In many respects he represented the heart of evangelicalism, living and working according to the Pietist creed: "In essentials, unity; in nonessentials, liberty; in everything, charity."

While few can match Henry for intellectual heft and output, the picture of late-twentieth-century evangelical higher education is more complete when it includes not just Henry's call for a comprehensive and highly rationalistic approach but also the conversional piety and lived experience that were foundational to Carl Lundquist's philosophy of Christian education. With its emphasis on a vital interior life with Christ at the center, on the interaction between the intellectual and the spiritual, on the link between the mission of the church and

---

[2]George K. Brushaber, interview with author, September 26, 2013, St. Paul, Minnesota.

the Christian college and on a hope-filled engagement with the world, Lundquist's vision is inseparable from his Pietism. Furthermore, the populist view that Lundquist championed, though less prominent than Henry's call for an world-class university aimed at intellectual elites, offers an equally worthy and transformative model for Christian higher education and cultural engagement.

CARL F. H. HENRY: MAKING EVANGELICALISM INTELLECTUALLY RESPECTABLE

Widely regarded as the intellectual shaper of modern evangelicalism, Carl F. H. Henry spent his adult life articulating a vision of what it meant to be an evangelical in a secular age. He was a prolific writer and scholar and, as a 1988 *CT* article stated, in his writings "the theological moorings of contemporary evangelicalism are anchored."[3] His book *The Uneasy Conscience of Modern Fundamentalism* (1947) signaled a change in the way evangelicals interacted with culture and established theological underpinnings for a new commitment to evangelical social engagement.[4]

Both for a dozen years at the helm of *Christianity Today* and for the decades of fruitful ministry that followed, Henry was at heart a professor of Christian philosophy. That was the position he held as a founding faculty member at Fuller Theological Seminary in Pasadena, California, before he took a leave of absence from academia in 1956 to become editor of *CT*.

Henry's "life work was devoted to making the movement intellectually respectable," wrote *CT* editor Ted Olsen in 2004.[5] Henry was instrumental in systematically defining what it meant to be evangelical through his writing, speaking and magazine editing. The author or editor of some forty books and dozens of essays and booklets, Henry also wrote regular editorials and countless articles for *CT*. And his daunting six-volume epistemology, *God, Revelation and Authority*, is considered among the most significant theological works in all of evangelicalism.[6] These efforts were ultimately about systematically edu-

---

[3]"CT at 30," *Christianity Today*, November 18, 1989, p. 20.

[4]Carl F. H. Henry, *The Uneasy Conscience of Modern Fundamentalism* (Grand Rapids: Eerdmans, 1947). For a discussion of Henry's call for social engagement, see David R. Swartz, *Moral Minority: The Evangelical Left in an Age of Conservatism* (Philadelphia: University of Pennsylvania Press, 2012), pp. 13-25.

[5]Ted Olsen, "Carl Henry's Dream," *Christianity Today*, February 1, 2004, p. 7.

[6]Carl F. H. Henry, *God, Revelation, and Authority*, 6 vols. (Waco, TX: Word Books, 1976–1983).

cating his readers and the wider evangelical community in what he would call a biblical and unifying "world-life view."

After leaving *CT* in 1968, Henry served as editor-at-large for the magazine, a lecturer-at-large for World Vision, and a professor at Eastern Baptist Seminary and Trinity Evangelical Divinity School, among other places. Throughout his career, Henry founded and directed the Institute for Advanced Christian Studies (IFACS), was instrumental in the formation of the Coalition of Christian Colleges (later the Council of Christian Colleges & Universities) and was involved in some aspect of leadership for many conclaves related to Christian higher education or evangelism worldwide. Said the late Kenneth Kantzer, *CT* editor from 1978 to 1982, "In Carl's mind, editing, lecturing, and preaching were all a part of his calling to education."[7]

Christianity Today: *The magazine as seminary.* From its beginnings, *Christianity Today* was envisioned by Billy Graham, Henry and other founders as a seminary of sorts for pastors who had not received adequate theological training as well as for a generation of fundamentalists who were woefully ignorant about the rational foundation for the faith they espoused. An outline for the magazine's founding stated the need for strong financial support from Christian businessmen because "this is primarily an educational program," and it needed to be sent free of charge to "tens of thousands who will never subscribe of themselves."[8] That educational mission was further clarified in a statement of goals that included overcoming "erroneous and weak training" by indirectly trying to become "a theological seminary." A brochure announced, "There is a realization that the period of three years in a theological seminary is not sufficient to prepare a student fully for the ministry." And *Christianity Today* would "supplement seminary training with sermonic helps, pastoral advice, and book reviews."[9]

Another of *CT*'s primary purposes was to "win a hearing for evangelical orthodoxy from non-evangelical scholars," wrote Olsen in 1987.[10] After one year as editor, Henry reported to the *CT* board that he wanted the magazine to do nothing less than steer the course of cultural debates by securing "the theo-

---

[7]Kenneth Kantzer, "The Carl Henry That Might Have Been," *Christianity Today*, April 5, 1993, p. 15.
[8]"Christianity Today," Collection 11, Box 5, Archives of the Billy Graham Center, Wheaton, Illinois.
[9]See "Policy Statement," Collection 11, Box 5, and "Memo to Contributors," Collection 11, Box 15, Archives of the Billy Graham Center.
[10]Olsen, "Carl Henry's Dream," p. 7.

logical respect and intellectual dignity necessary for effective conversation with liberal and neo-orthodox ministers." He continued, "It should be obvious from all of this, that our strategy is to raise up as wide a witness as possible for evangelical Christianity, without compromise with the liberal theology on one side, or concession to fundamentalist aberrations on the other."[11]

A rational defense of the faith. Over time, Henry gave less emphasis to social activism in light of the pressing need to buttress rational arguments for the faith. To that task he devoted himself through a wide range of educational efforts.[12] Christianity "stresses the importance of reason, not simply will or emotion," he argued, thus giving it "a stake in the arena of culture generally and in the realm of education specifically."[13]

But whether combating the erroneous thinking of theological liberals or addressing creeping secularism, Henry understood Christians to be at war with an alien culture. In the late 1960s he wrote, "We are engaged in battle for the minds and wills of men, and this demands the use of every legitimate weapon in our armory. We must dare to take the offensive, and to insist upon holding that offensive."[14] And in a 1972 newspaper article reporting on his role in the founding of IFACS, he said, "What we are concerned about is the battle for the minds of men. We feel basically called to an intellectual contribution in the war of ideas. This is our engagement."[15]

To Henry's way of thinking, the war being waged for hearts and minds would be won only through reason. In a 1958 editorial arguing for a Christian university as a "crucial key for unlocking and releasing this Christian contribution to social order," Henry makes no reference to regenerated hearts but focuses on reason as the avenue through which Christians must impact the culture. "For Christianity exalts God as Lord of the minds of men, and under

---

[11]Carl F. H. Henry, Report to the Board, May 28, 1957, Collection 3, Box 1, Archives of the Billy Graham Center.

[12]Even as Henry gained a wide following as editor of *CT*, he for the most part failed to push for "a new evangelical activism," says Richard Mouw. "Henry argued that the church has neither the 'competence' nor the 'authority' to pronounce on social specifics. The task of preaching, he insisted, was to offer general guidelines for faithful discipleship; the business of applying these guidelines to specific social situations was to be left to the individual"; Richard J. Mouw, "Awakening the Evangelical Conscience," *Christian History & Biography*, no. 92 (Fall 2006): 41.

[13]Carl F. H. Henry, "Christian Education and Culture," *Christianity Today*, November 10, 1958, p. 3.

[14]Carl F. H. Henry, "An Evangelical Protestant Strategy for the Late 1960s," undated, Collection 1, Box 15, Archives of the Billy Graham Center.

[15]UPI story of August 5, 1972, carried by papers across the country.

God seeks the spiritual and intelligible integration of all of life's experiences," he wrote. "Doubtless some religions degrade reason, but Christianity supports the intellectual integration of life and experience. The importance of reason is therefore an inescapable, enduring Christian emphasis."[16]

An "evangelical Harvard." In the best sense of the word, *CT* provided a bully pulpit for Henry to make his views known to a much wider audience. Through its pages he was able to further his educational mission and articulate a comprehensive and unifying world and life view. But as important as the magazine was in the "evangelical advance" that Henry felt called to lead, it paled in comparison to what he envisioned as the most essential weapon in the evangelical arsenal for combating the creeping humanistic worldview of contemporary culture: the establishment of a world-class evangelical university, an "evangelical Harvard." Henry floated this idea to Billy Graham a full year before *CT* got off the ground. And it was a vision he carried with him—unfulfilled—to his grave.

In an October 8, 1955, letter to Graham, Henry outlined his plan for a Christian university that would "attract students who would otherwise be inclined to go to the big established universities such as Harvard, Yale, etc."[17] Henry conceptualized this university as quite unlike the "established evangelical universities" of that day, institutions that he saw as having "abandoned the effective articulation of Christianity in relationship to the great cultural issues—education, economics, politics, art, and even theology—to the nonevangelical groups. Their passion has been evangelism, missions, and Christian education in the narrow sense, but not really Christian education in the large."[18] As historian Owen Strachan notes, the Christian university Henry mapped out was "to serve as a launching pad, not an endpoint, for bright young Christians," and he anticipated that many would choose it over the Ivy League schools.

---

[16]Henry, "Christian Education and Culture," p. 3.

[17]Quoting that letter, Owen Strachan writes that Henry described it as an institution "for preparing men professionally and for the pursuit of collegiate and post-collegiate studies leading to higher degrees, in an environment which so articulates evangelical Christianity in relationship to the cultural crisis in all the areas of study"; Owen Strachan, "Carl Henry's Grand Dream: A Gospel-Driven Christian School," Southern Baptist Theological Seminary website (September 13, 2013), www.sbts.edu/resources/towers/carl-henrys-grand-dream-a-gospel-driven-christian-school.

[18]Quoted in Owen Strachan, "Re-Enchanting the Evangelical Mind: Park Street Church's Harold Ockenga, the Boston Scholars, and the Mid-Century Intellectual Surge" (PhD diss., Trinity Evangelical Divinity School, 2011), p. 235.

Most importantly, said Henry, the school must have a faculty of "pure scholars" of Ivy League caliber who were "resolutely Christian."[19]

For years to come, Henry would propel forward various iterations of this vision for a Christian university. A 1960 editorial, one of several he wrote on the subject, asks, "Do We Need a Christian University?" and ends dramatically: "Perhaps it is too late for a Christian university. But of the need, the staggering need, there can be no doubt."[20] Over the next several decades, Henry would lobby again and again for a world-class evangelical university where "the mind of modernity" could be confronted in a systematic and rational manner. As late as 1989 he wrote about the need for evangelicals to enter into "pluralistic dialogue concerning American education" in an effort to demonstrate the intellectual validity of Christian claims:

> Unless Christian education publicly expounds its way of knowing God; and unless it strenuously proclaims universally valid truth; and unless it identifies the criteria for testing and verifying the knowledge-claims we make, then the Christian view of God and the world will survive as but a fading oddity in an academic world that questions its legitimacy and appropriateness.[21]

That his idea for an evangelical university never gained traction Henry attributed to a lack of vision on the part of evangelical leaders.[22] In meetings with "leading evangelical academicians" and "financially gifted evangelical laymen," Henry said, "the fortunes of a great evangelical university were debated, romanced, and eventually forfeited. The main obstacle was not money. Missing, rather, was a lack of consensus among potential supporters over whether American Christianity really needed a first-class university."[23]

He noted the confusion among American evangelicals over "what constitutes a university," citing Bob Jones, Oral Roberts, John Brown, Taylor, Seattle Pacific, Biola and Liberty among Christian colleges that understand the term to mean "an oversized college that offers some graduate courses alongside un-

---

[19]Ibid., p. 237.

[20]Carl F. H. Henry, "Do We Need a Christian University?" *Christianity Today*, May 9, 1960, p. 5.

[21]Carl F. H. Henry, "The Crisis of the Campus: Shall We Flunk the Educators?" *Faculty Dialogue* (Spring 1989): 35.

[22]In 1994, Henry looked back with pride at the response his initial 1960 editorial received: "Echoing conversations with evangelical academicians teaching in secular universities, the essay was publicized widely by *The New York Times*, national radio, and the religious press"; Carl F. H. Henry, *Gods of This Age or God of the Ages?* (Nashville: Broadman & Holman, 1994), p. 109.

[23]Ibid.

dergraduate studies" and one or two doctorates.[24] Clearly Henry had something of a different order in mind:

> This task is not adequately performed by any existing evangelical college or university on either the graduate or the undergraduate level. . . . [A] Christian university can set an example of human energy in the service of the true, the good, and the beautiful—in short, of man intelligently devoted to God and his revealed will.[25]

Henry's retelling of the circumstances that led to the death of his dream sounds somewhat dispassionate, but his words convey deep disappointment and perhaps some bitterness over the fact that the plan he had nurtured of evangelicals confronting "the mind of modernity" through a world-class university never came to fruition. "Evangelicals by and large responded more readily to evangelistic efforts with immediate tangible results than to long-range educational efforts seeking to challenge and alter the secular intellectual climate of our times," he wrote.[26] Henry, on the other hand, spent his lifetime intent on doing nothing less than intellectually challenging the climate of the times.

CARL H. LUNDQUIST: TRAINING "CITIZENS OF THE WHOLE WORLD"

Presenting a different perspective on Christian higher education was Henry's contemporary Carl H. Lundquist, an evangelical leader in his own right. Best known for his role as president of Bethel College and Seminary in St. Paul, Minnesota (1954–1982), Lundquist played leadership roles in a host of evangelical and higher education organizations, making important, behind-the-scenes contributions that have often been overlooked.

In addition to serving as president of the National Association of Evangelicals from 1978 to 1980, Lundquist was a contributor and resource scholar for *Christianity Today* and a board member of World Relief, the Baptist World Alliance and other evangelical and higher education organizations. Having already helped found what is now the Council of Christian Colleges & Universities and the Fellowship of Evangelical Seminary Presidents, Lundquist served as president of the Christian College Consortium after his retirement from Bethel in 1982. Before his death in 1991 he also traveled worldwide with his wife,

---

[24]Ibid., pp. 110, 113.
[25]Carl F. H. Henry, "The Need for a Christian University," *Christianity Today*, February 17, 1967, p. 8.
[26]Henry, *Gods of This Age or God of the Ages?*, p. 110.

Nancy, to lead devotional retreats on behalf of the Evangelical Order of the Burning Heart.[27]

Through his involvement in various evangelical causes and on behalf of Christian higher education, Lundquist provided foundational leadership to many emerging neo-evangelical organizations at a critical time in their development. Participating on a leadership level in some of the same initiatives as Henry, Lundquist was perhaps one of the evangelical leaders unwilling to get behind Henry's "big vision" for a world-class evangelical university that would "alter the secular intellectual climate of our times," as Henry put it.[28]

Though he expressed admiration for Henry and brought him to Bethel as a campus speaker from time to time, Lundquist would have at least taken a different approach than Henry to the task of bringing about change in the wider culture. Even as he challenged fellow evangelicals to think big regarding any undertaking for Christ, Lundquist placed great emphasis on personal piety, irenicism and humility as the starting points for any Christian endeavor. Motivated by a deep love for the world and an optimistic outlook, Lundquist often framed the issue of social involvement in terms of embrace of the world as opposed to the imagery of conflict and battle often found in Henry's prose.

Pietism did much to shape Lundquist's understanding of education and approach to cultural engagement, as can be seen in the following pillars of his educational vision.

A vital interior life with Christ at the center. As president of a Christian college and seminary for twenty-eight years, Carl Lundquist had ample opportunity to both articulate and implement a Christian philosophy of education in a way that Henry did not. Understanding Christian higher education on a practical and not merely a theoretical level, Lundquist held to a philosophy of education that was rooted in relationship and lived experience of Christ, with loyalties to any creed or commitment to orthodoxy of comparatively lesser importance. Known as a person with a deep devotional life, Lundquist wrote in 1959 that the unifying center of Christian higher education was "neither Truth nor the Pursuit of Truth but is Jesus Christ Himself. . . . It is in the light

---

[27]These and other involvements are outlined in James and Carole Spickelmier's recent biography of Lundquist, *Give First Priority to Jesus Christ* (St. Paul, MN: The History Center, 2013), p. 14.

[28]See James Patterson's account of involvement by both Henry and Lundquist in early initiatives for evangelical higher education; James A. Patterson, *Shining Lights: A History of the Council for Christian Colleges & Universities* (Grand Rapids: Baker Academic, 2001), pp. 27-36.

of our relationship to Jesus Christ, therefore, that students are recruited, teachers are selected, courses are constructed, personnel policies are adopted, discipline is handled, and student activities are planned."[29]

Like study, life together at Bethel was christocentric. "Whatever may be our secondary allegiances our primary loyalty is to Jesus Christ as Lord," Lundquist said at a 1970 faculty and staff retreat. "We love Him because He first loves us. He has become the supreme affection of our lives. As a result we enjoy a personal and intimate relationship with the Lord that adds the warm overtones of deep spiritual devotion to all of life." Acknowledging the school's pietistic heritage, he stated, "Bethel grew out of reaction to cold, formal religion in Sweden, however orthodox it may have been theologically. To our forefathers Christianity was more than a creed. It was Christ. It was life. We are both truest to our tradition and timeliest on the current scene when we continue to stress the genuine life that is in Christ." The university as community becomes "one" at the point of its "common love for the Savior and our commitment to Him," concluded Lundquist.[30]

The mutual enrichment of the spiritual and the intellectual. Because the "compelling idea" behind Bethel's existence was primarily a religious one, on the Christian campus there was no dichotomy between the sacred and the secular, said Lundquist: "Each interpenetrates the other. Piety alone cannot be substituted for rigorous learning experiences that will offer to the student as challenging and demanding an education as he could secure in a top-flight secular school."[31] That view was reiterated in a recent biography of Lundquist by his daughter and son-in-law, Carole and Jim Spickelmier, who emphasize that he was concerned both about "the spiritual tone of the campus" and its academic rigor.[32]

A personal relationship with Jesus Christ, not ideas or intellectual engagement, was the core of Christian higher education, from Lundquist's perspective. If the school had to make a choice between the ideals of academic

---

[29]Carl H. Lundquist, "1959 Presidential Report," in *1959 Annual—Baptist General Conference* (Chicago: BGC, 1959), p. 137.

[30]Lundquist, "Bethel as Community," *The [Baptist General Conference] Standard,* October 5, 1970, pp. 16-17.

[31]Carl H. Lundquist, "1965 Presidential Report," in *1965 Annual—Baptist General Conference* (Chicago: BGC, 1965), p. 119.

[32]Spickelmier and Spickelmier, *Give First Priority to Jesus Christ,* especially chap. 7.

competence and Christian dedication in its faculty, he said, the school would "compromise at the point of scholarship" before it would "at the point of Christian character." But he was quick to add, "We hope that we shall never have to make such a compromise. We want both. We believe that in the end the impact of one life upon another is probably greater than the impact of an idea or a method of teaching or a favorable physical setting."[33]

The link between the mission of the church and the Christian college. "Carl Lundquist was a church man first," said former Bethel president George K. Brushaber, who succeeded Lundquist at that post in 1982. "His passion was for the church man in the pew and individual churches in the denomination. . . . The school under Carl defined the denomination."[34]

Lundquist asserted in 1959 that the Christian college functioned best when it was rooted within a denominational framework and tied to the mission of the church. "It is recognized that evangelism and education are but two sides of the same coin," he said, "and both are included in the Great Commission."[35] Twenty years later, in articulating his philosophy of education, Lundquist highlighted the "enduring values" of the denomination's Swedish heritage that needed to be preserved for future generations. The emphasis on the personal and experiential was something to be highly valued, he said, and an "overarching contribution of our pietistic heritage to the new world. Rigorous scholarship is stressed and rewarded, but the results are to be laid at the feet of the Savior as an offering of love and devotion to Him."[36]

A hopeful engagement with culture. During the social unrest of the late 1960s and early '70s Lundquist expressed an optimistic outlook regarding the "concerns of the new generation," claiming that those concerns "make it a great day to be in Christian higher education." Encouraging students to engage the wider culture, Lundquist said that what he wanted to see on campus was "a positive Christian alternation between involvement *with* society and with-

---

[33]Lundquist, "1959 Presidential Report," p. 144.

[34]Brushaber, interview with author.

[35]Lundquist, "1959 Presidential Report," p. 137.

[36]Lundquist, "1979 Presidential Report," *1979 Annual—Baptist General Conference* (Evanston, IL: BGC, 1979), p. 100. At that time he outlined nine "controlling ideas" that he considered pivotal to his leadership of the school, having been "tested and refined through the years." They included understanding Christ as the intellectual center of the universe and education as the cutting edge of the church; the conviction that a denominational school should strengthen the whole church of Christ; and that to be truly Christian, a school must be characterized by integrity.

drawal *from* society." The tension, he said, was no longer between scholarship and devotion but between "activism and pietism," because for the Christian, "activism and pietism are complementary emphases." Lundquist's attitude toward "the world" was one of openness and welcome because "both Christian and non-Christian youth are talking about metaphysical matters. Schools like Bethel . . . are more important than ever to the well-being of America."[37]

Lundquist's view that piety and social action are interdependent makes him a model of "missional pietism," states historian Christopher Gehrz:

> Given the generational tensions gripping college campuses in 1969–1970, it is striking that Lundquist, though concerned that Bethel students not be "worldly" in their behavior, demonstrated considerable openness to and love for segments of "the world" that other conservative Christians regarded with disdain or outright hostility.[38]

In this respect, says Gehrz, Lundquist "affirmed the postfundamentalist evangelical desire to interact with culture rather than retreat from it," but he did so by emphasizing "that activism can only bear fruit if it is rooted in a Christ-centered, conversional piety."[39]

Lundquist noted the historical roots within the Baptist General Conference of social action and the importance of Henry's book, *The Uneasy Conscience of Modern Fundamentalism*, in reminding evangelicals of their "neglected mission" to address the social ills of the world. "Our basic goal at Bethel is the preparation of young people who will make a difference for Christ in the world. If they are to affect the structures of society later, they must be involved in its structures now and permeate them with Christian values," he said. "Bethel seeks to develop its own revolutionaries—young people who will seek to affect this world for Christ and to change it by the power of His Spirit."[40]

Rather than being threatened by student involvement in antiwar protests across from campus or by those who tested the limits on lifestyle issues, Lundquist welcomed student activism, provided there was an equal emphasis on withdrawal from society through a pietistic commitment to a life of devotion

---

[37]Carl H. Lundquist, "1970 Presidential Report," *1970 Annual—Baptist General Conference* (Evanston, IL: BGC, 1970), pp. 120-34. The quotations are from pp. 122, 124 and 131.

[38]Christopher Gehrz, "Missional Pietists: Lessons from Dale W. Brown and Carl H. Lundquist," *The Covenant Quarterly* 70 (August/November 2012): 42.

[39]Ibid., p. 45.

[40]Lundquist, "1970 Presidential Report," pp. 127-29.

and prayer. While Lundquist was known for his irenic and welcoming spirit, he also "unabashedly promoted abstinence and pietistic, holy living."[41]

Lundquist appeared to embrace the culture much more so than Carl Henry, who saw it as inhospitable to a Christian worldview. "In our school we emphasize that we are to penetrate the structures of society for Christ and be a part of the world," Lundquist said during a *Christianity Today* roundtable discussion with Christian college presidents in the fall of 1975. "The world setting itself is amoral, and many of its prevailing moods are neither good nor bad. It's simply the medium in which we work."[42]

In his silver anniversary report to the denomination, Lundquist described at length his vision for how students receiving the kind of Christian liberal arts education Bethel offered could have a positive influence on the wider culture:

> The liberally educated person . . . has become a citizen of the whole world at the same time that he has learned to live at home in an unseen world. All of this is the result of a Christocentric, liberal education which enables a students to relate to Jesus Christ all of the knowledge, appreciations, skills and motivations developed on campus and to apply them meaningfully to the purposes of God in His world. As the church concentrates on basic Christ-centered liberal education, it will enable its youth to make the most powerful impact for Christ upon all the structures of society.[43]

Lundquist's goal was to train citizens "of the whole world" who related to those outside the Christian community as "fellow creations of God." A liberal arts education developed under his leadership would be not only the means of liberation "from the chains of ignorance, provincialism, bigotry and narrowness," but would also set students free to become their "unique and creative best for the glory of God." Embedded in Lundquist's vision was an attitude of hopefulness and a commitment to cultural engagement attractive to a future generation of young evangelicals, many of whom are more drawn to the kind of deep personal piety and bottom-side-up activism Lundquist modeled than to the top-side-down intellectual engagement that Henry proposed.

---

[41]Paul L. H. Olson, "A University and Its Denomination: The Ties That Bind in the 21st Century" (EdD diss., University of Pennsylvania, 2005), p. 134. See Carl H. Lundquist, *Silent Issues of the Church* (Wheaton, IL: Victor Books, 1985).

[42]"Christian Educators Face the Issues," *Christianity Today*, November 7, 1975, p. 12.

[43]Lundquist, "1979 Presidential Report," p. 96.

Conclusion: Of Humility and Big Dreams

Lundquist was not naive as to how Pietism was viewed by fellow evangelicals influenced by the Reformed tradition (including Henry), but he stood firm in his conviction that Pietism made a unique contribution to evangelical higher education. "On many campuses with a strong Reformed doctrinal emphasis there is a built-in suspicion of Pietism which tends to downplay personal spiritual development in favor of a rigorous intellectual program," Lundquist wrote. "Thus there is a uniqueness about Bethel when compared to many schools with almost identical confessions of faith."[44]

Lundquist clearly saw the two emphases as complementary: "Understanding without devotion can be cold and formal. Devotion without understanding can lead to subjectivism and heresy. Each is incomplete without the other."[45] Henry seemed less inclined to be so generous in his assessment of Pietism. Despite his commitment to irenicism, he appears to have held little appreciation for pietistic contributions to the evangelical cause, and on at least a couple of occasions emphasized the link between Pietism and anti-intellectualism. For instance, in a 1958 editorial, he contended that "academic sterility" is a far greater threat to the faith than is rationalism: "Academic cretinism augurs not only a pietistic structure of anti-intellectualism but a stunted expression of the broader implications of revealed religion."[46] Almost twenty years later, he recalled that the neo-evangelicals of the 1940s and '50s "reached behind twentieth-century fundamentalism and appealed to a longer past. This longer look encouraged a revolt against pietism not simply disinterested in but even disdainful of serious intellectual pursuits."[47]

Henry's perspective illustrates Kurt Peterson and R. J. Snell's observation that "when Pietism is mentioned it is most often misunderstood and derided as the enemy of learning." They claim that Pietists were not anti-intellectual but "were suspicious of reason only when governed by the wrong master" and part of a desire "to hold everything, including the mind, captive to the word of God." A Pietist model of higher education does not "over think" itself, state Peterson and Snell. It "assumes the formation of not just minds but persons, not just

---

[44]Carl H. Lundquist, "The Best of the Past as a Gift to the Future," *The Baptist Pietist Clarion* (June 2007): 5.

[45]Ibid.

[46]Henry, "Christian Education and Culture," p. 6.

[47]Carl F. H. Henry, *Evangelicals in Search of Identity* (Waco, TX: Word Books, 1976), p. 30.

ideas but loves, and not just individuals but communities of friendship."[48]

Such a model was the one held by Carl Lundquist, known as a "true Pietist" because of the depth of his devotional and prayer life. His concern for the spiritual disciplines was balanced with his advocacy for education and the responsibility of Christians to be involved in society. Lundquist argued that the spiritual and academic were not "dichotomous" but that they should exist "in vital two-way interaction in which each enriches the other."[49] Or as George Brushaber put it, "Carl Lundquist cared about theology and theological precision more than most Pietists, but personal piety and the interiality of faith were most important to him. The passion of his heart was the grounding of students in biblical patterns of belief and practice."[50]

Henry "dreamed big," acknowledged Brushaber. "He saw a movement and thought this could be another Reformation. He was no small thinker." But while he was a brilliant man, his dream for an evangelical university "to compete with the Harvards of this world" was a wonderful but impractical one. "Carl Henry didn't understand faculty culture, shared governance, and the nuts and bolts of how you would put something like this together," Brushaber said. "By the early '70s the notion of a Christian university was only a memory, and there were no serious advocates for it."[51]

Lundquist's vision was "more communal and rooted" than Henry's, said Brushaber, who knew and worked with both men. "Carl Henry wanted to address Christianity with a capital 'C,'" he said. "The notion Henry had of building this cultural and intellectual center to which the whole world would come was not at all Lundquist's vision. Carl Lundquist was not an empire builder. He never aspired to be the leader of the evangelical world. There was a humility in him that would have made it very difficult for him to embrace a vision such as Carl Henry's."[52]

---

[48]Kurt W. Peterson and R. J. Snell, "'Faith Forms the Intellectual Task': The Pietist Option in Christian Higher Education," in *The Pietist Impulse in Christianity*, pp. 218, 221, 229.

[49]Carl H. Lundquist, "1963 Presidential Report," *1963 Annual—Baptist General Conference* (Chicago: BGC, 1963), p. 86.

[50]Brushaber interview with author.

[51]Ibid.

[52]Ibid.

5

Reconceiving the Christ-Centered College

Convertive Piety and Life Together

Roger E. Olson

◆

FROM A PIETIST PERSPECTIVE Christ-centered education begins with the experience of knowing Jesus Christ personally.[1] Such a model of Christian higher education values *transformation* over *information* without discarding or demeaning information and critical thinking.

As this book has emphasized, the main purpose of a Pietist approach to higher education is the shaping of Christian character, helping students become "whole and holy persons." Such transformation requires life-transforming encounters with God through Jesus Christ in the power of the Holy Spirit. Without setting aside critical inquiry or generous orthodoxy, it focuses on orthopathy and orthopraxy. The ultimate goal or telos of such Christian higher education is not mere knowledge or skill but character.

That means that Christian higher education is primarily about instilling certain dispositions in persons, dispositions that can be summed up in the word *integrity*—all of life and thought centered consistently around the person of Jesus Christ: his love, his justice, his peace, his care for persons. The ethos of such a Christian higher education community forbids duplicity, double stan-

---

[1]For a contrasting view of what "Christ-centered" means in the context of higher education, see Duane Litfin, *Conceiving the Christian College* (Grand Rapids: Eerdmans, 2004), particularly chap. 4.

dards, revenge, punitive treatment of persons, excessive competition, harassment and apathy. It promotes compassion, honesty, justice, fairness, redemptive treatment of persons, forgiveness, cooperation, respect and dedication.

THE PIETIST ETHOS IN HIGHER EDUCATION: CHRIST CENTERED, PERSON CENTERED

I have had the privilege of working and living in two Christian higher education communities that strived, and I trust still strive, to embody this Pietist ethos. During my fifteen years at the first one I observed in amazement how, for the most part and most of the time, the faculty, administration and staff worked together for the common good under the lordship of Jesus Christ. Our common experience of him and commitment to his lordship rubbed off on students as we modeled it before them. A concrete example of that was my coteaching with three other professors a required freshman course called Christianity and Western Culture for nearly fifteen years. The four of us prayed together, collaborated, critiqued ourselves and one another in love, and demonstrated before the freshmen how Christian colleagues can work and teach in harmony in spite of very different personalities and intellectual styles.

I've been teaching in a seminary now for as long as I was on the faculty of that Christian liberal arts college. Upon arriving at Bethel College I recognized a Pietist impulse at work in the way the curriculum was designed, the emphasis on spiritual formation, and the person-centered ethos of the community. At the center of everything about the seminary is Jesus Christ and personal experience of his living, transforming presence. Professors as well as students meet weekly for hour-long "covenant group" meetings in which we practice *lectio divina* and pray for one another, our community and the world. In my covenant group we sing hymns and tell stories of our spiritual journeys.

My point is that there exists a distinctive Pietist *ethos* that shapes some Christian colleges, seminaries and other Christian educational communities. Because the ethos is Christ centered, it is also *person centered*. To use an early Pietist phrase, it sees the purpose of existence as "for God's glory and the neighbor's good."[2] Therefore, the purpose of education is to glorify God and form persons in God's image—that is, to heal and make whole God's image in them.

---

[2] See Gary R. Sattler, *God's Glory, Neighbor's Good: A Brief Introduction to the Life and Writings of August Hermann Francke* (Chicago: Covenant Press, 1982).

I believe this ethos translates in many ways into the character of a Pietist-inspired institution of higher education. One way is that such an institution—or better, community—will be a safe place for sincere questioning. I believe a Christ-centered and Christ-serving college or university is one where community members feel safe entering into conversation with one another about constructing a Christian life and worldview that draws on and does justice to all the disciplines without prejudice. Vital higher education requires critical thinking and inquiry. A Pietist community of higher education should be one where people who dare to question "settled answers" intelligently and sincerely, without a spirit of iconoclasm or skepticism for its own sake, are affirmed rather than shamed into silence or punished.

One of the pathologies of Pietism, of course, is anti-intellectualism. Another is superspiritual otherworldliness. Yet another is legalism. None of these is necessary to true Pietism, but they are all manifestations of what I call Pietism "gone to seed"—Pietism that has lost its way and allowed certain dangers inherent in its spiritual emphasis to take over and control it. In reaction against these dangers, attempting to cure these pathologies, some respond to Pietism by throwing the baby out with the bathwater—something I continually warn against doing.[3] My argument here is that true Pietism is Christ centered and therefore person centered and therefore never anti-intellectual, otherworldly or judgmental.

A PIETIST UNDERSTANDING OF "THE LIFE OF THE MIND"

The life of the mind is part of the image of God, and exercising it even with critical questioning of settled traditions is part of transformation, growth in the image of God. God is the creator of the world and Christ is Lord of it, so superspiritual otherworldliness that ignores justice here and now is antithetical to Christ-centered piety. Judgmental legalism is by its very nature crushing to persons; true Pietism is grace filled and compassionate.

Another of Pietism's pathologies, however, is the tension it must negotiate between spirituality and intellectual honesty and excellence. Two things can happen within a Pietist ethos: it can lead to anti-intellectualism, or it can lead to dualism—a separating between the life of the spirit and the life of the mind so that they are never integrated. The challenge facing a Pietist-inspired com-

---

[3]As in Roger E. Olson, "Pietism: Myths and Realities," in *The Pietist Impulse in Christianity*, ed. Christian T. Collins Winn et al. (Eugene, OR: Pickwick, 2011), pp. 3-16.

munity of higher education is emphasizing equally and in a noncompetitive way both spiritual experience and critical, intellectual inquiry in all aspects and disciplines of the institution. This is part of the ongoing conversation and even debate that makes up the Pietist tradition. There is no easy solution; no rules or litmus tests can be given out.

The reason this is a tension that often turns into debate is that true Pietism, as opposed to liberal Pietism, holds to a cognitive content of Christianity. For true Pietism, going back to its roots in Philipp Jakob Spener, August Hermann Francke and others who founded the movement, Christianity is not only a feeling. It is that, but it cannot be reduced to that. True Pietists did not and never have tossed aside Christian orthodoxy or the Bible as authority for faith and practice—even as they held that transforming experience of God is primary for defining true Christianity.

It is simply a misunderstanding of Pietism to assume, as some have, that since person-transforming spiritual experience of God is what's permanent and most important in Christianity, there is no firm, definite, nonnegotiable cognitive content to Christianity. That would be like assuming that since persons are more important than rules, rules are unnecessary. Communities must have rules, but from a Pietist perspective they serve persons, not the other way around. So it is with beliefs and doctrines. They serve persons, not the other way around. But they are necessary. From a Pietist perspective, doctrines have a ministerial function, not a magisterial one.

CONTROVERSY WITHIN COMMUNITY

Okay, but that still leaves a question unanswered. What happens in a Pietist community, especially one dedicated to critical inquiry—"science" broadly understood—when a person not only questions but denies a settled, nonnegotiable doctrine? Sooner or later, every Pietist community faces this issue.

Of course, there's no Pietist formula for handling heresy. There's no Pietist rulebook that addresses the problem and tells how to approach it. So we are left to draw on Pietist impulses—the Pietist ethos, if you will—to discern how best to handle it.

It seems to me that if the person pronouncing the heresy is part of the community, the community itself has to take some responsibility for failing to nurture him or her in the right way. But it also has to consider the possibility that the heretic is right and the community's tradition is wrong. Finally, being person centered, not rule or doctrine centered, the community ought to express to itself and the world around it that, even though this is not what the community believes, it values the person enough to keep him or her as a vital member and move on with dissent in its midst.

I am told that the Baptist General Conference (BGC), a denomination founded by Swedish Pietists, ran into this very issue during its formative years. A leading pastor named A. P. Ekman denied the doctrine of the atonement. John Alexis Edgren and other Conference leaders gently remonstrated with him. When Ekman persisted they affirmed him as a valued member anyway, prayed that God would help them deal wisely with the disagreement, and went their separate ways without excommunicating him.[4] This story used to be often told by BGC leaders as an example of Pietist "irenicism." Eventually, however, as the BGC was affected by fundamentalism and then entered into the wider "generic evangelicalism" of the American evangelical movement, the story became something of an embarrassment. The point is, however, that authentic Christian Pietism, as a movement and ethos, always held firmly to the doctrine of the atonement while at the same time making room for those who had their doubts.

This Pietist irenic ethos was put to the test at the Christian college where I taught in the 1990s. Some constituents of the college and seminary judged that a professor had expressed heretical opinions and ought to be fired. Great pressure was put on the administration to do just that. The administration organized a "Day of Theological Clarification." The "jury" was composed of all the tenured professors of theology of the college and seminary. Some who were retired were invited to serve on it. Most of us disagreed with our colleague's controversial opinion, but we voted unanimously to keep him among us. The same result happened when the denomination took up the issue of what to do with him. I would say the institution and denomination passed the test with flying Pietist colors.

A PIETIST EPISTEMOLOGY?

Finally, is there a Pietist way of knowing, of investigating, of thinking about the phenomena of heaven and earth—the things we study and teach in higher

---

[4]The "atonement controversy" is covered (with obvious admiration for Edgren's handling of it) by L. J. Ahlstrom, *John Alexis Edgren* (Chicago: Conference Press, 1938), pp. 149-57.

education? I do think Pietism affects, colors and influences the *ways* we go about our investigations, but I don't believe in a "Pietist epistemology" as such. How does it affect, color and influence our ways of studying and thinking about heaven and earth?

I judge that there is real tension between classical foundationalism and Pietism. At best the two fit uncomfortably together. Pietism is not an epistemology, but it is a *posture*—a posture toward reality. So is classical foundationalism. I know I tread on thin ice here, so I'll tread lightly.

It seems to me that classical foundationalism *tends* to treat knowledge as objective; perspective is set aside, bracketed out. Only that counts as "knowledge" that can be proven objectively, or at least intersubjectively, using logic working from indubitable truths of reason or experience. "Faith" is ruled out as irrelevant at best and corrupting of the search for truth at worst.

While classical foundationalism may work well, as an ideal, in the so-called hard or experimental sciences such as physics, it seems less appropriate in the search for truth in the human sciences. Postmodern thought is showing us that even in the so-called hard or experimental sciences, however, something like faith, at least perspective, is inescapable. Cold, hard rationalism is at best an ideal. There is no "view from nowhere."

But Christian Pietism says there ought not to be a view from nowhere. Not only does such not exist; for the Christian it ought not exist. Kierkegaard's "passionate inwardness," faith in Jesus Christ as Lord of all, a transformed perspective on reality that puts God at the center, is part and parcel of the transformation wrought by the Holy Spirit in conversion.[5] Conversional piety is the ongoing process of being transformed in mind as well as in character—to see everything in the light of God as Creator and Redeemer.

This Christian pietistic perspectivalism plays itself out, I think, in various ways, depending on the discipline. But all have in common "seeing the world *as*" God's good creation, loved by God and being redeemed by Jesus Christ, who calls us into being, created cocreators of a new creation with God through the Holy Spirit. They also have in common *love* for God's creation and *hope* for new creation—for redemption, for the promised liberation of creation from bondage to decay—and *faith* that our efforts, together with God's grace and

---

[5]For an introduction to the great Danish philosopher, see C. Stephen Evans, *Kierkegaard: An Introduction* (Cambridge: Cambridge University Press, 2009).

power, can make a difference penultimately, even if only God can liberate creation fully and ultimately.

Put another way, Christian Pietism is a posture that "sees" all disciplines taught in the university as servants of the *missio dei*—of God's mission in the world to heal it and draw it to himself.

"Integration of faith and learning," then, from a Pietist perspective, is not so much subordinating every discipline to a rigid, detailed, rationally coherent worldview as regarding every discipline as a servant of the mission of God and therefore dedicated to healing, to making whole, to bringing harmony out of chaos and peace out of strife.

The issue for mathematics, for example, is not what difference Christian doctrine makes for how it's practiced but what difference Christian faith, as participation in the mission of God, makes for viewing mathematics' purpose. Why *be* a mathematician? A Pietist would answer, "For God's glory and the neighbor's good"—and creation's healing.

In my own opinion, there are certain theories, ways of seeing reality *as*, that Christianity rules out. They may not be as obvious in mathematics as in, say, the social sciences, but they are probably somewhere in every discipline *as it is practiced by secular theorists*. I believe a true Pietist cannot embrace social Darwinism—a common alternative view of life's meaning and purpose that infects both the "right" and the "left" in the modern world. Not so much an epistemology as a posture, Pietism does not require any one theory in any discipline. But I think it tends to conflict with rationalism and finds certain points of congeniality with postmodernism.[6]

In summary, a Pietist will always shine the critical light of faith in God as Creator and Redeemer on every theory and adopt and adapt only those that fit with the mission of God into his or her practice and teaching of his or her discipline.

---

[6]See Roger E. Olson, "Pietism and Postmodernism: Points of Congeniality," *Christian Scholar's Review* 41 (Summer 2012): 367-80.

PART TWO

CHANGED PEOPLE
CHANGING THE WORLD

Pietists and Their Neighbors' Good

One shows oneself as a Christian so far as one is a
true person of prayer before God and practices love toward
neighbor. Otherwise it is all empty talk.

AUGUST HERMANN FRANCKE,
"THE DUTY TO THE POOR" (1697 SERMON)

6

The Common Priesthood
Seeking the Common Good

Dale G. Durie

◆

WITH THE SIMPLE MOTTO "For God's glory and neighbor's good," German Pietism offered a grand vision of the Christian's potential impact in the world. All believers, taught pastors such as Philipp Jakob Spener and August Hermann Francke, could bring glory to God and affect their neighbor for good. While such a notion may not seem radical in our day, it was in the late seventeenth and early eighteenth centuries, and it became part of the shared language of a movement that inspired reform in the European church and pockets of significant change within European culture.

As those who teach and learn at a school with a pietistic heritage, we desire to see movements like this one today. We desire to lift up this grand vision such that we are "salt and light" and "world changers."[1] Yet we, and the faith communities we call home, often fail to see how our work, play and service could actually be participation in the mission of God in the world (*missio Dei*). We might say "Amen" on Sunday to the notion that we have a purpose to play in God's mission, but on Monday it is swallowed up by the realities of life. A movement like the one Spener participated in seems far from a possibility in our faith communities, our neighborhoods and our workplaces.

The failure to see purpose in our work and effect change in our world

---

[1]To name two of Bethel University's "core values" ("Values," Bethel University website, www.bethel.edu/about/values).

should not, however, lead us to throw up our hands. It should push us to dig deeper and to look closer at what inspired this movement and its mantra. The vision of "God's glory and neighbor's good" stems from the Pietist commitment to two crucially important principles: the common priesthood and the common good. And maybe, if we are captured by this theology, we might recast this vision in such a way that it again launches movements of change in our own time.

The Common Priesthood in Scripture

The common priesthood finds its origins in the Garden, before the fall. It's important to see how crucial the common priesthood is throughout salvation history so we can understand why its recover today is so important. Wheaton scholar John Walton points out that Genesis 1–2, when understood in its ancient Mesopotamian context, depicts a temple dedication, with humanity analogous to the priests in the "temple" of the Garden. Speaking of these ancient ceremonies, Walton notes, "During the seven days, the functions of the temple would be proclaimed, the furniture and functionaries installed, the priests would take up their role and at the end, the deity would enter and take up his rest."[2] Walton concludes, "With the mention of God's rest on day seven, we can see that Genesis 1 is thinking of the cosmos (the universe) as a temple. God is creating his dwelling place, putting people into it as his images (representatives), and taking up his place at the helm to maintain the order he established."[3]

Central to day six of most temple dedications was the installation of priests. In the creation account, on day six God creates people as image bearers (Gen 1:26-27), an act that had an obvious priestly connotation in its ancient context, as Walton explains:

> In the ancient world an image was believed in some way to carry the essence of that which it represented. An idol image of deity, designated by the same terminology used here, was used in worship because it contained the deity's essence . . . the deity's work was thought to be accomplished through the idol. . . . In

---

[2]John H. Walton, from a handout given at a postdoctorate week of study on Genesis. A similar outline is available as John H. Walton, "Genesis 1 as Ancient Cosmology" (March 2010), www.bibleinterp .com/articles/genesis1357910.shtml. For a fuller development of these ideas, see Walton, *The Lost World of Genesis One: Ancient Cosmology and the Origins Debate* (Downers Grove, IL: InterVarsity Press, 2009).

[3]Walton, Genesis handout.

Mesopotamia a significance of the image can be seen in the practice of kings setting up images of themselves in places where they wanted to establish their authority.[4]

He concludes, "The image of God in people provides them the capacity not only to serve as God's vice-regents (his representatives containing his essence), but also the capacity to be and act like him."[5] Israel's God, unlike other gods, granted jurisdiction for ruling to people, giving all "people the mission of bringing order to their world just as God brought order to the cosmos."[6]

Humanity's common priesthood is also made clear in the Genesis 2 telling of the creation story. Here God puts Adam and Eve in the garden to "work it" and to "take care of it" (Gen 2:15 TNIV[7]). These terms are used elsewhere by Moses to refer to priestly service in the tabernacle (see Ex 3:12; Num 3:7-10; 8:15). People, then, serve as priests in God's temple by drawing out the latent potential in creation ("work it") and by protecting the purity and emerging beauty of the garden ("take care of it").

Of course this beautiful picture of a common priesthood working for the common good was defaced by rebellion. Walton, in summarizing Genesis 1–3, observes that

> God created everything just right for people, but sin came through disobedience and brought corruption, impacting not only individuals, but permeating families and society and eventually all of creation. . . . Since people had distanced themselves from God and knowledge of God had become distorted and corrupted, reclamation was necessary.[8]

This reclamation project of families, societies and all of creation was first launched through the covenant people of God whom we call the Israelites. The priestly echoes of Genesis can be heard as God covenants with Israel: "I will make you into a great nation, and I will bless you; I will make your name great, and *you will be a blessing*. I will bless those who bless you, and whoever curses you I will curse; and *all peoples on earth* will be blessed through you" (Gen 12:2-3, italics mine).

---

[4]John H. Walton, *Genesis*, NIV Application Commentary (Grand Rapids: Zondervan, 2001), p. 130.
[5]Ibid., p. 131.
[6]Ibid., p. 136.
[7]Unless otherwise specified, all biblical quotations in this chapter are from the TNIV.
[8]Walton, *Genesis*, p. 37.

The priestly sounds of Genesis also echo in the covenant at Mount Sinai.

> Then . . . the LORD called to (Moses) from the mountain and said, "This is what
> you are to say to the house of Jacob and what you are to tell the people of Israel:
> 'You yourselves have seen what I did to Egypt, and how I carried you on eagles'
> wings and brought you to myself. Now if you obey me fully and keep my cov-
> enant, then out of all nations you will be my treasured possession. Although the
> whole earth is mine, you will be for me a *kingdom of priests* and a holy nation.'"
> (Ex 19:3-6)

As a kingdom of priests, Israel was to be a blessing to all nations. Through them
the whole earth was to be blessed, as God intended in the Garden.

Yet Israel failed in its mission. It rejected its identity as a kingdom of priests,
leaving such work exclusively to the office of priest (Ex 20:18-20). Later, Israel
demanded a king to rule it like all the other nations, rejecting YHWH as its
king (1 Sam 8:7). And eventually, due to open rebellion, the bright light intended to draw nations to God is instead sent into captivity among the nations
(Jer 29). In exile, ironically, Israel does serve as a light to the nations, but not as
the beacon of hope God intended.

Driven by a desire for a kingdom of priests serving the common good, Jesus
came as a high priest in the service of God to aid God's people. The author of
the book of Hebrews writes,

> Since the children have flesh and blood, he too shared in their humanity so that
> by his death he might break the power of him who holds the power of death—
> that is, the devil—and free those who all their lives were held in slavery by their
> fear of death. *For surely it is not angels he helps, but Abraham's descendants.* For
> this reason he had to be made like his brothers and sisters in every way, in order
> that he might become a merciful and faithful *high priest in service to God*, and
> that he might make atonement for the sins of the people. Because he himself
> suffered when he was tempted, he is *able to help* those who are being tempted.
> (Heb 2:14-18, emphasis mine)

The apostle Peter also saw the vision of a high priest empowering a royal priesthood:

> As you come to him, the living Stone—rejected by human beings but chosen by
> God and precious to him—you also, like living stones, are being built into a spir-
> itual house to be *a holy priesthood, offering spiritual sacrifices acceptable to God
> through Jesus Christ.* . . . [For] you are a chosen people, *a royal priesthood,* a holy

nation, God's special possession, that you may declare the praises of him who called you out of darkness into his wonderful light. (1 Pet 2:4-5, 9, emphasis mine)

Jesus, the one true High Priest, made possible a royal priesthood that is able to return to the mission of the Garden: to be a light to the nations and a blessing to all people, serving the common good.

THE COMMON PRIESTHOOD AND PIETISM

And so it was that after Jesus' departure the new covenant people of God sought to live out this vision. For a number of centuries the mission of the Garden was mostly central as the church fulfilled Jesus' words to "make disciples of all nations" (Mt 28:19) who are "the salt of the earth" and "light of the world" (Mt 5:13, 14). God's people often suffered for doing good (1 Pet 4:12-19); strived to live out the fruit of the Spirit, against which there is no law (Gal 5:22-26); were careful to do what is right in the eyes of everyone (Rom 12:17); and sought to live at peace with everyone, as far as it depended on them (Rom 12:18).

A few centuries after Christ, however, the church in the West faltered greatly in its priestly mission to be a blessing to the nations. With the rise to power of the Roman emperor Constantine, Western Christianity transitioned from a persecuted minority to a celebrated majority. The effect to the common priesthood was dramatic as church leaders entered into collusion with the state. "The church recognized its subjection to the Emperor without complaint," wrote historian Alexander Flick, "and permitted him to appoint and dispose its officers, to call and dismiss synods and councils, like Arles (314) and Nicaea (325), and almost to replace the Holy Ghost itself in determining the proceedings."[9] With subsequent emperors the pope (and his priests) "slowly assumed more and more power until Innocent III (1198–1216) taught Europe to think of the popes as world rulers."[10]

All of this, of course, left behind the notion of God's people as a royal priesthood. As church and state spawned their new child, power and authority came to rest with fewer and fewer people: the clergy.

In reaction to the centralizing of the church's power with the clergy alone

---

[9]Alexander C. Flick, *The Rise of the Medieval Church* (New York: G. P. Putnam's Sons, 1909), p. 292.
[10]Bruce L. Shelley, *Church History in Plain Language*, 3rd ed. (Nashville: Thomas Nelson, 2008), p. 161.

(and their abuse of that power), Martin Luther, and later the Pietists, made a radical break with tradition by reemphasizing the common priesthood. In his 1520 work *The Babylonian Captivity of the Church* Luther wrote, "Let everyone, therefore, who knows himself to be a Christian, be assured of this, that we are equally priests, that is to say, we have the same power in respect to the Word and the sacraments."[11] While many in the later Middle Ages had earlier decried clerical corruption and sought reform, Jonathan Strom emphasizes that

> Luther sought to abolish the clerical estate altogether by arguing that all Christians are equally priests; he disallowed the special status of the clergy noting: " . . . We are all consecrated priests through baptism; as St. Peter says in 1 Pet 2:9, 'You are a royal priesthood and priestly nation.'"[12]

For Luther, wrote Dale Brown, "the priesthood constituted a service in which each believer was a Christ or a priest to his or her neighbor."[13]

As the German Lutheran pastor Philipp Jakob Spener sought "better times" for the church in the wake of the Thirty Years' War, he attached special importance to the common priesthood, making its "establishment and diligent exercise" his second proposal in *Pia Desideria* (1675).[14] Brown sees Spener as building on Luther when he "asserted that the name 'priest' is a general name for all Christians and applies to ministers no differently than to other Christians."[15] Strom suggests that Spener "gave the common priesthood the greatest prominence in the seventeenth century, and his interpretation of it became a centerpiece in his attempts to revitalize Christianity."[16]

Two years after writing *Pia Desideria*, Spener spelled out his interpretation of the common priesthood. Concerning the 1677 tract entitled *The Spiritual Priesthood*, Strom notes,

> Here we have the three-fold office of the common priesthood: *sacrifice, prayer and blessing, and the Word*. Spener derived the authority of the spiritual priesthood

---

[11]Quoted in Jonathan Strom, "The Common Priesthood and the Pietist Challenge for Ministry and Laity," in *The Pietist Impulse in Christianity*, ed. Christian T. Collins Winn et al. (Eugene, OR: Pickwick, 2011), p. 43.

[12]Ibid.

[13]Dale W. Brown, *Understanding Pietism*, rev. ed. (Nappanee, IN: Evangel, 1996), p. 42.

[14]Philip Jacob Spener, *Pia Desideria*, trans. Theodore G. Tappert (Philadelphia: Fortress, 1964), p. 92.

[15]Brown, *Understanding Pietism*, p. 42.

[16]Strom, "Common Priesthood," p. 47.

directly from Christ as the one high priest. Again, echoing Luther, he argued all Christians have become spiritual priests through baptism and regeneration.[17]

Spener's understanding of the common priesthood, however, did not lead to a withdrawal from society and the common good. Spener biographer K. James Stein comments that

> Spener taught that the Christian life is devoted to world-formation, that is, to the well-being of society. . . . The earth must be cultivated . . . the reborn must join in labor aimed at supplying their own and their neighbor's needs.[18]

For Spener, then, a common priesthood working for the common good was the grand theology behind the grand vision that launched the grand movement we call Pietism.

"Handles" of the Common Priesthood

But this theology was not an ivory tower notion. No, it had handles: a common priesthood realized through *sacrifice, prayer and blessing, the Word in community,*[19] *and work for the common good.* By these handles the vision was not only held up by Spener and subsequent leaders but also taken hold of so as to launch a movement.

Sacrifice. In *The Spiritual Priesthood* Spener imagines a series of ten questions that need answering about sacrifice. From his answers it is clear that he imagines the priestly role to require an all-consuming commitment by Christians. It will impact their desires "so that they no longer desire to serve themselves, but him who has bought and redeemed them." It will lead them to separate "from the world and its uncleanness," and to use their bodies "*alone* for the glory and service of God." It will make them "holy *temples* and abodes of God."[20] For Spener, this sacrifice comes about by "allowing our *reason* to be brought into captivity to the obedience of Christ . . . ; by surrendering our *wills* to the divine will in true submission and obedience . . . ; and by making an acceptable *sacrifice* of our *spirits and souls* in true *repentance.*"

---

[17]Ibid., p. 48.

[18]K. James Stein, *Phillip Jakob Spener: Pietist Patriarch* (Chicago: Covenant Press, 1986), p. 238.

[19]Spener does not list community as an office, but as his 1677 tract was intended to justify the reading of Scripture in conventicles (small groups), community is assumed and at points directly addressed. We'll return to this point shortly.

[20]Philipp Jakob Spener, *The Spiritual Priesthood* (1677), reprinted in *Pietists: Selected Writings*, ed. Peter C. Erb (New York: Paulist Press, 1983), p. 52. Italics original.

In this all-consuming sacrifice we become willing to receive whatever "is pleasing to him," and to "lay down our *lives* for his glory, if it be his *will*."[21] And to "How often and when should we make such offerings to God?" Spener answers, "*Always,* through our whole life. For although we surrender and offer ourselves to God with body and soul once for all when we first yield our hearts to his service, nevertheless this purpose should be repeated, and sacrifices of this kind should be brought by us to God the Lord daily and even hourly."[22]

For Spener, these sacrifices do not make "atonement for our sins" nor are they "altogether pure." "No," Spener writes, "Christ alone has made satisfaction for us by his sacrifice" and "by virtue of the holy sacrifice of Jesus our sacrifices are also sanctified and acceptable to God for his Son's sake."[23]

Prayer and blessing. In addition to sacrifice, Spener also sees the priestly practices of prayer and blessing to be handles by which we take hold of our priestly role. As priests we not only have the authority to pray for and bless others, but also our very words can be words that can change things for the common good:

> As the high priest of the Old Testament blessed the people . . . and prayed for them . . . , so Christ also, as the true High Priest of the New Testament, laid his blessing upon us . . . and prayed for us and still prays of us. . . . In like manner it is the duty of Christians not only to offer *prayers to God for themselves,* but also *to make intercession for their fellow men* . . . and to *bless them.* . . . For Christ's sake such prayer and blessing are not in vain, but effectual.[24]

While prayer and blessing were activities primarily reserved for the clergy, Spener breaks with tradition and extends them to all Christians, as they are all priests able to affect the common good.

The Word. Followers of Christ also lay hold of and live out the common priesthood by utilizing their authority to read the Word of God for themselves and with others. Spener argues, "As the priests were occupied with the law of God (Mal. 2:7), so also is it the office of spiritual priests to let the *Word of God* dwell richly among them (Col. 3:16). . . . They shall use it for *themselves* and

---

[21]Ibid., pp. 52-53. Italics original.
[22]Ibid., p. 53. Italics original.
[23]Ibid.
[24]Ibid., p. 54.

among or with others . . . all have both the *right* and *command* to read them (John 5:38)."[25]

The reading and understanding of the Scriptures by anyone, educated or uneducated, is possible because of the "enlightenment of the Holy Spirit, by whose inspiration the Scriptures were first recorded."[26]

The right and command to read the Scriptures, Spener suggests, should not lead Christians to "be so busy with the Word of God as to neglect secular affairs."[27]

> It is, indeed, their greatest joy to be occupied with their God and his Word, as the one thing needful. . . . But as they still live in the world and need to work for the support of their bodies, and are also placed by God in certain positions for the general good, when they have bodily work and business, they do so diligently according to the ability that God gives, avoid all idleness, and so prove even in such service their obedience to God and their love to their fellow men.[28]

It is clear that the neighbor's good is always near at hand in Spener's mind. The common priesthood is for the common good. And as such, if we truly desire to serve as members of the common priesthood working for the common good, we must be people of sacrifice, praying and blessing with our words and inviting others to dwell richly in the Word with us.

Community. Embedded in the invitation to dwell in the Word is the assumption of community. Pietists quickly became known for gathering in conventicles to read and apply Scripture and to support one another in a spirit of love. Two years before writing in depth about the common priesthood, Spener had argued for *ecclesiolae in ecclesia* ("little churches within the church") in *Pia Desideria*:

> Thought should be given to a *more extensive use of the Word of God among us.* . . . It should therefore be considered whether the church should not be well advised to introduce the people to Scripture in still other ways than the customary sermons on the appointed lessons. . . . In addition to our customary services with preaching, other assemblies would be held in the manner in which Paul describes them in 1 Corinthians 14:26-40. One person would not rise to preach (although this practice would be continued at other times), but others who have been

---

[25]Ibid. Italics original.
[26]Ibid., p. 56.
[27]Ibid., p. 59.
[28]Ibid.

blessed with gifts and knowledge would also speak and present their pious opinions on the proposed subject to the judgment of the rest, doing all this in such a way as to avoid discord and strife.[29]

While conventicles are mostly assumed in *The Common Priesthood*, Spener does touch on the authority that the common priesthood gives all believers to call and lead such communities. To the question, "May a number also meet together [to read Scripture]?" Spener responds,

> They may mutually edify each other when *occasion* arises. In the same way it cannot be wrong if several good friends sometimes meet *expressly to go over a sermon* together and recall what they heard, *to read in the Scriptures*, and *to confer* in the fear of the Lord how they may put into practice what they read.[30]

Notably, given his context, Spener also believed this priestly authority was to be exercised by men *and* women:

> Since God dignifies believing women also with his spiritual gifts . . . the exercise of them *in proper order* cannot be forbidden. The apostles themselves make mention of those godly women who worked together with them and edified their fellow men; and far from censuring them for this, they accorded them love and praise for it.[31]

Given this authority, a female colleague, Johanna Eleonora Petersen, emerged as a leader from within Spener's own *collegia pietatis*. Petersen would go on to form a conventicle of adult women who gathered to read and reflect on Scripture in community. In addition, she helped run a boarding school, teaching Scripture, devotional works and even Greek to a small group of girls, and later took up preaching.[32]

Work for the common good. "A frequent stereotype of Pietistic Christianity," observes Dale Brown, "portrays it as almost exclusively preoccupied with inward devotion and private moral scruples." Brown couldn't disagree more:

> On the contrary, the Pietist milieu resulted in a desire to transform the living conditions of the poor and oppressed, reform the prison system, abolish slavery,

---

[29]Spener, *Pia Desideria*, pp. 87-89.
[30]Spener, *Spiritual Priesthood*, p. 63.
[31]Ibid., p. 62.
[32]For a concise introduction to Petersen, see Michelle A. Clifton-Soderstrom, *Angels, Worms, and Bogeys: The Christian Ethic of Pietism* (Eugene, OR: Cascade, 2010), chap. 3.

break down rigid class distinctions, establish a more democratic polity, initiate education reforms, establish institutions, increase missionary activity, obtain religious liberty, and propose programs for social justice.[33]

A piece of Pietism's commitment to the common good came from what James Stein describes as Spener's teaching "that the Christian life is devotion to world-formation, that is, to contribution to the well-being to society." In particular, Stein notes that Spener saw world formation as coming through work:

> Spener could sound quite Lutheran on the work ethic. Each person is called to his or her profession by God. All work can be done in obedience to God and for the benefit of one's neighbor. . . . If [the reborn] want to live to the Father's glory, they must eat and drink. Therefore, they must work.[34]

Influenced by Spener, August Hermann Francke went so far as to offer six reasons why Christians should be diligent in work:

> (1) God commands us to work (Gen. 3:19); (2) humanity is made to find fulfillment in work "just as the bird is made to fly"; (3) God has decreed that we work for our daily bread (2 Thess. 3:10-12); (4) work is a means of suppressing our aptitude for sin; idleness is the beginning of vice; (5) believers should not be a burden to others, especially not to unbelievers; (6) we should work so that we have the means to help the needy (Eph. 4:28).[35]

Of special concern for Spener and Francke was the Christian's responsibility to work toward meeting the needs of the poor, both individually and through the government. Long before he came to wider attention for *Pia Desideria*, Spener was preaching on the need for local officials to remember their duty to the poor.[36] Francke insisted that "Christian rulers should see that every poor person be sufficiently served that they are cared for and that grants be properly distributed. If the poor can work, they should be expected to do so; if not, they should be given as much as they need."[37] Work, then, provides the Christian the opportunity for not only personal fulfillment but also participation with God on the mission of world formation for the common good.

---

[33]Brown, *Understanding Pietism*, pp. 86-87.
[34]Stein, *Philipp Jakob Spener*, p. 238.
[35]Quoted in Douglas H. Shantz, *An Introduction to German Pietism: Protestant Renewal at the Dawn of Modern Europe* (Baltimore: Johns Hopkins University Press, 2013), p. 138.
[36]Stein, *Philipp Jakob Spener*, p. 239.
[37]Quoted in Shantz, *Introduction to German Pietism*, p. 139.

CATCHING THE VISION FROM A PIETIST UNIVERSITY

I teach at the Christian liberal arts university from which I graduated. As a student I came to Bethel as a grandson of fundamentalism and a son of evangelicalism. On my dad's side my grandparents were a pastor and pastor's wife, and on my mom's side they were missionaries. My parents were missionaries for almost fifty years. This spiritual heritage passed on many things that I embrace today: a love of the Scriptures; whole-hearted, whole-life devotion to Jesus; a passion for the least reached; and so on.

But I caught a few other things from my spiritual heritage too: the sacred and secular are separable; callings are for ministers and missionaries; and saving souls is the only real mission of God in the world. As I came to live in and learn from a pietistic community I was quickly confronted with a different way of viewing God and the mission of God in the world. Let me offer two examples.

I came to college practicing what William Shannon calls spiritual apartheid. This is the belief that God is more present and active in certain times and places than in other times and places. It is "the mentality that sets God apart from creation."[38] As such, I had erected a wall between the sacred and the secular. In my way of thinking, God was at work on Sundays, at church, through the pastor and maybe at chapel. Monday through Saturday and between chapels we held on for dear life until we could go where God was most at work: church. Then my sophomore year I lived with a group of guys who had gotten to know one another the year before. Not terribly consistently, but occasionally, we would pray together and talk about the Bible or a message from chapel. With a growing sense of desire, we held each other accountable in areas of our lives (especially mine) that were in desperate need of change. These kinds of "God moments" happened in other places, too: professors' offices; in the hall; after football practice. Gradually, without me fully knowing it, the wall between the sacred and secular was being torn down. I was starting to believe God could be at work in every moment and in every place, in the same way God was at work on Sundays. Church, I was learning, could happen anywhere.

The second example had even greater influence on me: she was a soph-

---

[38]William Shannon, *Silence on Fire* (New York: Crossroad, 1991), p. 31.

omore majoring in math and computer science, which was fine, but when I asked her why she chose those majors she said, "I guess I sensed God calling me to them." We met the previous spring on a blind date set up by our roommates. This conversation took place the next fall, and I tried to help her see that only ministers and missionaries had "callings from God." I don't think I said it out loud, but I was thinking, "The rest just settle for a way to make money so they can support ministers and missionaries who do the real work of God in the world: saving souls." She kept pushing back, however, insisting that her studies, and someday her work, could have a worth of their own. They could be as valuable to God's kingdom as any other kind of work; they could change the world for the better. After three more years of drinking Pietism's Kool-Aid, and more than twenty-five years of marriage, I have become convinced that the math and computer science major was right. Every Christ follower has a calling to participate in the mission of God, and the mission of God includes the common good.

Casting the Vision at a Christian Liberal Arts University

My personal conversion to a more pietistic perspective has led me to cast Pietism's vision in my classrooms.[39] I teach that every major is a "ministry major" and that every activity can be an act of worship. In doing so I am guided by the following implicit principles, which I occasionally make explicit:

- We are priests serving in God's temple: the universe.
- Priestly service requires us to sacrifice the leadership of our lives to God.
- We have the priestly authority to pray and bless others.
- We have the authority to make church happen anywhere and at any time.
- Our work can be participation in world formation for the common good.

If indeed the common priesthood was the theology behind the vision that launched the movement we call Pietism—if a common priesthood realized through sacrifice, prayer and blessing, the Word in community and work for the common good as the handles by which the vision was held up and taken hold of—then I suggest we too can hold up and invite others to lay hold of this

---

[39]I have the advantage of teaching a course titled Vocation and Calling: A Biblical Perspective, yet I try to bring these themes into all my courses.

vision so as to launch movements for the common good. We can be brokers of hope, believing that the common good can indeed happen now, in part, even as it will happen in full when Christ returns.[40]

---

[40]I would like to acknowledge Roy (Doc) Dalton, former professor of history at Bethel, who first modeled and taught me of Pietism. His life of piety was one I found worth imitating, and his pietistic approach with students continues to shape me as a Bethel professor today.

7

Pietism and the Practice of Civil Discourse

Christian T. Collins Winn

◆

O N JANUARY 3, 2011, media consultant Mark DeMoss, a conservative Repub-
lican and evangelical Christian, announced that he was shutting down the
"Civility Project." DeMoss, who had served as an adviser on Mitt Romney's 2008
presidential bid, launched the project with Lanny Davis, a liberal Democrat
who is also Jewish, with the hope of promoting a "more civil exchange of ideas."
In the letter announcing the closure, DeMoss said that "our only aim in
launching this project two years ago was to call people from all races, walks of
life, and religious and political persuasions to graciousness, kindness, common
decency and respect—civility—toward all people, and particularly those with
whom we may disagree."[1]

The keystone of the project was the thirty-two-word civility pledge: "I will
be civil in my public discourse and behavior. I will be respectful of others
whether or not I agree with them. I will stand against incivility when I see it."
Though DeMoss and Davis were able to get thousands of signatures from
people across the United States, they could secure signatures from only three
of the 535 sitting members of Congress, and no sitting governors. This left
DeMoss perplexed: "I must admit to scratching my head as to why only three
members of Congress, and no governors, would agree to what I believe is a

---

[1]The original Civility Project website is no longer online, but DeMoss's letter can be found at https://
web.archive.org/web/20110124090419/http://www.demossnews.com/resources/civility_project.pdf.

rather low bar."[2] The dismissive tone with which the project was treated by politicians and pundits alike, coupled with personal attacks against DeMoss and Davis, ultimately led to its demise.

The significance of the end of the Civility Project is magnified when it is placed next to the shooting of U.S. Representative Gabby Giffords in Tucson, Arizona, a mere five days after DeMoss's letter. In the wake of Ms. Giffords's shooting, politicians and leaders from across the political spectrum echoed President Barack Obama's call for a more concerted effort to "usher in more civility in our public discourse."[3] After the 2012 election cycle, it is fair to say that the jury is still out on how successful those efforts have been.

When Giffords was shot I was in Dublin, Ireland, coleading a Bethel University course titled Conflict, Reconciliation, and the Church, which studies "The Troubles"—as the Northern Irish conflict is called—seeking to understand the complex processes that lead to social breakdown and violence, the role that churches and communities of faith play in such processes and, conversely, the difficult task of transforming such communities of faith into centers of healing and reconciliation. We had already been in Dublin for three days and were bound for Belfast on January 9. Most of the students had read about "The Troubles,"[4] but truthfully it was hard for them to enter into the conflict. This is partly because most of them came from more sheltered environments, but also because they assumed there was no real correlate in the U.S. context to the kind of political violence that had torn apart the social fabric of Northern Ireland for many decades. Setting aside for a moment the fact that most of these students had come of age under the aegis of terror alerts and a heightened sense of security in the U.S. because of the events of 9/11, seeing the events unfold around the shooting of Representative Giffords from a distance *may* have reinforced in our students the need to take peacemaking more seriously than they had previously.

It certainly underlined for my colleagues and me a sense of the responsibility and mission that educators have in cultivating the virtue of civil discourse. As citizens of a democratic republic, we know that deliberation and argument

---

[2]Ibid.

[3]Quoted by Mark DeMoss, "Don't Expect Civility," *Politico*, January 17, 2011, www.politico.com/news/stories/0111/47677.html.

[4]By this point in time the students had read Aaron Edwards and Cillian McGrattan, *The Northern Ireland Conflict* (Oxford: Oneworld Publications, 2010).

have a rightful place; and we know that our differences don't just enrich our lives, but they also lead us into conflict and division. Different walks of life, different stories and experiences, different commitments and different views of the world are not easily reconciled, if at all. And this is not simply a description of a national or international situation; it also holds true within communities of faith, particularly in the Christian church. Followers of Jesus can be found across the political and theological spectrum.

In distinction from the broader culture, however, it is legitimate to ask whether our differences really ought to divide us. Does Scripture not call us to be one, even as Jesus was one with his Father (Jn 17:20-23)? If we answer this question in the affirmative—that enfolded in the call of Christ is a call to unity— then we must *also* acknowledge that the unity of which the Bible speaks is not mere uniformity. Unity in Christ does not mean sameness; it can and does mean legitimate difference. And this leaves us with the challenge of how to live together in such a way that we make space for real and legitimate differences, without severing the bond of faith that holds us together.

It is here that the virtue of civil discourse becomes important. By the term *civil discourse* I mean to name a set of practices and a sensibility for engaging in public discourse, both within Christian communities and beyond in the larger public square. As Richard Mouw has argued, however, "civility" and its correlate "civil discourse" have often been subject to misunderstanding, interpreted as simply being polite. Drawing on classical Greek notions, Mouw argues,

> To be civil was to genuinely care about the larger society. It required a heartfelt commitment to your fellow citizens. It was a willingness to promote the well-being of people who were very different, including people who seriously disagreed with you on important matters. Civility wasn't merely an eternal show of politeness.[5]

Civility, then, wasn't just being nice. Rather it referred to a general sensibility whose concern was the larger common good. Such a sensibility, however, requires conviction and commitment, and thus Mouw opts for the useful term *convicted civility* in his discussion.[6]

Mouw draws on a variety of thinkers as he attempts to articulate what con-

---

[5]Richard J. Mouw, *Uncommon Decency: Christianity Civility in an Uncivil World*, rev. ed. (Downers Grove, IL: InterVarsity Press, 2010), p. 14.
[6]See ibid., pp. 11-20.

victed civility looks like, being especially attentive to his own Reformed tradition. In this chapter, I want to offer a fourfold way of thinking about civil
discourse through consideration of one of the key influences on Bethel University: the theological tradition of Pietism.

WHAT HAS PIETISM TO DO WITH CIVIL DISCOURSE?

Pietism is a renewal tradition born in German-speaking lands in the late seventeenth century that came to have a substantial influence on most of the
Protestant world in Europe, North America and, by extension, Asia and
Africa.[7] As made clear elsewhere in this book, Pietists emphasized a living
relationship with Jesus Christ, a transformed life lived out in service to the
neighbor, the importance of communal and individual engagement with
Scripture through conventicles or small groups, and the cultivation of an
irenic, or peaceable, spirit. Their vision quickly spread into Scandinavia by the
early eighteenth century and, along with the Baptist and Holiness traditions,
was a key impulse among the Swedish immigrants who, in 1871, founded a
seminary in Chicago that would eventually evolve into Bethel University, now
located in St. Paul, Minnesota.

Aside from this historical connection, however, the Pietist tradition is especially germane to the question of civil discourse because it was born and came
of age in the midst of conflict. The period in which Pietism was born was
marked by social, religious and political division. The Thirty Years' War, fought
largely in German-speaking lands from 1618 to 1648, had managed to pit
Christian against Christian, and the cultural aftermath in the life of the church
was nothing short of disastrous. As Philipp Jakob Spener lamented in 1675,
"Not a few stake almost everything on polemics. They think that everything has
turned out very well if only they know how to give answer to the errors of the
papists, the Reformed, the Anabaptists, etc."[8]

From the start, Spener called for a more careful, loving and irenic tone in

---

[7]For a discussion of the German context, see Douglas H. Shantz, *An Introduction to German Pietism: Protestant Renewal at the Dawn of Modern Europe* (Baltimore: Johns Hopkins University Press, 2013). For the larger trans-Atlantic context in which Pietism should be understood, see W. R. Ward, *Early Evangelicalism: A Global Intellectual History, 1670-1789* (Cambridge: Cambridge University Press, 2006); and idem, *The Protestant Evangelical Awakening* (Cambridge: Cambridge University Press, 1992).

[8]Philip Jacob Spener, *Pia Desideria*, trans. Theodore G. Tappert (Philadelphia: Fortress, 1964), p. 49.

the life of the church and the broader culture,[9] and he developed a program of reform that offered practical suggestions for the revitalization of the Christian community. For these reforming efforts Spener was often attacked and vilified by his opponents and was drawn into numerous theological controversies over the course of his career. In one year alone, 1695, no less than fifteen separate works were published against Spener.[10] Nevertheless, by all accounts Spener acquitted himself well, putting his theoretical call for a different approach to controversy to the test time and time again.[11]

SPENER'S PRACTICES OF CIVIL DISCOURSE

In light of the history and emphases of Pietism, I would like to suggest four overlapping practices or dispositions that can be helpful as we consider what it means for us to be civil in our differences.

The first is what we might call a *spirit of good faith*. In all of the many controversies in which Spener was embroiled, he consistently exhibited good faith. He did not back away from conflict, but neither did he fail to take seriously the arguments of his opponents. He wanted to be understood and he wanted to understand, even if his opponents did not always grant him the same kindness. Spener came to debate committed to being what one recent commentator has called a "sincere arguer," that is, one committed to the reasonable exchange of ideas.[12] This notion captures well the fact that, from a Pietist point of view, civility should not be understood as the avoidance of conflict, or the absence of argument. It is, rather, a genuine commitment to dialogue and argument because at base the Pietist is concerned with understanding not only him- or herself, and not only the opposing side, but also the truth of the matter. In this search for the truth, one must make every effort to think through one's own position, to express it clearly and to listen to one's dialogue partner *in*

---

[9]In his innovative *Pietismus und Aufklärung: Theologische Polemik und die Kommunikationsreform der Wissenschafte an Ende des 17. Jahrhunderts* (Göttingen: Vandenhoeck & Ruprecht, 1997), Martin Gierl argues that the Pietist movement—he focuses especially on Spener and the Radical Pietist Gottfried Arnold—can be seen as a "communicative event" whose aim was to shift the tone of theological and social discourse in late-seventeenth-century German-speaking lands.

[10]K. James Stein, *Philipp Jakob Spener: Pietist Patriarch* (Chicago: Covenant Press, 1986), p. 136.

[11]For a discussion of the difference of Spener's approach to controversy see Gierl, *Pietismus und Aufklärung*, pp. 307-14.

[12]Scott F. Aiken and Robert B. Talisse, "Civility in Argument," 3 *Quarks Daily*, August 20, 2012, www.3quarksdaily.com/3quarksdaily/2012/08/civility-in-argument.html.

good faith, trying to understand where they are coming from. If after this disagreement remains—which is entirely possible since sincerity in argument is no guarantee of truthfulness—nonetheless, the bonds of community and goodwill will remain and the possibility of future fruitful exchanges will be more likely.

By extension, the second element of a Pietist approach to civil discourse is a genuine openness to being taught, or what one might call *humility*. Spener said that he was "willing to yield to anybody, no matter how simple-minded, who will show me something better and more advantageous for the discharge of my pastoral duties and whatever else has to do with edification . . . [for] all of this is God's cause, not ours."[13] As Martin Brecht has pointed out, this humility comes through especially in Spener's personal correspondence, where one sees a person committed to finding the truth *without* the prior assumption that he is already in total possession of it.[14] Engagement of any kind, but especially in the fields of theological and political discourse, requires the humility to realize that we are not God, that we ourselves are also pilgrims on the way.

Perhaps another way of saying this is that we need each other, that the pursuit of truth is a fundamentally communal endeavor. The Pietist twist on this, which was certainly novel in its day, was the willingness to countenance the possibility that God speaks the truth not only through my friends but also through my adversaries, and therefore I must be willing to be taught even by those with whom I disagree.

The third element that marks a Pietist approach to civil discourse is the overarching concern of *love for one's neighbor*. For the Pietists love of neighbor undergirded the practices of good faith and humility, and Spener stressed the intimate connection of truth and love:

> From all this it becomes apparent that disputing is not enough either to maintain the truth among ourselves or to impart it to the erring. *The holy love of God is necessary.* If only we Evangelicals [i.e., Protestants] would make it our serious business to offer God the fruits of his truth in fervent love, conduct ourselves in a manner worthy of our calling, and show this in recognizable and unalloyed love

---

[13]Spener, *Pia Desideria*, p. 86.
[14]Martin Brecht, ed., *Geschichte des Pietismus*, 4 vols. (Göttingen: Vandenhoeck & Ruprecht, 1993), 1:368-70.

of our neighbors. . . . There is no doubt that God would *then* allow us to grow more and more in our knowledge of the truth.[15]

As Carl Lundquist, the former President of Bethel University, put it, "Truth, in fact, is troth—*a way of loving*. And it is motivated not only by curiosity and the desire to be in control but by compassion."[16] Progress in the truth is made possible in and through genuine love, and therefore a civil discourse marked by a concern for truth will also be marked by love of neighbor. For the Pietists "love" was no mere emotion but the practice of real and genuine care through acts of service. From the Pietist point of view, to practice good faith and humility when engaged in controversy or argument is itself the practice of love of neighbor. For in both the practitioner assumes, affirms and embraces the humanity of the other, and sees their adversary as loved by God and deserving of respect, care and hospitality.

The fourth and final element refers to the larger framework within which our first three aspects are placed. We might call it *the hopeful commitment to God's peace*. At Bethel University we often speak about the "irenic spirit of Pietism," by which we mean to denote a commitment to peace or peaceableness. As Virgil Olson describes it, "The irenic spirit was the Pietist's response to the brutality of the religious wars, persecution of religious belief by political institutions and incivility of the theological wars. It was expressed in the phrase 'in essentials unity, in non-essentials liberty, in all things charity.'"[17] As Paul Olson demonstrated in his 2005 dissertation, it is precisely the irenic spirit of Bethel that has enabled the university to foster a limited though significant form of theological pluralism, and to weather the controversy that necessarily comes with such pluralism.[18]

Unfortunately, however, the term *irenic* has not always been understood, and some have been led to assume that being a Pietist means simply being nice to one another. This misunderstanding is obviated when we view the notion of "the irenic spirit" within its proper and original eschatological context, the Pietist

---

[15]Spener, *Pia Desideria*, p. 102. Emphasis mine.

[16]Quoted by Christopher Gehrz, "Recovering a Pietist Understanding of Christian Higher Education: Carl H. Lundquist and Karl A. Olsson," *Christian Scholar's Review* 40 (Winter 2011): 147.

[17]Virgil A. Olson, "History of Swedish Baptist Pietism: A Significant Influence on Early Leaders of the Baptist General Conference," *Baptist Pietist Clarion* (June 2007): 5.

[18]See Paul L. H. Olson, "A University and Its Denomination: The Ties That Bind in the 21st Century," (EdD diss., University of Pennsylvania, 2005).

theology of hope. As Michelle Clifton-Soderstrom notes, "The hope of the Pietists inspired a resuscitation of personal faith and widespread renewal in the church."[19] Pietistic work for the revitalization of Christianity was not rooted in optimism but in the conviction and hope that the work of God in the life, death and resurrection of Jesus Christ was continuing to unfold in history in the power of the Spirit, and that this work was a work of healing.[20] More specifically, it was the work of the healing of the nations, or what the Bible calls God's peace, or *shalom*. And though the final appearing of God's *shalom* was in the future, through our participation here and now penultimate appearances of *shalom* could emerge. Spener's own hope was that through the practical act of loving the neighbor, with whom one might intensely disagree, God would act to bring about some measure of the *shalom* that will someday renovate the cosmos itself.

When seen from this perspective, the "irenic spirit of Pietism" is really more of a challenge than a possession. It asks us, Are we committed to God's peace, God's *shalom*? We all know only too well, and some of us perhaps more than others, that the practice of good faith, humility and genuine neighbor love is hard work, at which we fail daily and in which we are often afflicted by the failures of others. What hope does is to call us to begin again at the beginning. To turn around, and to start over once more—to practice good faith, humility and love—in the hope that God's peace may break into our common life now.

THE ROLE OF CHRISTIAN HIGHER EDUCATION IN BRINGING ABOUT CIVIL DISCOURSE

As a complement to the work of churches, mosques and synagogues, higher education can also play a constructive role in cultivating the practices of civil discourse outlined above.[21] The reason, I would argue, is that higher education, and particularly Christian higher education, is not only engaged in shaping the ways that students think but also interested in cultivating whole persons. Cultivation of whole persons can occur through formal and informal interaction

---

[19]Michelle A. Clifton-Soderstrom, *Angels, Worms, and Bogeys: The Christian Ethic of Pietism* (Eugene, OR: Cascade Books, 2010), p. 73.

[20]See Spener, *Pia Desideria*, pp. 76-86.

[21]I deliberately include here communities of faith that move beyond the Christian sphere because, though Christians would argue that God's peace and hope are rooted in the event of Jesus Christ, nevertheless the hope generated in other religious communities can also be productive of a culture of civility.

via a variety of actors, but I am especially concerned here about faculty interaction with students.

The practices of civil discourse I have outlined above are probably best conveyed to students through a kind of intellectual and/or spiritual modeling on the part of professors. That is, faculty pass on these different practices best as they display them to students in their own work in the classroom and beyond. Modeling how to engage, think with and seek to understand those with whom one may disagree should be central to the practice of a Christian university, but it requires that faculty themselves are not only committed to such a vision of intellectual practice and mission but also are equipped and supported by their institutions in such an endeavor.

I would suggest that this requires at least two things: first, the transformation of the general education curriculum, and second, institutional support in the form of faculty development. The general education curriculum of the average Christian university continues to revolve around a "Western-centric" approach to knowledge. This is problematic on a variety of levels, but it also hampers the process of cultivating the kinds of practices outlined above. Notwithstanding the fact that most students do not come to university with a grasp—let alone mastery—of the Western canon, the fact that they are not exposed to narratives and sources that lie far beyond the purported Western canon means that educators miss a golden opportunity for transformative and critical learning experiences. I am thinking here of the pedagogical process to which my students were exposed in Northern Ireland.

Almost none of my students had a personal connection to the Northern Ireland narrative of violence, but through readings, film, music, discussion and direct experiential encounters, they were brought face to face with an alien culture and society and were given the opportunity to ask critical questions such as, What if this were my society? What if I were in this situation? How would I respond? These kinds of empathetic questions require that students enter into a reality and thought world that is radically different from their own to contemplate basic human problems such as violence, identity and belonging, the role of faith in civic life and so on. Such intellectual skills are part of the bedrock of the kind of practices I enumerated earlier. To enter into the thought world of another requires good faith, humility and some level of care or concern for understanding others.

I am not suggesting that all students go to Northern Ireland or even that they must take courses that physically place them in another culture—though this would be good![22] Rather, the same process of transformation and critical engagement can also occur as students read texts, hear music or watch films that come from cultures remarkably different from their own. For this to happen, though, many Christian universities will need to open up their general education curriculum to include more exposure to unfamiliar sources and narratives.

For such curricular changes to be effective, however, faculty will need to be supported by their institutions. If students are going to pick up on the modeling that faculty are purportedly doing, then the faculty need to be doing the modeling. Without denying that many professors are very gifted teachers, exposure to different pedagogical strategies through institutionally supported faculty development is essential. Faculty are finding themselves stretched more and more not only by the full-time responsibilities of teaching, scholarship and service, but also by the need to work extra jobs or teach overloads because of lack of pay. So if universities really want to produce students who will be able to make a difference in the current climate through a witness of peaceableness and civility, then they will need to provide the resources to help train and develop the kind of faculty necessary for producing such students.

CONCLUSION: RECOVERING HOPE FOR CIVIL DISCOURSE

This, of course, is where hope comes in. The dissolution of the Civility Project, the attack on former representative Giffords and other episodes all evince an underlying lack of hope in our society. Christian universities have an opportunity to play a central role in rekindling this hope. The question, of course, is whether they will grasp this opportunity. Though there are reasons for pessimism, I continue to believe there are even more reasons to hope that Christian universities can live out their mission by offering a space in which civil discourse is valued, cultivated and practiced for the common good of the larger society. While the practices I have outlined are certainly not able to

---

[22]On the contributions of off-campus programs like Bethel's to intercultural learning and something like Mouw's "convicted civility," see Naomi Ludeman Smith, "(Re)Considering a Critical Ethnorelative Worldview Goal and Pedagogy for Global and Biblical Demands in Christian Higher Education," *Christian Scholar's Review* 42 (Summer 2013): 345-73.

address all of the root causes of the general rancor that afflicts our faith communities and the larger society, the practices of civil discourse—good faith, humility, genuine love, and hope in God's own peace—can contribute to the rebuilding of the bonds of trust and hope needed for human communities to thrive. May God grant us the faith, love and, above all, hope necessary for the task in front of us.[23]

---

[23]This chapter originated as the 2012 convocation address at Bethel University. Thanks to Deb Harless for the invitation to deliver that address.

8

Love My (Religious) Neighbor

A Pietist Approach to Christian
Responsibility in a Pluralistic World

Marion H. Larson and Sara L. H. Shady

Before you learn to do it with your hands,
you have to learn it in your heart.

EDNA ADAN, *HALF THE SKY*

◆

EDNA ADAN, who is featured in *Half the Sky: Turning Oppression into Opportunity for Women Worldwide*,[1] is known for her dedicated service to women's health in Somaliland. As the first trained nurse-midwife in Somaliland, Edna built and now runs a women's maternity hospital, trains women in villages to perform proper and sterile midwife practices, and fights for women's health throughout the world. Edna describes her work with a passion that goes well beyond her academic training and cultural understanding. In her perspective, the development of the mind is not the only thing necessary to be of service to humanity. One must also cultivate the heart.

As educators at a Pietist university, we seek to integrate Edna's perspective

---

[1] *Half the Sky*, directed by Maro Chermayeff (New York: New Video Group, 2012), DVD. See also Nicholas D. Kristof and Sheryl WuDunn, *Half the Sky: Turning Oppression into Opportunity for Women Worldwide* (New York: Vintage, 2009), pp. 123-30.

into our work with students, believing that we must teach both minds and hearts. Within the context of growing religious diversity in the twenty-first century, educating students to serve in a religiously diverse world is a necessity. Such preparation, we believe, must be deliberate in addressing the issue of religious diversity as a crucial part of developing intercultural competence.

It can be challenging to do this, however, within the context of an explicitly Christian university. How do we best prepare students to constructively work with persons who believe differently, when their college campus is limited to members of the same religion? How do we facilitate and cultivate opportunities for constructive interfaith engagement when our students are ignorant about other traditions, afraid of having conversations about faith with religious others and not sure that interfaith engagement should be a Christian responsibility? Navigating these issues requires that we think creatively about how to help students better understand their own views on spirituality as well as how to interact with others who hold views on spirituality that are different from their own.

We believe there are several aspects of a Pietist ethos consistent with and supportive of this type of interfaith education. One place where this can be found is in the work of August Hermann Francke, an eighteenth-century Pietist theologian, pastor and teacher who was deeply inspired to put the work of Philipp Jakob Spener into practice. In his book *God's Glory, Neighbor's Good*, Gary Sattler situates Francke and the larger Pietist tradition against the backdrop of Spener's six pious desires. We believe three of these desires have direct application to the issue of educating students for service in a religiously diverse context. Specifically, Spener's desires "that love might be practiced in everyday life, that Christians might have a better idea of how to behave in controversies with heretics and unbelievers, practicing love in controversy, too, and that theological schools might stress piety as well as scholarship."[2]

In this chapter we connect these three Pietist themes with the work of leading contemporary theologians who address the issue of Christian responsibility in a religiously diverse world, with a particular focus on Brian McLaren and Miroslav Volf. For both McLaren and Volf, true Christian practice calls us to learn to meaningfully love *all* of our neighbors, even the religious other.

---

[2]Gary R. Sattler, *God's Glory, Neighbor's Good* (Chicago: Covenant Press, 1982), p. 12.

Learning to build and navigate relationships with persons of different faith traditions should never entail abandoning our own religious commitments. Instead the strength of those commitments should prompt us to seek and sustain constructive relationships with all people we encounter. We believe we can prepare students for this sort of cultural engagement, promoting Spener's desire for an active view of faith, a central commitment to love of neighbor and an irenic spirit.

"THAT THEOLOGICAL SCHOOLS MIGHT STRESS PIETY AS WELL AS SCHOLARSHIP"

The historical context into which Pietism emerged was one characterized by theological orthodoxy. Post-Reformation theologians focused primarily on defending true belief, and from a Pietist perspective, this was done at the expense of preparing pastors who could serve as well as teach. Spener believed theological education should engage both the mind and the heart; living a life of Christian devotion dedicated to spiritual growth and service to others was just as important as possessing right belief.

An important aspect of interfaith education is that it allows students to grow in spiritual maturity while actively learning to practice "being Christian" in a diverse world. This is consistent with the Pietist ethos, stressing an active, living faith. As Sattler explains, "For Lutheran orthodoxy [of the seventeenth and early eighteenth centuries] faith was a noun, something (a body of propositions) with which one agreed. For Francke faith was a verb, a way of being which was the necessary outworking of intellectual and emotional assent to the claim that Jesus is Savior."[3] As Christian educators, affirming faith as a verb implies a responsibility to extend learning beyond mere intellectual activity to actual engagement with the people living beyond the borders of our campuses.

In order to provide this type of engagement for our students, we have regularly taken students off campus to a variety of events where they will encounter people from different faith traditions in meaningful ways. For example, we often design service projects where our students will work together with students from other religious backgrounds. After working a few hours, we share a meal together and talk about the different ways service is motivated by re-

---

[3]Sattler, *God's Glory, Neighbor's Good*, p. 105.

ligion. Additionally, we encourage students to attend off-campus interfaith dialogues, where they are seated at tables with persons from diverse religious backgrounds and participate in discussions on a variety of topics ranging from theological to personal or political.

A fairly common experience shared by many of our Christian students participating in interfaith dialogue for the first time is surprise at the diversity of religious beliefs they encounter and the sincerity with which those views are held. As one of our evangelical students noted after his first dialogue, "I always thought that everyone in America was either a devout Christian or a devout atheist. I've never met people before who take other faiths seriously." Engaging students in interfaith dialogue can be an incredibly powerful tool for moving them beyond the learning that takes place through reading books about other faiths or through classroom discussion. While we can often accomplish a great deal by having students encounter different views through texts, films and speeches, a greater depth of learning can come from personal experience. After all, as Robert Wuthnow observes, I must consider new ideas heard directly from my religious neighbor "differently than if I simply read about them in a book or considered them in the abstract."[4] We believe this is the type of direct learning our students need to have in order to fully engage the world beyond our campuses. At interfaith dialogues, our Christian students have had the opportunity to, for example, hear firsthand the story of a man who was ostracized in high school for being Jewish, or of a woman who converted to Islam because of the emphasis on peace in that tradition only to find that she was subsequently perceived as dangerous. While listening to members of the Baha'i tradition, which most of our students never knew existed, many not only learned about the principles of this faith but also about the experience of being misunderstood or ignored by society at large. Students also learn that many Muslims, Jews, Buddhists and Christians share similar values, such as justice and equality.

Specific to the role of educators at Christian colleges, we are not merely trying to develop good citizens, but like Spener we are also seeking to help our students develop spiritual maturity that goes beyond intellectual growth. Engaging students in direct interaction with people of other faith traditions

---

[4]Robert Wuthnow, *America and the Challenges of Religious Diversity* (Princeton, NJ: Princeton University Press, 2007), p. 291.

creates an opportunity for spiritual growth and learning outside of the "campus bubble" that is characteristic of our Christian college. They develop religious literacy as they learn more about traditions that differ from their own. Hearing people from other faith traditions talk about their faiths, instead of learning about other religions indirectly, helps our students recognize which of their assumptions about that faith tradition are accurate, and which are stereotypical, misguided or wrong. They also come to understand that just as not all Christians think alike, so also not all Muslims, Jews, Buddhists, Hindus or Baha'i think alike. Students who have participated in interfaith dialogues also become the bearers of what philosopher Miriam McCormick calls "responsible belief," having a clearer understanding of why they believe what they believe (and why others don't), and they learn firsthand lessons about how to live out the Christian responsibility of hospitality: to welcome the stranger in their midst and love the neighbor who is different from their usual neighbors.[5]

Even while recognizing this call to welcome and love, some of our evangelical students are concerned that their very participation in interfaith dialogue will imply that they agree with everything they are hearing—that the distinctives of Christianity will be lost in the process. But this isn't necessarily true. It *is* possible to listen, seek to understand and even come to appreciate aspects of another religion without compromising commitment to one's own. In these efforts toward hospitality without compromising Christian faith, differentiating between theological and civic issues can be essential. Topics such as salvation or the divinity of Christ, for example, are theological issues likely to elicit significant disagreement between people of different faiths. These conversations are crucial, particularly within the Pietist tradition, where conversion and regeneration are emphasized. At the same time, however, the Pietist emphasis on practice over belief suggests that individuals can disagree over theological issues while still seeking to come together with people of other faiths by emphasizing the similarities, in what theologian Miroslav Volf calls our "socially relevant knowledge of God," that is, the emphasis that many religions place on love of God and love of neighbor.[6] In other words, one doesn't need to uphold theological pluralism in order to promote civic pluralism.

---

[5]Miriam McCormick, "Responsible Believing," in *Toward a Pedagogy of Belief and Doubt,* ed. Sydney Watts (Richmond, VA: Teagle Foundation, 2008), p. 32.
[6]Miroslav Volf, *Allah: A Christian Response* (New York: HarperOne, 2011), p. 14.

Affirming civic pluralism allows us to put faith into action by working for the common good. As Brian McLaren explains, interfaith engagement is actually a living version of religion, which "[at root] means reconnecting or rebonding broken relations—with God, with neighbor, with stranger and enemy, with nonhuman life, with all creation."[7] For McLaren, active engagement with others in a pluralistic context actually deepens and strengthens one's faith because it challenges us to really live out what Jesus identified as the central commands of Christianity: "'You shall love the Lord your God with all your heart, and with all your soul, and with all your mind.' This is the greatest and first commandment. And a second is like it: 'You shall love your neighbor as yourself'" (Mt 22:37-39). McLaren asks, "Could it be that our core doctrines are even more wonderful and challenging than we previously imagined, asking us not simply to assent to them in the presence of our fellow assenters, but to practice them in relationships with those who don't hold them? Could our core doctrines in this way become 'healing teachings'?"[8] This sentiment is echoed in Francke's sermon *Duty to the Poor*: "One shows oneself as a Christian so far as one is a true person of prayer before God and practices love toward neighbor. Otherwise it is all empty talk."[9]

"THAT LOVE MIGHT BE PRACTICED IN EVERYDAY LIFE"

The Pietist emphasis on faith as action, not mere assent, is also reflected in the Pietist understanding of Christ's command to love our neighbors. The emphasis is clearly seen in the writings of Johanna Eleonora Peterson, who said that Christian faith must join love of God with love of neighbor. Petersen was a prolific writer in the German Pietist movement, completing several books on spiritual life as well as biblical commentaries and an autobiography.[10] She is also known for her service to others, including ecumenical engagement with Jews living in her own community. As Michelle Clifton-Soderstrom describes her, "[Petersen] never lived as though her faith was private. . . . She found God by loving her neighbors and praying for her enemies. . . . She lived a life of

---

[7]Brian McLaren, *Why Did Jesus, Moses, the Buddha, and Mohammed Cross the Road? Christian Identity in a Multi-faith World* (New York: Jericho Books, 2012), p. 249.

[8]Ibid., p. 163.

[9]Quoted in Sattler, *God's Glory, Neighbor's Good*, p. 158.

[10]Johanna Eleonora Petersen, *The Life of Lady Johanna Eleonora Petersen, Written by Herself*, ed. and trans. Barbara Becker-Cantarino (Chicago: University of Chicago Press, 2005).

ongoing conversion to God, and in doing so she was receptive to others."[11]

As Peterson reminds us, love isn't just an intellectual perspective or emotional disposition: it is active. In the context of interfaith interactions, what might this love look like?

Love listens and receives. We demonstrate love of our religious neighbor when we listen with a generous spirit, willing to receive and learn. This may sound obvious, but it can be much more difficult than it seems. Particularly for those convinced of the truth of Christianity, "listening" often consists of looking for flaws in what the other person has to say, mentally preparing for ways to demonstrate the superiority of Christianity over the other person's religion. But this kind of selective listening is far from loving. Especially when communicating with religious neighbors in situations of great need, Anthony Gittins, a theologian and cultural anthropologist who explores the intersections between faith and society, reminds Christians that

> we must never forget that we go to real people living in real situations amid real problems, but that these people have real wisdom and real aspirations; to overlook these truths would lead to our patronizing others and ultimately treating them as no better than objects.[12]

Instead of objectifying others through selective listening, we ought to practice humility, a genuine openness to being taught.

At the very least, we Christians can demonstrate our willingness to be taught about other religions by listening to our religious neighbors provide an insider's perspective on what it's like to be, say, Jewish or Muslim or Buddhist. Such listening can help us come to "see others through their own eyes," not just our own, as we pay "receptive attention to their own story about who they see themselves to be," says Volf.[13] "Receptive attention" includes practicing what Volf calls "hermeneutical hospitality" as we seek to "enter sympathetically into others' efforts to interpret their sacred texts."[14] The goal of such attentive listening, says theologian Volker Küster, is to "understand the religious other in

---

[11]Michelle A. Clifton-Soderstrom, *Angels, Worms, and Bogeys: The Christian Ethic of Pietism* (Eugene, OR: Cascade, 2010), pp. 68-69.

[12]Anthony J. Gittins, *Gifts and Strangers: Meeting the Challenge of Inculturation* (New York: Paulist, 1989), p. xi.

[13]Miroslav Volf, "Living with the 'Other,'" *Journal of Ecumenical Studies* 39 (Winter–Spring 2002): 19.

[14]Miroslav Volf, "A Voice of One's Own: Public Faith in a Pluralistic World," in *Democracy and the New Religious Pluralism*, ed. Thomas Banchoff (Oxford: Oxford University Press, 2007), p. 280.

a way that the other can recognize himself or herself in my perception."[15] But our listening shouldn't stop there: "Love demands that we try to see . . . [our religious neighbors] as they see themselves *and* to see *ourselves* as *others* see us."[16] Of course, we may not always like what we hear when we learn how our religious neighbors perceive Christians, but we cannot hope to mend old wounds if we don't even know what those wounds are. We cannot hope to love our neighbors if we don't know what love looks like to them.

Christians can also learn from their religious neighbors by listening to the insights and experiences gained from various spiritual disciplines and practices common to numerous religions. For example, at an *iftar* (community meal breaking fast during Ramadan) in a local Islamic center, one Muslim student talked with our students about the way in which the Ramadan fast helped him develop deeper compassion for those who never have enough to eat. At another interfaith event, a Jewish woman who had recently lost her mother reflected on the soul formation she was experiencing as a result of saying *kaddish* (prayers for the dead) in community with others who had experienced similar losses yet who sought to honor God amid their grief. Not only do we Christians stand to gain much as we listen to such stories, but we also demonstrate love by "respecting the image of God in others and seeing their potential contributions as being of equal value to ours."[17] Volf sums up this attitude toward our religious neighbors when he says,

> So what is a Christian way to see oneself in relation to others? It is very simple. Commanded, as Christians are, to love their neighbor as themselves, their stance should be that of discerning generosity toward others—toward them as persons as well as toward their beliefs and practices.[18]

Love fights religious prejudice. We show love to our religious neighbors when we listen attentively and show our willingness to learn from them. Such

---

[15]Volker Küster, "Toward an Intercultural Theology: Paradigm Shifts in Missiology, Ecumenics, and Comparative Religion," in *Theology and the Religions: A Dialogue*, ed. Viggo Mortensen (Grand Rapids: Eerdmans, 2003), p. 179.

[16]Miroslav Volf, "Your Scripture Meets Mine," *The Christian Century* (October 19, 2004), p. 43. Emphasis added.

[17]Elizabeth Conde-Frazier, "From Hospitality to Shalom," in *A Many Colored Kingdom: Multicultural Dynamics for Spiritual Formation*, ed. Elizabeth Conde-Frazier, S. Steve Kang and Gary A. Parrett (Grand Rapids: Baker Academic, 2004), p. 172.

[18]Volf, *Allah*, p. 94.

listening is also crucial if we are to demonstrate love by fighting prejudice against religious others. This is the case, says Volf, because "the best way to fight prejudice is by knowledge—not just knowledge of people's beliefs and practices, but knowledge of their feelings and hopes, their injuries and triumphs as well."[19] If Volf is right, then Christians have a lot of learning to do, both about other religions in general and about individual religious neighbors we encounter. It also means that we need to be deliberate in seeking out such encounters and then in counteracting falsehoods and misperceptions expressed by fellow Christians about other faiths.

Of course, this is easier said than done, in part because each of us has preconceptions about other religions that get in the way. For example, many Christians describe Christianity as a religion of grace, whereas they describe other religions (such as Islam) as more "legalistic," centered on human efforts to please a demanding God. As one of our evangelical students noted, "To Muslims, Allah . . . is a severe reckoning force. Christians believe in an all-powerful God, yet he is gentle to his beloved; he is a true Father." Christians holding such an understanding of Islam tend to hear comments about Allah's greatness or power or holiness as confirmation of their views—even though they themselves might speak of Christians as worshiping a powerful and holy God whose judgments are at times described in the Bible as fierce. Their preconceptions about other religions make it difficult for them to see the many parallels between their own Christian beliefs and those held by their Muslim neighbors. These preconceptions tend to magnify differences and contribute to the religious prejudice that leads to violence. It is worth remembering that religious violence is not unique to the twenty-first century. The irenic spirit central to the Pietist tradition emerges from the context of religious warfare in Reformation Europe. For the Pietists love of neighbor meant loving Catholics, Lutherans and Calvinists despite their differences.

We can start fighting prejudice simply by reminding ourselves that preconceptions can distort and by recognizing our human tendency to focus on what makes our beliefs look good and what makes the beliefs of others look inferior. Failing to recognize this tendency makes it impossible for us to interact lovingly with our religious neighbors. Speaking as a Christian, Volf ad-

---

[19]Ibid., p. 203.

dresses his Muslim neighbor when he says that "my distorted image of you dishonors you; I do you injustice by clinging to it. . . . If I care for you, I will want my image of you to do you justice."[20] We demonstrate love of our religious neighbors, then, when we seek to be "truthful about the other as well as about ourselves"—and when we speak truthfully about our religious neighbors to fellow Christians.[21]

Love follows the Golden Rule. We demonstrate love for our religious neighbors by listening and learning, as well as by fighting religious prejudice. Although there is much to be learned by listening to others, at times Christians also wish to speak of their faith in hopes that others may be attracted to Christ. There is a long and vibrant history of missions among Pietist Christians, motivated by love of Christ and love of neighbor and frequently accompanied by acts of service. A. H. Francke, for example, promoted medical missions in India, keenly aware of the responsibility Christians had to "be mindful of the well-being of the people in their care."[22] Many Christians throughout the history of the church have seen missionary efforts as the primary way to show love for religious neighbors.

Love certainly might (and often does) motivate mission work, but Volf argues that many of our religious neighbors don't see mission work and various evangelistic efforts as reflections of love. There may be numerous reasons for this, of course, some of which (such as failure to listen and learn or failure to combat religious misinformation and prejudice) we have already discussed. In addition to these reasons, Volf identifies what he describes as a failure to be guided by the Golden Rule when we speak of Christ to our religious neighbors.

The "Golden Rule" of witnessing tells us to "witness to others in the way you think others should witness to you."[23] It seems obvious, then, that we would avoid tactics such as those used by street corner preachers who point fingers at passersby, shouting insults and accusations. It also seems obvious that we would oppose various scare tactics that some Christian youth groups use in order to impress teenagers with the seriousness of sin and the horrors of hell.

---

[20]Ibid., p. 205.

[21]Ibid., p. 206.

[22]Christoffer H. Grundmann, "Pietism, Revivalism, and Medical Missions: The Concern for the Corporeality of Scripture in A. H. Francke, P. Parker, and G. Dowkonnt," in *The Pietist Impulse*, ed. Christian T. Collins Winn et al. (Eugene, OR: Pickwick, 2011), p. 297.

[23]Volf, *Allah*, p. 211.

Perhaps less obvious, though, is our tendency to "compare the best practices of one's own faith with the worst practices of the other faith," says Volf.[24] This, too, demonstrates a violation of the Golden Rule, a failure to love our religious neighbor as we love ourselves.

The "Golden Rule" of witnessing also tells us to "witness to others only if you are prepared to let them witness to you," says Volf.[25] Many of our religious neighbors take their spiritual lives and religious practices seriously, just as Christians seek to do. Our failure to listen with care and attention to what they have to say demonstrates a lack of regard—a lack of love. Christian missionaries are often "professional 'givers,'" says Anthony Gittins, but they may not always acknowledge the desire and rights of others to give as well. "In our concern for all we 'do' for others, are we perhaps insensitive to what the others (try to or might like to) do for us?" he asks.[26] McLaren reimagines Christian missions in a similar way. He explains,

> Sharing is never a one-way street. It is always about receiving as well as giving. In generosity, we freely share our treasures with people of other faiths, *without requiring them to convert.* And in the same spirit, we gratefully receive the treasures generously offered to us by other faiths—*without needing to convert.*[27]

This is particularly important to keep in mind if we hope to demonstrate love for neighbors from religions—such as Islam—that take their own call to missions very seriously.

Love takes responsibility. Even if we seek to treat our religious neighbors with respect and love, listening attentively so that we can learn and receive at least as much as we might hope to give, we still will at times offend without meaning to do so. And we will almost certainly encounter neighbors who have been hurt by other Christians. (This reality provides yet another reason why it is so important for Christians to take the time to have actual conversations with our religious neighbors, for we might not otherwise learn about the pain that has been done to others in the name of Christianity.) Unfortunately, even the best of intentions can't guarantee a good outcome. In such circumstances, love of neighbor includes coming to take responsibility for the harm that we—and

---

[24]Ibid., p. 212.
[25]Ibid., p. 207.
[26]Gittins, *Gifts*, p. 104.
[27]McLaren, *Why Did Jesus*, p. 262.

others—have done in the name of religion. As Spener writes in *Pia Desideria*, "Let us therefore be diligent in investigating even more deeply our own shortcomings and those of the rest of the church."[28]

"That Christians Might . . . Practice Love in Controversy Too"

Living for "God's glory and neighbor's good" is often easier to think about than to practice. According to McLaren, the biggest obstacle to establishing and sustaining healthy relationships with persons of different faith traditions is fear. As he explains, "Your greatest obstacle will be in you and mine will be in me. In the end, it is not the threats of others that cause me to shrink back, but rather my own fear."[29] As educators we must train students to engage difference with courage and civility.

McLaren recognizes that fear of other religions is not only problematic because fear might prevent us from entering into dialogue with those who believe differently. Additionally, fear can easily harden into religious hostility and conflict. According to McLaren, Christians in contemporary America suffer from what he calls "Conflicted Religious Identity Syndrome."[30] This label describes the tension between wanting to love my neighbor and at the same time being afraid that such love betrays my commitment to the truth of my own faith tradition. At root is often a belief that Christianity actually requires opposition toward other faiths, leaving believers without a clear understanding of how to be a genuine Christian without taking a hostile stand regarding other views.

The Pietist ethos advocates that we approach conflict with an irenic spirit. This means neither that we find peace simply by avoiding disagreement, nor that we must embrace all views as equally true. Rather, having an irenic spirit means we speak our view of the truth with love and sincerity, and charitably respect the other's point of view as well. Once again the Pietist ethos reminds us that *how we act* is just as important as *what we believe*.

Francke describes an irenic approach in his "Scriptural Rules of Life." First he emphasizes that our actions should be of more priority than our words: "Do not force yourself to speak much. But if God gives you opportunity to

---

[28]Philip Jacob Spener, *Pia Desideria*, trans. Theodore G. Tappert (Philadelphia: Fortress, 1964), p. 37.
[29]McLaren, *Why Did Jesus*, p. 52.
[30]Ibid., p. 15.

speak, speak with respect, after mature consideration, gently, as much as you have certainty, with loving sincerity."[31] Second, not only should our own actions serve as a witness to our faith, but also citing examples of virtue within our own tradition can be far more effective than engaging in theological debate. As Francke advises, "Do not let good—and especially living—examples of virtue and [ones] which bear witness to divine providence, omnipotence, goodness, justice, escape your memory, for one can edify much with that."[32] Finally, he recognizes that we will not always be able to reach agreement in conflict. When disagreement remains, we should avoid taking a hostile position toward the other:

> If you have presented the truth clearly and with good arguments, be satisfied. You will gain little with further quarrelling. Your opponent will consider the matter more if he sees that you are certain of your subject and will not quarrel. Should he learn nothing more from you, at least he may learn gentleness and modesty from your example.[33]

Consistent with this Pietist mindset, McLaren's solution to the tension regarding our relationships to other faiths requires that we change how we think about our own Christian identity. Rather than believing that our faithfulness to Christianity is demonstrated by hostility toward different views, our faithfulness can be made manifest in the way we bear witness to Christ through our love of others. McLaren explains,

> My understanding of Jesus and his message leads me to see each faith tradition, including my own, as having its own history, value, strengths, and weaknesses. I seek to affirm and celebrate all that is good in each faith and tradition, and I build intentional relationships of mutual sharing and respectful collaboration with people of all faith traditions, so all our faiths can keep growing and contribute to God's will being done on earth as it is in Heaven.[34]

For McLaren, this switch from "hostility" to "solidarity" actually puts us more in line with the central teachings of Christianity. This affirms the core identity of Christians as those who love God and neighbor above all else.

---

[31]Quoted in Sattler, *God's Glory, Neighbor's Good*, p. 200.
[32]Quoted in ibid., p. 201.
[33]Quoted in ibid., p. 203.
[34]McLaren, *Why Did Jesus*, p. 69.

As educators it is crucial that we avoid teaching other religions from the perspective that they are "the enemy." As McLaren explains,

> When we increasingly understand who we are in relation to an enemy—whether that enemy is legitimate, innocent, or imaginary—we develop an increasingly hostile identity. Such an identity teaches us to see *sameness as safety* and *otherness as danger*. It is characterized by duality: us and them, right and wrong, good and evil, light and darkness. It promotes a mentality of us *versus* them, us *apart from* them, us *instead of* them, us *without* them, us *over* them, us *using* them, us *in spite of* them, us *oppressed* by them, or us *occupying* them, but never us *for* them or us *with* them.[35]

Preparing our students to live constructively in the midst of religious diversity requires that we help them learn to look for truth and goodness even beyond the boundaries of their own view of Christian truth. This can mean asking them to listen charitably before critiquing, to make sure they really understand how someone from a different faith views the world. This listening stage provides the space for students to identify points of commonality, in addition to the differences, between views. From these points of commonality one builds the solidarity to maintain a spirit of love and to be an agent of peace, even in controversy. "We don't need to agree," says Volf; "we just need to be civil rather than mean-spirited as we disagree."[36]

CONCLUSION

Michelle Clifton-Soderstrom begins her book on Pietist ethics with a reference to familiar words from the apostle Paul: "The only thing that counts is faith working through love" (Gal 5:6). As Christian educators at a Pietist institution, this is a central theme of our commitment to developing whole and holy persons. We desire to cultivate students with mature faith commitments ready to take their academic skills to serve others in the world at large. The twenty-first-century context in which these students will live and serve is increasingly diverse—a "highly connected, interdependent, and religiously mixed world. As a rule, many religions inhabit a common political space."[37] This means that, increasingly, interfaith interactions will become part of our

---

[35]Ibid., p. 63.
[36]Volf, *Allah*, p. 262.
[37]Ibid., p. 236.

lives. In these interactions with our religious neighbors, we must, says Volf, "avoid inconsistency. The way you think about others and act toward them should not clash with the beliefs about God you espouse and seek to commend to them."[38]

---

[38]Ibid., p. 74.

PART THREE

RESPONSES

Views from the Natural and Health Sciences

The heavens are telling the glory of God;
and the firmament proclaims his handiwork.
Day to day pours forth speech,
and night to night declares knowledge.
There is no speech, nor are there words;
their voice is not heard;
yet their voice goes out through all the earth,
and their words to the end of the world.

PSALM 19:1-4

Religion that is pure and undefiled before God, the Father,
is this: to care for orphans and widows in their distress,
and to keep oneself unstained by the world.

JAMES 1:27

9

Pietist Values in Science and Science Education

Richard W. Peterson

◆

THE SETTING WAS A MEETING of faculty leaders in the chair's office of a large and prestigious physics department while planning a national conference, and the conversation drifted to a discussion of that state's undergraduate institutions with demonstrated success in nurturing students for graduate work. It was noted with some surprise the many exemplary students coming from one or two rather modest schools with continuing strong Christian identities, and the unanswered question was posed, "How is this possible, as they seem to start with weaker students?" A student's likelihood for success in undergraduate or graduate-level physics is often not well predicted by ACT or GRE scores but depends as much on students' self-image and confidence, sense of calling and belonging, and their subsequent "grit" in facing the many bumps lying ahead.[1] In faculty discussions about how a student may be doing in physics, it is a tradition in my own department to balance an awareness of their conceptual understandings with "Has the student turned the corner?" in terms of being able to see themselves anew as truly belonging and called into their chosen field. This is not only an issue of psychology, but for many students of faith this is where "the rubber hits the road" in practically integrating their faith's foundation and an academic discipline.

---

[1]Lauren Aguilar, Greg Walton and Carl Wieman, "Psychological Insights for Improved Physics Teaching," *Physics Today* 67, no. 5 (2014): 43.

Within such an academic venue a student's human experience and an increasing awareness of their foundational professional calling often rise in priority along with their cognitive abilities and conceptual maturity within the discipline. The lasting impact of undergraduate science education (or the quality of a course's instruction) is only approximated by tests of conceptual understanding and problem solving. Disabilities and human limitations may in fact become strengths when encountered within the context of really knowing "who you are" and where you are called to service. The importance of personally "turning the corner" is found in the "convertative" perspective introduced above by David Williams:

> By *convertative* I mean that when one's whole person is involved, one experiences a kind of movement analogous to the movement from sickness to health. The life of the mind becomes more than a mere analysis of propositions. The inquirer needs to see something they did not before and feel the change that has been wrought by having considered the world in a different way. Pietism's central theological notion maintains that an encounter with the transcendent will leave one altered in all senses of what it means to be a person and this experiential emphasis is carried into the realm of academic inquiry.[2]

Similarly, Minnesota humorist and storyteller Kevin Kling has observed that many of us are better enabled by the perspective "I am, therefore I think" than by the familiar "I think, therefore I am."[3]

The quest for enabling a student's transcendent calling and personal identity is not unique to Christian institutions of pietistic heritage, yet for those of us under that umbrella this goal rises naturally in importance and should stimulate our best efforts as research mentors and teachers. The following sections of this response will touch on particular facets of this perspective, both in terms of actually doing physics and also regarding how we try to teach and mentor such an area of science—considering both where we seem to do well, and where we often seem to come up short.

DELIGHT IN DISCOVERY

The modern scientist of pietistic background and faith will often find the per-

---

[2]Quoted from p. 45 above.
[3]Kevin Kling, *On Stage with Kevin Kling* (St. Paul: Minnesota Historical Society Press, 2013), p. 4.

sonal experience of research bringing them closer to the Creator, and they may find such an engaging experience with God's world trumping concern about many details regarding how God has acted in scientific history. To be the first person to observe or really understand a certain phenomenon is fundamentally an occasion for personal delight, wonder and thanksgiving. Never does a person of faith feel closer to their source of strength and sustenance. William D. Phillips, a 1997 Nobel Prize winner in physics, said at an impromptu press conference at that time, "There are many people I want to thank, and I'd also like to thank God for giving us such a wonderful and interesting universe to explore."[4] This thankful reaction of wonder and delight within the process of science is also emphasized in Andy Crouch's description of colleagues sharing in his wife's work as an experimental physicist:

> If there is one personality characteristic of the vast majority of scientists I have met, it is delight. There is something about science that attracts people who are fascinated and thrilled by the world. . . . In many scientists, delight is matched by wonder—a sense of astonishment at the beautiful, ingenious complexity to be found in the world. This is not the "wonder" that comes from ignorance—"I wonder how a light bulb really works?"—but a wonder that comes from understanding.[5]

Astonishment is no small deal in science, and the nineteenth Psalm affirms that such an encounter with the transcendent is marvelously complementary to our more rational embrace of God's laws and corresponding scientific workings throughout the history of the universe. Thus in an academic environment that especially values the personal "Wow, this is really cool!" experience of delight, it is crucial for science teachers and research mentors to plan for, treasure and celebrate such "aha!" moments. As any science teacher enters the classroom or laboratory, an undergirding goal remains, "How can we celebrate and demonstrate today's phenomenon so as to passionately proclaim the pure wonder (and sometimes mystery) of the very big or tiny facets of our universe?" Doing this well may profit by PowerPoint bullets being mercifully turned off, as we use language and our human senses to personally delight in a sustaining universe.

---

[4]Quoted in Larry Witham, "Putting Faith in Science," *Washington Times*, Oct. 22, 2001.
[5]Andy Crouch, "What I Wish My Pastor Knew About . . . The Life of a Scientist, Part 1," *The BioLogos Forum*, blog, April 29, 2013, http://biologos.org/blog/what-i-wish-my-pastor-knew-about-the-life -of-a-scientist-part-1.

Feeling Small and Low

The traditional Shaker dance tune "Simple Gifts" proclaims,

'Tis the gift to be simple, 'tis the gift to be free
'Tis the gift to come down where we ought to be

The practice of science at its best builds on and reinforces a modest and humble demeanor, as does the irenic heritage within Pietism. In science we often perceive our work as physically only a small speck in a big, beautiful and complex universe. The awesome universe we study and try to embrace (on both large and small scales) has its own natural ways of escorting us to "where we ought to be."

Crouch reminds us that scientists (like their artistic counterparts) are a very human lot, often exhibiting a public persona quite the opposite of humility. Still, he observes, "If intellectual humility is essentially a willingness to admit what you do not and cannot know, science cultivates humility like few other pursuits can— because in few other pursuits do you so often find out that you were wrong."[6]

It is also clear that the endeavor of science does not aim to obtain absolute truths. In a memorable segment of Jacob Bronowski's 1973 BBC documentary series *The Ascent of Man,* he stands in the ashes of Auschwitz, where many of his family died, and reminds us of the inherently uncertain and temporal basis of this precious cooperative human endeavor we call science:

Science is a very human form of knowledge. We are always at the brink of the known; we always feel forward for what is to be hoped. Every judgment in science stands on the edge of error and is *personal.* Science is a tribute to what we can know although we are fallible. In the end, the words were said by Oliver Cromwell: "I beseech you in the bowels of Christ: Think it possible you may be mistaken."[7]

Likewise, Kathy Nevins has reminded us of the implications of a humble and personally vulnerable pietistic posture for our classrooms.[8] For institutions seeking to build on this heritage, it is important to champion highly interactive teaching atmospheres that build on an openness to continually learn from each other. Nowhere is such a posture more important than in science classes fea-

---

[6]Crouch, "What I Wish My Pastor Knew."
[7]Jacob Bronowski, "Knowledge or Certainty?" *The Ascent of Man,* film series, BBC and Time-Life (1973).
[8]See pp. 57-59 and 63-66 above.

turing a great diversity in student backgrounds. The impact (good and bad) of science and technology in our world may sometimes be judged in a most insightful manner by those students who find the details of science and engineering difficult, boring or irrelevant to their lives. Teachers who have spent years nurturing their own science majors will still often admit to being most enriched by these humbling and insightful interactions with a diversity of students who bring new perspectives and human experiences.

Surely some of the tempering strength of the process of science is reflected in its consensus-seeking openness to the correction of fellow workers. In this fashion the global science community traditionally seeks to function almost like a giant brain that is open to input and peer review from fellow workers as it seeks consensus. While sometimes failing to achieve such ideal openness to correction, the science enterprise may still come closer than many facets of society—including discussions within the church.

Earlier in this book, David Williams asks, "Could the conventicle have an academic use?"[9] For three decades Bethel University physics/engineering has been very visible nationally while fostering intense group projects in advanced laboratories that bravely blur the boundary between undergraduate research and academic assignments. Students and faculty members strive to humbly work and grow together while documenting progress on challenging mini-entrepreneur projects, and in recent years faculty members from around the US have come to the Bethel campus to be immersed in the subject matter and approaches of these conventicle-like endeavors. Walls come down between students and faculty as problems are addressed that would be quite intractable within a traditional academic laboratory. This approach has its inherent limitations and risks, but it builds on a pietistic heritage as lives are changed. Graduating students often affirm that this type of experience provided a crucial, transcendent encounter with themselves and one small part of the universe.

SCIENCE: BLESSING OR CURSE?

In the aftermath of World War II, Robert Oppenheimer created quite a stir by simply observing, "Physicists have known sin." In reaching this conclusion it seems the post-Nagasaki Oppenheimer was less burdened about work on two

---

[9]Quoted from p. 47 above.

atomic bombs to help end WWII (a project he had broadly supported and skillfully led) than the human attitudes, egos and motivations of the hundreds who worked feverishly behind the fences of the Manhattan Project. While to many Christians the accusation of sin in science may sound like no big surprise, it does bring to mind those desired virtues of the early Pietists that are listed above by Roger Olson: "compassion, honesty, justice, fairness, redemptive treatment of persons, forgiveness, cooperation, respect and dedication."[10] So it is that those who aspire to teach and mentor must take a long, reflective look at their work and its broad ramifications for the earth itself and its present and future living populations, and we must help our students do the same. In such a context we are reminded of the comments of Albert Einstein to Caltech science and engineering students in 1931, as he threw out a humanitarian high calling for the "creations of our minds," equations and diagrams of young scientists to provide blessing to all people:

> It is not enough that you should understand about applied science in order that your work may increase man's blessings. Concern for man himself and his fate must always form the chief interest of all technical endeavors, concern for the great unsolved problems of organization of labor and the distribution of goods— in order that the creations of our mind shall be a blessing and not a curse to mankind. Never forget this in the midst of your diagrams and equations.[11]

While we all come up short on that challenging list of pietistic desired values and actions, it is clear that both Einstein and Oppenheimer found from life experiences that scientists have special responsibilities that follow from their own gifts, abilities and positions of power. Scientists and engineers simply cannot function as amoral advisors in a technical world that affects us all.

It is interesting to contemplate how early Pietists might view the lives and work of scientists of Christian faith today. For example, they might enjoy meeting three Nobel Prize winners of the last half-century in the area of optical physics who have been articulate about their Christian faith and its impact on their lives: Charles H. Townes (1964), Arthur L. Schawlow (1981) and William D. Phillips (1997). Phillips, for example, notes,

> I am a physicist. I do mainstream research; I publish in peer-reviewed journals;

---

[10]Quoted from p. 101 above.
[11]Quoted in "Einstein Sees Lack in Applying Science," *New York Times*, Feb. 17, 1931.

> I present my research at professional meetings; I train students and postdoctoral researchers; I try to learn from nature how nature works. In other words, I am an ordinary scientist. I am also a person of religious faith. I attend church; I sing in the gospel choir; I go to Sunday school; I pray regularly; I try to "do justice, love mercy, and walk humbly with my God" [Mic 6:8]. In other words, I am an ordinary person of faith.[12]

Phillips is well known to enjoy conveying his laser cooling research through fun, demonstrated lectures for young people and their physics teachers. Townes and Schawlow also wrote and spoke with passion, humor, humility, irenic spirit and conviction to show the public what scientists are really like—and not like. Clearly these inspiring and brilliant folks have seemed to pass many of the tests of desired pietistic virtues.

But where do modern scientists find their biggest challenges in meeting foundational pietistic expectations? Too often in the public eye the world of science seems an isolated haven well beyond the priorities, woes and joys of regular people. This "out-of-touch" reputation is only enhanced by the seemingly scary expectations of the fabled, totally committed professional lifestyle of those in the sciences. Indeed, almost any science professor of recent years has probably been troubled by gifted students electing to try another career because of what appears to be a near-burnout lifestyle expectation for academic scientists who seek tenure and grants . . . and yet more grants. Scientists seem to necessarily work within a very high-pressure, isolated and sometimes prestigious world that may threaten parallel efforts on their part toward pursuing justice and peace, outreach to the less privileged, and even a compassionate mentoring of students—or being able to devote quality time to their families. If science is so given to isolation and competition, is it even a worthy Christian calling?

In teaching liberal arts science classes or those for science and engineering majors, it is important to extend ourselves in honestly emphasizing that science is a very human enterprise and should build on strong interactions with the needs of a hurting world. Conveying such needs is not where science education has often excelled. On the other hand, both of the physicists who have received the Nobel Peace Prize—Andrei Sakharov (1975) and Joseph Rotblat (1995)—spoke, wrote and lived costly lives to emphasize this human side of science.

---

[12]William D. Phillips, "Does Science Make Belief in God Obsolete?" Big Questions Essay Series, John Templeton Foundation, www.templeton.org/belief/essays/phillips.pdf.

Rotblat simply concluded his Nobel address with, "Above all, remember your humanity."[13] We are also challenged by the plea from a post–World War II high school principal as reported by Haim Ginott:

> Dear Teacher, I am a survivor of a concentration camp. My eyes saw what no man should witness: Gas chambers built by learned engineers, children poisoned by educated physicians, infants killed by trained nurses, women and babies shot and burned by high school and college graduates. So I am suspicious of education. My request is: Help your students become human.[14]

Scientists and teachers must not be isolated from the full mix of human struggles as they reach out to the disenfranchised and in care of God's creation—including the resources of our vulnerable planet Earth—lest we become what Einstein called "a curse to mankind." Of course, such hands-on avenues of service will take different forms in each scientific discipline and for the gifts, personality and calling of each worker. The scientific community has too often fallen short in skillfully celebrating the sustaining delights of discovery and applications with the broader public. Tragically too many folks simply do not have a clue about what we do and how work in the sciences may joyfully enhance our lives of faith. In addition, we may often be hindered in our quest to serve and teach by undue homage to power structures that visibly entice through the many godlike idols within our professional world of publication, grants and research. Whether in the physical or social sciences (or in the humanities or theology), Philipp Jakob Spener would likely plead with all twenty-first-century scholarly workers to more often come down from their ego- and jargon-shrouded towers and humbly seek to be an enabling portion of the blessing envisioned in Deuteronomy:

> See, I am setting before you today a blessing and a curse: the blessing, if you obey the commandments of the LORD your God that I am commanding you today; and the curse, if you disobey the commandments of the LORD your God, but turn from the way that I am commanding you today, to follow other gods that you have not known. (Deut 11:26-28)

---

[13]Joseph Rotblat, "Remember Your Humanity," 1995 Nobel Acceptance and Lecture, www.nobelprize.org/nobel_prizes/peace/laureates/1995/rotblat-lecture.html.

[14]Quoted in Haim G. Ginott, *Teacher and Child: A Book for Parents and Teachers* (New York: Macmillan, 1972), p. 317.

10

A Pietist Approach to Nursing Education in a Christian University

Nancy L. Olen

◆

I T HAS BEEN A PRIVILEGE to read and reflect on the rich history that is mine, having been educated at North Park University as an undergraduate and having taught at Bethel University for nearly twenty-five years. Both schools are historically pietistic academic institutions. This chapter will explore my responses to the concepts presented above that seem particularly relevant to nursing education in Christian universities today. I have chosen to reflect on the pietistic vision, the notion of whole person transformation through dialogue and experiential learning, and the meaning of being salt and light in the multicultural world of health care today.

FOR GOD'S GLORY AND NEIGHBOR'S GOOD

"God's glory and neighbor's good," the famous motto of the eighteenth-century German Pietist leader August Hermann Francke, resonates with the long history of nursing.[1] Historically, most nurses understood their practice as a call from God to serve him and society. The aim was to serve all, but especially the vulnerable, the widows, orphans, prisoners and the poor. These nurses were

---

[1] Gary R. Sattler, *God's Glory, Neighbor's Good: A Brief Introduction to the Life and Writings of August Hermann Francke* (Chicago: Covenant Press, 1982).

motivated by obedience to God, by altruism and by empathy for those who suffered. Similar concerns moved Francke to found homes for orphans and widows among the other institutions of Halle.[2] That city's acclaimed pharmacy sent medicines to the Pietist mission at Tranquebar, India, the beginning of a longstanding Pietist passion for global health care missions.[3]

Just like the Hebrew midwives, Christian nurses today willingly glorify God by serving others. In the first chapter of Exodus we read that Hebrew midwives defied the laws of the Pharaoh and allowed baby boys to live. "So God dealt well with the midwives; and the people multiplied and became very strong" (Ex 1:20).

Christian nurses willingly glorify God by serving others. We believe that all persons, regardless of age, intellect, physical strength or social usefulness bear the image of God. To assess and design unique and creative nursing interventions, we do this best when we are consciously aware of God's image marked on even the most debilitated person. With that perspective, we can become instruments of God's divine healing, knowing that our efforts make a difference for the recipient of nursing care. The nurse is a servant of God's mission in the world, dedicated to maintaining and restoring health. We desire that each person, family or community becomes all that God intended. A recent graduate of the Bethel nursing program joined the United Nations outreach to South Sudan to serve people in need of health care. She exemplifies glorifying God by serving others.

Nursing author Mary Elizabeth O'Brien writes that when a nurse, nurse educator, nurse administrator or nurse researcher stands before a client, student or staff member, God is also present because each is created in his image. Because God is present, the ground on which that nurse stands is holy ground. It is in the act of serving others that a nurse can truly encounter God.[4] Jesus' famous parable in Matthew 25 supports this assertion: "'I was sick and you took care of me.'... Then the righteous will answer him ... 'And when was it that we saw you sick...?'... And the king will answer them, 'Truly I tell you, just

---

[2]Ibid., pp. 60-67. See also Francke's 1697 sermon, "The Duty to the Poor," in ibid., pp. 155-85.

[3]See Christoffer H. Grundmann, "Pietism, Revivalism, and Medical Missions: The Concern for the Corporeality of Salvation in A. H. Francke, P. Parker, and G. Dowkontt," in *The Pietist Impulse in Christianity*, ed. Christian T. Collins Winn et al. (Eugene, OR: Pickwick, 2011), pp. 296-306.

[4]Mary Elizabeth O'Brien, *Spirituality in Nursing: Standing on Holy Ground*, 3rd ed. (Sudbury, MA: Jones and Bartlett, 2008), pp. 7-8.

as you did it to one of the least of these who are members of my family, you did it to me'" (Mt 25:36-37, 39-40).

WHOLE-PERSON TRANSFORMATION THROUGH DIALOGUE AND EXPERIENTIAL LEARNING

Christian nursing education is committed to shaping a whole and holy person. As Roger Olson argues above, the goal is not just to disseminate information but to transform students—into people who love God with heart, soul, mind and strength and who love their neighbors as themselves. We work to prepare nurses who are knowledgeable, confident in their identities and able to articulate their purpose in work and their commitment to service. The stamp of God's image on every individual provides us the potential to be like and reflect him.

In 1961 I was a student of nursing at the Swedish Covenant School of Nursing in Chicago. Following a class in pathophysiology, my teacher, Delores Johnson, sought me out in the library. She invited me to have coffee with her and then asked my forgiveness for her response to a question of mine that seemed to demean me. She went on to say that regardless of my lack of knowledge and experience, she believed she had no right to treat me in a disrespectful way. I remember being speechless and uncertain how to respond to such a gracious teacher.

In order that students profoundly understand the truth of Scripture, faculty members themselves are challenged to live out their theory in their practice. As the apostle James asked, "What good is it, my brothers and sisters, if you say you have faith but do not have works? Can faith save you? If a brother or sister is naked and lacks daily food, and one of you says to them, 'Go in peace; keep warm and eat your fill,' and yet you do not supply their bodily needs, what is the good of that? So faith by itself, if it has no works, is dead" (Jas 2:14-17).

Here Jesus is our model, as his teachings touched on all dimensions of life. Using teaching methods aimed at active learning, he discussed social relationships, moral concerns, money management, social and economic justice, and many other aspects of living together. His ministry integrated cure and prevention, and he invested heavily in health promotion—as seen in the beatitudes (Mt 5:3-12), in which he outlined a radical program of personal internal discipline oriented toward whole-person transformation.

Students are transformed, certainly in their personal devotional life, but especially in the day-to-day experiential learning in clinical sites. Even more than in chapel time or lecture classes, students and faculty members exchange stories of faith and questions of doubt. It is at the bedside of dying persons that the real meaning of *spirit* is discussed. It is in memory care units, serving people with dementia, that the biblical promise that nothing "will be able to separate us from the love of God in Christ Jesus our Lord" (Rom 8:39) can be explored. It is in the sharing of time and resources with a young, indigent family that the true meaning of Christian community becomes a reality. The deep communication between student and teacher, between junior and senior faculty member, or between nurse and client transforms each when we recognize one another as fellow learners and fellow pilgrims on the journey of life.

In over twenty years of teaching at Bethel, my faculty colleagues have covenanted to live together in a community centered on Jesus Christ. We have attempted to promote peace, to appreciate each other's differences and to support one another as we desire to grow more like Christ Jesus. We have agreed to promote honesty, compassion, mercy and justice. We have worked hard to maintain person centeredness over content centeredness and to avoid competitiveness.

Education of such a whole-person orientation that is geared toward total transformation requires a great investment of time, energy and spiritual resources. My own student experience returned to me many times over the years when I was tempted to disregard or diminish a student of mine who had much to learn. Asking for and granting forgiveness was a reality for which I was thankful.

BEING SALT AND LIGHT IN THE MULTICULTURAL WORLD OF HEALTH CARE

Health care today is multicultural. Cultures are not good or bad in themselves; they are the reality in which we live and work. Knowledgeable nurses who have a personal relationship with Jesus Christ recognize themselves to be members of a common priesthood with all other believers. They know they have been blessed to be a blessing to all they encounter. They pray for creativity and wisdom to address the complexity of the world's health problems and the brokenness of the health care systems in which they work. They value working together with the entire health care team. But how do the teachings of Jesus make a difference in such diverse societies as we find worldwide today?

Just this past week, I sat with a family of another cultural heritage. Their ninety-four-year-old father was hemorrhaging internally. The surgeon suggested that because of his age and fragile condition, nothing more should be done. The family voiced their beliefs that precisely because of his age and fragile condition he was so very valuable, and therefore everything possible should be done to give him a chance to live. As I encouraged the family to express their values, the surgeon listened with care. He agreed to perform the surgery in spite of what he believed would be a poor prognosis. The elderly man lived for thirty-six hours post operatively. During that time, three estranged members came and were reconciled to him and the others. The wife and daughter later thanked the health care team profusely for the miracle of healing that they believed had occurred in the life of that man.

When faced with cultural restrictions and ethical dilemmas, nursing educators can encourage students of nursing with the words that are often (but erroneously) attributed to Saint Francis of Assisi: "Preach the gospel at all times and if necessary, use words." Nursing, as a practice profession, is uniquely prepared to build the kingdom of God, with or without words. Our greatest strength is being present with broken people.

To complete what is left unfinished in God's world challenges nurses to go to the whole world to heal the sick, feed the hungry, clothe the naked, shelter the stranger and serve without thought of being served. The goal of nursing is to promote, maintain and restore wholeness in all people, and to make God's image seen and alive in them again.

CONCLUSIONS

Multiple theoretical perspectives are used to understand nursing knowledge and practice today. The framework of Pietism is a useful lens that supports us in our search for God's truth in nursing. The Bethel nursing department's mission statement reflects accurately the heritage of its founders when it expresses its mission to develop "nurses who bring a Christ-like presence to healthcare and are prepared to serve a diverse and changing society."[5]

---

[5]Department of Nursing, Bethel University, www.bethel.edu/undergrad/academics/nursing.

The early Pietists had a strong commitment to learning and to the devotional life. They also gave of their finances and energy to care for communities of vulnerable persons—orphans, the elderly and new immigrants. Christian nursing education can be encouraged by these leaders of the past to prepare persons to live for Christ on the holy ground of today's complex health care world.

PART FOUR

PROBLEMS AND PROPOSALS

Putting the Pietist Vision into Practice

I have often vacillated between the biblical realism of Anabaptism and the
optimism of the Pietist spirit. . . . I would love to give priority to being
faithful. At the same time I am concerned about being effective.
I want to heed the commandment to love the world because
of loving the world so much I want it to
be what God wants it to be.

DALE W. BROWN,
ANABAPTISM AND PIETISM

Day by day and with each passing moment,
Strength I find to meet my trials here;
Trusting in my Father's wise bestowment,
I've no cause for worry or fear.

LINA SANDELL,
"DAY BY DAY," TRANSLATED BY A. L. SKOOG

11

Intellectual Virtue and the Adventurous Christ Follower

Raymond J. VanArragon

◆

PIETISM IS KNOWN FOR ITS EMPHASIS on Christian experience and practice. A Pietist does not wish to be an armchair Christian, a Christian with a finely tuned set of theological views that do not have any significant impact on the way she lives her life. In fact, a Pietist thinks, the impact of one's Christian faith *should* be significant. Armchair faith is no faith at all.

At Bethel University, this emphasis on active faith is often captured in the call to be "adventurous Christ followers."[1] Adventure, of course, goes beyond mere activity: it smacks of daring and danger. And so the phrase "adventurous Christ follower" calls to mind a person who makes a daring career choice, serving in a nonprofit organization in some far-flung part of the globe or starting a new business with some overtly Christian emphasis. Peril and danger lurk: these adventures can end in failure and even disaster. Nonetheless, an adventurous Christ follower takes risks, follows where the Spirit appears to lead, and, more generally, makes life choices that put concern for security and comfort somewhere behind concern for following God's direction.

But these are not the only kinds of adventure that an active Christian—a Pietist—will engage in. Christ followers will also encounter *intellectual* ad-

---

[1]One prominent example: current Bethel president Jay Barnes's inaugural address was titled "Becoming an Adventurous Christ-follower," *Bethel Focus* (Spring 2009), www.bethel.edu/publications -archive/focus/spring-2009/departments/in-focus.

venture, in universities and beyond, and these adventures bring their own re-
wards and their own dangers. In this chapter I want to explore some of the
dangers. In particular, I want to explore some ways in which, as I see it, adventurous Pietists can acquire tendencies away from certain important intellectual
virtues and toward their vicious counterparts. To that end, I'll begin by discussing virtues themselves, differentiating intellectual virtues from moral ones.
Then I'll turn to intellectual virtues related to a concern for truth and an appropriate open-mindedness, discuss how pietistic tendencies of adventurous
Christ followers can make them susceptible to the corresponding vices, and
conclude with some reflections on ways to maintain these virtues and the importance of doing so.

INTELLECTUAL VIRTUES

What are virtues? Virtues are character traits or dispositions that are in some
way fitting or appropriate and whose acquisition and exercise contribute to
living a good human life. There are different kinds of virtues, and a distinction
is often drawn between moral and intellectual virtues. Moral virtues are states
of character whose end is the promotion of what is good, or the elimination of
suffering, or some such thing. Generosity and benevolence, for example, are
moral virtues that promote the good of others. Intellectual virtues, on the other
hand, are virtues aimed at acquisition of true belief, at the promotion of
knowledge and understanding. The line between the two is probably difficult
to draw: oftentimes morally virtuous behavior includes pursuit of the truth, as
when successful philanthropy requires understanding of where funds can best
be directed. Indeed, it could be argued that intellectual virtues are just a subset
of moral ones, since truth, knowledge and understanding are themselves good![2]
But we can nonetheless keep in mind a rough distinction between the two
kinds of virtues.

When we think of intellectual virtues, we typically think of traits such as
studiousness and inquisitiveness, or the competent exercise of such skills as
reasoning, calculation and rational reflection. And there are virtues in these
areas. But the category of intellectual virtue might be legitimately expanded to

---

[2]For more on the distinction between intellectual and moral virtues, see Jason Baehr, *The Inquiring
Mind: On Intellectual Virtues and Virtue Epistemology* (New York: Oxford University Press, 2011),
especially pp. 206-22.

include more mechanical, less intentional processes, such as vision, hearing and memory. A person who sees well and processes visual information accurately has a kind of intellectual virtue, since this attribute enables her to reliably acquire true beliefs about the world around her. So we can think of intellectual virtue quite broadly, to include the exercise of both active and passive intellectual capacities.

One final point about intellectual virtue applies to virtues more generally and is made most famously by Aristotle in his *Nicomachean Ethics*: corresponding to most virtues are vices that represent extremes, where the virtue is the mean between them.[3] The following illustration will make this clear. With eating there are two extremes with respect to quantity: eating too much and eating too little. Both dietary habits are vicious (not in the sense of being nasty or cruel but in the sense of exemplifying vice). The virtue lies somewhere in between, at the mean, and of course involves eating the proper amount. Other more explicitly moral virtues usually have the same structure. Generosity, for example, involves an appropriate selflessness with respect to one's possessions, where the extremes are stinginess and, on the other side, a kind of carelessness that can lead to complete loss of possessions and inability to make selfless use of anything. There are also vices opposed to intellectual virtue. In the next sections we'll turn to a couple of intellectual virtues and explore how adventurous Pietists may be prone to particular vices connected with them.

Concern for Truth

The first intellectual virtue I want to discuss has to do with a concern for truth.[4] There are in fact numerous virtues connected with such concern, but here we shall simply point to some highlights. A person with a virtuous concern for truth *values* truth appropriately: she keeps the pursuit and maintenance of true beliefs as a central goal, and she strives to ensure that the way she lives is appropriately guided by what is true.[5]

Concern for truth fits with Aristotle's framework for the virtues: it admits of

---

[3] Aristotle, *Nicomachean Ethics*, trans. Terence Irwin, 2nd ed. (Indianapolis: Hackett, 1999).

[4] By *truth* I mean nothing controversial. What is true is simply what accurately describes reality, the way the world really is.

[5] As former Bethel president Carl H. Lundquist stated, "It is not enough to know that truth is. It must be manifested in its seeker"; Lundquist, "1962–1963 Presidential Report," *1963 Annual—Baptist General Conference* (Chicago: BGC, 1963), p. 87.

a mean, but it also admits of nonvirtuous extremes. On one extreme we have excessive concern for truth. This kind of vice can take a variety of forms. One example is the person obsessed with accumulating knowledge about trivial topics who, in pursuit of that end, ignores other essential elements of human life. Such a person is concerned about truth, all right, but not in a virtuous way: the truths are insignificant, and the concern inordinately distracts from other matters of real importance. Another example is a person who is dedicated to the fine points of theological debate but who makes no effort to ensure that his theology properly affects his behavior. (This form of vice has always been of great concern to Pietists.[6]) In both examples the concern for truth is vicious in the sense that it is out of balance and detracts from living a fully virtuous life. On the other extreme we have a person who demonstrates insufficient concern for truth. Such a person may have little interest in learning or in expanding his understanding of reality, and he does not care to have his actions guided by such understanding in any case. Both extremes are vicious; the virtue (or virtues) lies somewhere in between.

Here I will focus on the second extreme—insufficient concern for truth—and I will give two reasons that our Pietist adventurer may tend in that direction. The first reason comes from Pietism itself. As Christopher Gehrz notes, Pietists tend to emphasize the importance of a heart transformed by the experience of conversion and regeneration, and hence they do not attach "special importance to the examination of philosophical presuppositions and theological propositions."[7] Jenell Paris expands on the same point earlier in this volume when she writes that, "For Pietists, faith is heartfelt, experiential and not heavily doctrinal.... Faith is a way of life, not an ideology or a set of control beliefs."[8] According to Mark Noll, this priority of Christian living over belief has historically led Pietists into trouble. It is worth quoting at some length from his book *The Scandal of the Evangelical Mind:*

---

[6]An example can be found in the life of August Hermann Francke (1663–1727). Prior to his conversion, as Douglas Shantz puts it, "Even theological study contributed to his misery. He could define faith and new birth, but had no experience of them"; Shantz, *An Introduction to German Pietism: Protestant Renewal at the Dawn of Modern Europe* (Baltimore: Johns Hopkins University Press, 2013), p. 105.

[7]Christopher Gehrz, "Recovering a Pietist Understanding of Christian Higher Education: Carl H. Lundquist and Karl A. Olsson," *Christian Scholar's Review* 40 (Winter 2011): 140.

[8]Quoted from p. 76 above.

The intellectual problem of Pietism lay in its excesses. Pietists had rediscovered the truth that Christianity is a life as well as a set of beliefs. The difficulty arose when some Pietists began to view Christian faith as only a life, without a concern for beliefs at all. This led into fascination with practice, deep involvement in spiritual experience, and absorption in the psychological dimensions of the faith. Objective realities of revelation were sometimes almost totally eclipsed. . . . At its extreme, the Pietist emphasis on religious life gave very little attention to self-conscious Christian thought.[9]

Noll's complaint, in short, is that Pietism's emphasis on experience and action led to an intellectually vicious and damaging lack of concern about Christian truth. (He goes on to describe Pietism's link to theological liberalism. I shall return to a similar point below.)

So one reason that Pietists may tend toward the vice of insufficient concern for truth has to do with their strong emphasis on experience and practice.[10] Of course such an emphasis in itself is altogether laudable. A second praiseworthy pietistic inclination relates to Pietists' desire for significant engagement with those with whom they disagree. This inclination can lead to similar danger.

To see this, note first that there are contexts in which concern for the truth quite properly does not take center stage, or at any rate in which the tendency not to emphasize it is altogether understandable. Such contexts occur regularly in healthy and robust relationships. In general, when we maintain relationships, even friendships, with people with whom we disagree, the fact of our disagreement and the truth of the matter is not something we tend to focus on. Much of this tendency can stem from moral virtue. We love the friend and wish her good; but then it can be painful to think that she is mistaken about something really important. In addition, it can seem wrong somehow to think of that person as lacking something significant that you have: in an important sense friendship is a relationship between equals, and focusing on this perceived lack can create an obstacle to that sort of equality.

---

[9]Mark A. Noll, *The Scandal of the Evangelical Mind* (Grand Rapids: Eerdmans, 1994), pp. 48-49. Note that Noll is not targeting all Pietists with this indictment, and in particular not the great German Pietists such as Philipp Jakob Spener and August Hermann Francke, both of whom displayed a robust concern for Christian truth.

[10]Pietism in its radical forms tended to exhibit the related vice of pursuing truth in the wrong way— by overemphasizing personal interpretation of Scripture and deemphasizing other sources of Christian belief such as reason, tradition and the church. See Shantz, *An Introduction to German Pietism*, chap. 6.

Further still, concerns about propriety can prevent one from discussing or calling any kind of serious attention to the disagreement. So there are a number of factors that tend to push concern for the truth aside in loving relationships among people who disagree.

All of these factors can be relevant in the lives of those adventurous Pietists who quite properly emphasize active love and building relationships with religious others. The kind of stance that tends to deemphasize disagreement can slide into the tendency to think that the truth about the matter on which you disagree is unimportant. In this way, love of the other can lead to insufficient concern for the truth.

I am not saying that this *will* happen to our adventurous Pietist, only that it can, and that a focus on experience and action over belief, together with the adventurous spirit that leads our Christ follower into deep and profound engagement with others, can incline her toward this particular intellectual vice.

OPEN-MINDEDNESS

Let's move to the second virtue: open-mindedness. It is clear that open-mindedness admits of extremes: some people are utterly dogmatic in their beliefs and refuse to take seriously any point of view that differs from their own, while other people are tossed about, holding to one position one day and a different one the next. Virtuous open-mindedness is somewhere in between.

Open-mindedness is a virtue emphasized by Pietists. It is connected with the "irenic spirit" for which Pietists are well known, and, as Christian Collins Winn points out, it is a central element in a Pietist approach to civil discourse. As he says, the Pietist is a "sincere arguer" who enters dialogue with a *"genuine openness to being taught."* This openness was typical of Philipp Jakob Spener, who Collins Winn says was "committed to finding the truth *without* the prior assumption that he is already in total possession of it."[11]

The big question is, what beliefs is a virtuous person willing and able to set aside? On which is he open to correction and amendment? About which topics does a virtuous Pietist exhibit genuine openness to being taught? The answer can't be "all of them." Consider some examples. Most of us are not open to alternative views about things that we've seen with our own eyes. We are not

---

[11]Quoted from pp. 127-28 above.

open to the suggestion that we are in the Matrix and that most of our beliefs about our sensory environments are mistaken. Likewise, most of us believe that discrimination on the basis of race or gender is wrong, and we are not particularly open to being taught otherwise. And we are not, on either account, intellectually vicious.

But why is it virtuous not to be open-minded with respect to these beliefs, to be unwilling to set these beliefs aside? That's a difficult question, but an important part of the answer is that those beliefs are *true*, and the cognitive faculties that produced the beliefs are trustworthy. My vision is reliable, as is my moral sense (at least on basic issues of equality): both faculties are intellectually virtuous in the sense that they reliably get me in touch with the truth. Moreover, when those faculties function properly some of the beliefs they produce are quite properly held very firmly: a person who only *tentatively* believes that discrimination is wrong has a moral compass that is not working very well. Trusting these faculties by believing their outputs and being closed to opposing views is perfectly consistent with the dictates of intellectual virtue. (This is not to say that our ordinarily reliable faculties ought never to be doubted: sometimes our visual beliefs and our beliefs about morality should be open to amendment. But not in the cases just described.)

My suggestion is that it is likewise entirely consistent with intellectual virtue not to be particularly open-minded with respect to the essentials of Christian belief.[12] (As Pietist Carl Lundquist, former president of Bethel University, said in a sermon in the 1950s, "We need to be mindful in our search for truth that our Savior has set some limits. There also is no virtue in having an open mind toward that which God has closed."[13]) Why? In short, because those Christian beliefs are *true* and are generated from a reliable source, namely, the Holy Spirit, who has guided and continues to guide the church to ensure that these truths are known.[14] A person can quite properly hold those beliefs very firmly, not taking seriously

---

[12]By "essentials of the Christian faith" I mean such claims as that God exists and is Creator of the heavens and the earth; that God is a Trinity; that God became incarnate in the person of Jesus Christ who walked the earth about two thousand years ago; and that Christ's sacrificial life and death make possible our salvation.

[13]Carl H. Lundquist, "The Limits of Tolerance," undated chapel address [1955?], Carl H. Lundquist Papers, box 32, The History Center: Archives of the Baptist General Conference and Bethel University.

[14]Readers may note that similar themes are found in Alvin Plantinga, *Warranted Christian Belief* (New York: Oxford University Press, 2000). Indeed, Plantinga's work has influenced much of the argument here.

the possibility of giving them up, while maintaining the intellectual virtue of open-mindedness. Virtuous open-mindedness is open-mindedness aimed at the truth; open-mindedness that involves setting aside (and perhaps giving up) beliefs that are produced by reliable vision, reliable moral sense or the Holy Spirit does not contribute to fulfillment of that fundamental intellectual goal.[15]

Nonetheless, I think, it can be tempting for an adventurous Pietist to miss out on the virtue and become excessively open-minded. To see how this can happen, consider the story of John Hick, a British philosopher whose views in philosophy of religion have been highly influential. Hick was raised a Christian but gave up Christian belief, a process he sets out in a story about his religious development. He describes how, as a young professor at the University of Birmingham in England, he lived in a community with many religious groups represented and became involved in a number of community-relations organizations. These organizations had foes, including the Neo-Nazi National Front, a group of racist thugs who threatened Hick and assaulted some of his friends. As Hick reports, "In all this I found myself in active comradeship with Muslims, Jews, Hindus, Sikhs, Marxists, and humanists, as well as with fellow Christians."[16] That was the context for his eventual epiphany.

> In the course of this work I went frequently to Jewish synagogues, Muslim mosques, Sikh gurudwaras, Hindu temples, and of course, a variety of churches. In these places of worship I soon realized something that is obvious enough once noticed, yet momentous in its implications. This is that although the language, concepts, liturgical actions, and cultural ethos differ widely from one another, yet from a religious point of view basically the same thing is going on in all of them, namely, human beings coming together within a framework of an ancient and highly developed tradition to open their hearts and minds to God, whom they believe makes a total claim on their lives and demands of them, in the words of one of the prophets, "to do justice, and to love kindness, and to walk humbly with your God" (Micah 6:8).[17]

---

[15]One might argue that the fact that so many people disagree with Christians on religious matters gives us reason to reconsider—and give up—Christian belief. But of course many people disagree with us on the issue of racial and gender discrimination, too. For further discussion of this complicated issue, see Philip L. Quinn and Kevin Meeker, eds., *The Philosophical Challenge of Religious Diversity* (New York: Oxford University Press, 2000).

[16]John Hick, "A Pluralist View," in *Four Views on Salvation in a Pluralist World*, ed. Dennis L. Okholm and Timothy R. Phillips (Grand Rapids: Zondervan, 1995), p. 38.

[17]Ibid.

The position that Hick came to as a result of all this, and the position he endorsed with amendments for the rest of his life, was that there is an ultimate divine reality, beyond human conception, to which all the major world religions are culturally conditioned responses. Differences between religions, he argued, are only surface deep; at their heart, all religions are fundamentally the same.

Now Hick was not a Pietist, at least not by description, but his engagement with the world fits well with what we might expect from an adventurous Christ follower. He was an active Christian, something of a pioneer in interfaith relations. And yet a certain kind of open-mindedness led him away from Christianity to a position that sees all religions as essentially equal. Much of his open-mindedness stemmed from moral virtue: he was by all accounts a wonderfully kind and generous man, and his interfaith engagement was undoubtedly praiseworthy. Furthermore, his feeling of solidarity with religious others, generated in part by the violent opposition of bigots (and the apathy of much of the Christian community at the time) is both laudable and understandable. Still, his open-mindedness crossed to the level of intellectual vice.[18] It led him to reject Christian belief and, as many critics have pointed out, to overlook vast differences between religions in order to portray them all as fundamentally the same.

The result, as seen in the writings of John Hick, can be full-blooded loss of Christian faith. If Christianity is mainly about opening one's heart to God, and members of other religious groups are by all appearances similarly open, well, maybe our religions are all fundamentally the same. Focus on Christian practice to the neglect of belief can lead to setting aside belief too easily and can lead a person too quickly to adopt a belief system that may preserve the practice but leave it without a foundation. (I shall return to this point below.) In addition, the same kind of profound engagement with those with whom we disagree—which arouses feelings of camaraderie and equality—that can lead to a lack of concern about the truth on the point of disagreement can also make

---

[18]It is important to note that Hick would not agree with the suggestion that the position at which he arrived resulted from intellectual vice. He would attribute it to intellectual virtue since, naturally, he thought that his reasoning led him to the truth. (He defended his position in numerous books, including *A Christian Theology of Religions* [Louisville, KY: John Knox, 1995].) This point leads to a second: to a considerable degree, what traits and processes are in fact intellectually virtuous depends on what is true. In our discussion we are working from the assumption that the central claims of Christian faith are true, but a person who rejected that assumption would attribute Christian belief to some form of intellectual vice.

a view that puts all religions on equal footing seem attractive. The result can be full-blooded loss of Christian faith.

THE REASON FOR THE ADVENTURE, AND MITIGATING THE RISKS

We have seen that adventurous Pietists can fall prey to intellectual vice. But this danger should not discourage them from adventure! Here I will reflect on our motivation for adventure—and how the vicious tendencies I have described may in fact undercut that motivation. Then I will conclude with some simple steps to help mitigate the risks.

As I have said, at Bethel University we aim to produce adventurous Christ followers, a goal shared by other Christian institutions of higher education, even if they state it differently. To achieve this, we promote adventure as part of the educational experience itself: not only do our students find themselves engaging seriously with writings of non-Christians in the classroom, but they also now more than ever encounter non-Christians outside the classroom, both locally and abroad. Why do we do this? The reasons are both intellectual and moral—intellectual in the sense that we as an educational community want to learn more about other people, their practices and their traditions, and moral in the sense that we want to get to know them and engage significantly with them and in so doing promote understanding and reconciliation in a world that desperately needs it. Those reasons are excellent, and the results can be exhilarating. Living out our Christian faith in crosscultural and interreligious engagement can be a source of renewal and revitalization; our faith can be strengthened when put into action in contexts well removed from our places of spiritual comfort.

Now what would be the problem if all this adventure instead resulted in what I have labeled a loss of intellectual virtue? What would it matter if we were to say that the truth isn't important so long as we understand each other? What if we became so open-minded as to exclaim, with John Hick, that all religions are fundamentally the same? This would be regrettable, I think, not only be-cause both claims are false but also because the essentials of the Christian faith give us the motivation to pursue these engagements in the first place. For-getting this fact places our adventures in something of a vacuum, in which we participate in them merely for generic moral reasons. Our engagement then lacks a solid foundation. On the other hand, our Christian faith gives us a framework into which a rich set of reasons can fit: we worship a God who created the world and who demonstrated profound love for this world by entering it in the person of Jesus Christ and by dying for us. This God commands us to exercise the very same active love, a command that we seek to fulfill in part by going out into the world, engaging with others, and promoting understanding and reconciliation. In that context, our adventures make sense; they make less sense without it.[19]

So Christian institutions of higher learning should seek to promote intellectual virtue and discourage intellectual vice, a considerable challenge in the face of the adventures on which we send our students and ourselves. But what then can we do to offset the risks—risks that may result in our losing sight of the truth and depriving ourselves of a robust motive for engaging in adventure in the first place? Recognizing that there are no guarantees here, I want to make two suggestions, both of which should serve as reminders rather than new information.

A first suggestion relates to the seductive pull of seemingly open-minded views like that of John Hick. To many people his views seem safe and seem to imply that everyone is right; but these are illusions. We need to be up front about the fact that intellectually there is no safe ground, no position without risk. No matter where we stand, we could be mistaken. Being open to alternative views can lead one to truth, but it can also lead one to falsehood. And Hick's pluralist stance is no better on this score: his belief that all religions are equally in touch with the truth could itself be mistaken. (And, of course, Christians believe that it is.) In addition, his stance is in fact not nearly as magnanimous as it may appear: it implies not that most religious people's beliefs are true but that they are mostly false.[20] We can find it disconcerting to disagree on such important matters with people we love and admire—and our students can feel the discomfort when involved in intercultural engagement. But such disagreement is practically unavoidable. We do no one a service when we pretend otherwise.

A second suggestion is that we pray, read the Bible, study the creeds and explore writings of great heroes of the faith. (We should also promote these

---

[19]It is a bit difficult to see how Hick's "divine reality," something beyond all human conception, can serve as a source of motivation to pursue understanding and reconciliation.

[20]For an excellent discussion of this point and its consequences, see Alvin Plantinga, "Pluralism: A Defense of Religious Exclusivism," in *The Philosophical Challenge of Religious Diversity*, ed. Philip Quinn and Kevin Meeker (New York: Oxford University Press, 1999), pp. 172–92.

practices among our students.) Doing this can help us to keep the truth regularly in mind and facilitate the working of the Holy Spirit to seal the truth upon our hearts and minds. The great Pietists of the past emphasized the importance of Bible reading for the sake of promoting Christian living, as when Spener wrote,

> Thought should be given to a *more extensive use of the Word of God among us*. We know that by nature we have no good in us. If there is to be any good in us, it must be brought about by God. To this end the Word of God is the powerful means, since faith must be enkindled through the gospel, and the law provides the rules for good works and many wonderful impulses to attain them. The more at home the Word of God is among us, the more we shall bring about faith and its fruits.[21]

My suggestion is that we employ similar means in our effort to cultivate rich and steadfast Christian belief.

In Christian higher education we desire to produce not merely morally upstanding citizens but also adventurous Christ followers. To that end we should seek to equip ourselves and our students with intellectual virtue, and to recognize that what motivates our adventurous engagement is the love of God shown in Christ, a love that we cannot help but emulate in our pursuit of truth, understanding and reconciliation.[22]

---

[21]Philip Jacob Spener, *Pia Desideria*, trans. Theodore G. Tappert (Philadelphia: Fortress, 1964), p. 87. Italics original.

[22]My thanks to Chris Gehrz and the audience at Bethel University's "Not Ready for Primetime" library forum for helpful comments on an earlier draft of this paper.

12

Organizational Identity and the Pietist Ethos

Joel S. Ward

◆

JOHN HENRY NEWMAN'S proposal that a university be organized around theology advances an important question for the practice of faith in the Christian liberal arts college. In his book *The Idea of a University*, Newman responds to an educational environment not unlike the current situation in American higher education. The university, in Newman's time, suffered from disciplinary proliferation resulting in a disagreement regarding the purpose of the institution. The salient question was the organization and union of the expanding information horizon so that students might receive a true university education. Newman suggested that theology function as the umbrella of the curriculum, organizing each discipline as it relates to another.[1] He argued that without a mediating discipline the university would devolve into an un-productive community of competitors. The student would be adrift trying to navigate the reason and trajectory of an educational enterprise.

In many regards Newman's analysis has proven correct. In large research universities with theology reduced in status or even eliminated, individual de-partments and even faculty members are driven to think competitively about their work and colleagues. In many public institutions scholarship follows funding. The market, however defined, performs as an organizing principle

---

[1]John Henry Newman, *The Idea of a University*, ed. Frank M. Turner (New Haven, CT: Yale University Press, 1996).

demonstrated by the growing inclination to make the prospective student lofty promises about job placement.

The amplification of competitiveness under the current constraints of the national economy provokes many institutions to attempt to heighten their advantage by adopting marketing strategies. Curricular initiatives believed to better attract the college-bound student take administrative and financial precedent. However, Newman's bid proposes an alternative to providing an education driven by enrollment numbers and encourages a more serene and prudent view of higher education.

Can theology, defined as a particular set of beliefs and practices, help frame and differentiate an educational mission? I propose renewing the practices of a theological heritage as a missional coordinate for rearticulating organizational identity. This proposal operates in contrast to a market research and positioning approach that has often preceded "organizational recasting."[2] Organizational recasting positions an organization's identity by recalling important communicative practices, thereby reasserting the contemporary relevance of the organization's unique value proposition. Before discussing faith practices as a principle of organizational identity we look first at the relationship between organizational identity and member identification. Following this general outline we will apply these categories to a more specific case of theological heritage, Pietism, and how it might function in a Christian liberal arts institution of higher education.

ORGANIZING IDENTITY

Organizational identity is broadly defined as a coherent set of messages that create and shape the external perception of an organization.[3] The public expression of organizational identity typically resides with managers who communicate about the organization both internally and externally. However, organizational identity has been shown to correlate closely with how members individually identify with an organization and in turn how the organization

---

[2]See Jeremy Langett, "Through the Story: Organizational Recasting and the Necessity of Narrative-Driven Internal Branding" (PhD diss., Duquesne University, 2010).

[3]Bey-Ling Sha, "Exploring the Connection Between Organizational Identity and Public Relations Behaviors: How Symmetry Trumps Conservation in Engendering Organizational Identification," *Journal of Public Relations Research* 21 (July 2009): 295-317.

relates to stakeholders.[4] This interaction is typically called organizational identification: the degree to which a member depends on the organization for his or her own individual identity. Consequently, organizational identity emerges more as a synthesis of identifying member practices rather than only official messages derived from the organization's mission. Communicative practices occurring both internally and externally shape the overall culture and character of an organization's identity.

Organizational identity is constructed dynamically between the original communicative practices of members and the corporately adopted principles that shape and form member communication. For example, American higher education's reassessment of faculty members' official relationship to the organization is demonstrated in the shift away from tenure and toward multi-affiliated adjuncts or temporary, nontenured faculty.[5] This newer norm in higher educational institutions will likely have a noted impact on colleges' and universities' organizational identities. Since every member's practices, full or part time, bear on the organization's externally perceived identity, a larger number of part-time members will unquestionably influence the coherency of the educational enterprise.

A coherent and therefore stable organizational identity depends on the agreement of members' declared roles in an organization, the cooperative practices in which they engage, and members' perceptions of the organization's official mission congruent with their held beliefs. Both member tenancy and positive identification influence all elements of organizational identity. From an organizational management perspective, the question rests on how to construct messages inside the organization that encourage compliance with organizational goals and encourage cooperative behaviors even if the employment commitment from the organization becomes tenuous.

Management's conservative impulse is supported by the fact that member identification increases cooperative practice and supports the organization's mission. Members who positively identify with an organization help establish

---

[4]Shelly L. Brickson, "Organizational Identity Orientation: Forging a Link Between Organizational Identity and Organizations Relations with Stakeholders," *Administrative Science Quarterly* 50 (December 2005): 576-609.

[5]Brenda S. Sonner, "A is for 'Adjunct': Examining Grade Inflation in Higher Education," *Journal of Education for Business* 76 (September/October 2000): 5-9.

missional fidelity and legitimate public relations messages.[6] How an organization is constituted by member identification comprises the basis of many contemporary integrated marketing paradigms advocating conceptual identification along with cooperative practice. In product marketing this means a transition from simple product satisfaction to product *experience* satisfaction. In either case, an organizational mission tangibly articulated and practiced by its members can create and foster missional coherency and stability. In marketplace terms, organizational identification management consists of overseeing a brand. Attempting organizational identification management in similar fashion can result in several undesirable outcomes in which the member (1) adopts completely the provided identity with loss of individuality, (2) completely rejects the provided identity along with organizational membership or (3) becomes ambivalent and therefore implicitly oppositional to stated organizational goals.[7]

Organizational mission officially articulated is not a sure prediction of organizational identification or of a coherent organizational identity. Even a member's silent ambivalence can prevent organizational identification among other members. The dialectic between individual member practice and officially stated organizational mission persists in every organization. In our case the mediation of this dialectic should be considered carefully. Newman's original proposition foresees the competitive impulse present in the dialectic between a universal mission and intraorganizational competition. In periods of organizational crisis a strong temptation persists for managers to control organizational identity even at the risk of weakening member identification. Conservation commonly means retrenchment around an official mission statement without objective assessment of what contributed to missional drift. Alternatively, core mission objectives are procedurally abandoned in an attempt to quickly redirect the organization's trajectory in line with populist market trends. The current higher education economy has institutions demonstrating both of these responses, with renewed attention, for example, on core curriculums and continued interest in online education opportunities.

In times of crisis a judicious mediation of this dialectic is important for

---

[6]Sha, "Exploring the Connection," pp. 295-317.

[7]Michael G. Pratt, "The Good, the Bad, and the Ambivalent: Managing Identification Among Amway Distributors," *Administrative Science Quarterly* 45 (September 2000): 456-93.

achieving synthesis and cooperation between organizational identity and members' organizational identification. Straining the relationship between an organization's management and organizational members furthers a suspicious competitiveness that weakens the corporate support of an organization's mission and raises doubts about the organization's continued legitimacy. Organizational identity, organizational identification and members' individual identities constitute a complex nexus that requires prudent negotiation. Shifting or renewing an organization's mission cannot be accomplished without members' renewed identification and cooperation with the proposed method of mediation. Arguments for or against change must be accompanied by a means of arbitration that functions authoritatively for all stakeholders.

THE LIBERAL ARTS DENOMINATED

That Christian liberal arts institutions must distinguish themselves in the current educational economy does not require ample justification. Recent economic erosion in the landscape of American higher education has reintroduced questions regarding the role of the liberal arts institution in the personal and professional development of a student.[8] The financial challenges faced by both small colleges and larger universities have greatly affected schools' dependence on annual enrollment for operating costs, even as better-endowed institutions have adjusted expectations regarding future fiscal stability. Higher education institutions have made new attempts to substantiate the legitimacy of their programs, and in the collection of small liberal arts colleges, this has resulted in an entrenchment around the idea of education for the person, not the professional. Rather than compete with the postgraduation placement promises made by academically prestigious schools or the considerably lower cost of state universities, liberal arts colleges have argued that their more intimate atmosphere is better equipped to provide a student-tailored educational experience.[9]

---

[8]See, among many other examples, Eric Hoover, "A Liberal-Arts Leader Weighs Costs and Quality," Head Count (blog), April 10, 2012, http://chronicle.com/blogs/headcount/a-liberal-arts-leader -weighs-costs-and-quality/29924; and Eric Kelderman, "The Liberal Arts Confront Fiscal Reality at Edinboro U," *The Chronicle of Higher Education,* October 14, 2013, http://chronicle.com/article /The-Liberal-Arts-Meet-Fiscal/142279.

[9]Michael Delucchi, "'Liberal Arts' Colleges and the Myth of Uniqueness," *Journal of Higher Education* 68, no. 4 (July–August 1997): 414-26.

Christian liberal arts institutions adopt similar kinds of classification since religiously informed liberal arts curriculum has long focused on the personal development of the student in conjunction with professional preparation. Colleges with theological heritage often self-identify as this type of academic institution, claiming to be better equipped to educate the "mind, body and spirit" with smaller class sizes and a residential student body.[10] The religious affiliation of many small liberal arts colleges strengthens the association between the liberal arts and whole-person education since Christian institutions are explicit about faith integration in core and discipline-specific curricula.

Promotional messaging at colleges and smaller universities has made the tailored-student-experience claim too profusely. Previously localism and denominational affiliation distinguished comparably sized schools claiming the benefits of the small-college communal atmosphere.[11] Educational institutions separating from church origins is a well-documented theme in American higher education, followed closely by schools remaining true to their theological heritage without strong denominational affiliation.[12] More recently this trend has been mirrored in Christian churches, many of which are dropping denominational names for broader, more ambiguous titles[13] even though, by and large, American churches remain denominationally divided.[14] Mourning or championing the dissolution of denominationalism is not my intent. Instead our focus here is on the more general loss of organizational form, institutional affiliations that provide the basis and power behind educational purpose.

How smaller liberal arts colleges should respond to the current economic circumstances and garner alternative financial support remains functionally unanswered. The relaxing relationship between schools and their theological heritage poses an important question for a coherent organizational identity and

---

[10]Hugh Hawkins, "The Making of the Liberal Arts College Identity," *Daedalus* 128 (Winter 1999): 1-11.

[11]David B. Potts, "American Colleges in the Nineteenth Century: From Localism to Denominationalism," *History of Education Quarterly* 11 (Winter 1971): 363-80.

[12]James Tunstead Burtchaell, *The Dying of the Light: The Disengagement of Colleges and Universities from Their Christian Churches* (Grand Rapids: Eerdmans, 1998).

[13]For example, the Baptist General Conference (of Swedish Pietist origin) adopted the "missional name" Converge Worldwide in 2008 in order to better "articulate the mission and message of Jesus in a more effective way"; see James and Carole Spickelmier, eds., *New Century/New Directions, 2001–2010: The Baptist General Conference/Converge Worldwide* (Arlington Heights, IL: Harvest, 2012), chap. 9.

[14]Brian Steensland et al., "The Measure of American Religion: Toward Improving the State of the Art," *Social Forces* 79 (September 2000): 291-318.

for organizational messages modeling an educational institution's mission. Institutions wanting to boost enrollment must attract students from a student
pool that may not strongly identify with a particular denomination.[15] Whereas
previously colleges and universities attracted students who recognized the
school as denominationally affiliated, the new shape of the Christian church
complicates this relationship.[16] Responsive or reactionary, the distinctiveness
of denominational heritage has become less important for external and internal
messaging about a school's identity and how the educational experience offered
to students is particular to a theological and oftentimes ethnic heritage.[17]

Schools with denominational history articulating less distinctive missions
appear to mimic the dissipation of Christian denominationalism. Church organization focuses away from local, ethnic and historical origins and more
toward broadly defined missional communities. This outward orientation, or
what American religious historian Sydney E. Mead calls "revivalism," focuses
on "life and works" rather than "faith and order" as the steering purpose of a
church's organizational activity. In other words, member identification with
church organizations has become more closely aligned with organizational
outcomes (e.g., events, increased membership, enhanced programming) rather
than doctrinal orthodoxy. Mead credits this theme in the broader Protestant
church of North America for promoting a kind of schizophrenia, leaving the
church more likely to adopt sociocultural norms for agenda setting rather than
turning to its theological tenets to guide church organizing.[18]

Mead's analysis of American Protestantism poses a difficult problem, not
just for American denominationalism but also for small colleges that may rely
on denominational affiliation for support and distinction. Maintaining organizational identity parallel to the vicissitudes of society, economy and individual
member activity is not a question that colleges and universities face alone, even

[15]Phil Davignon, Perry L. Glanzer and P. Jesse Rine, "Assessing the Denominational Identity of American Evangelical Colleges and Universities, Part III: The Student Experience," *Christian Higher Education* 12 (October–December 2013): 315-30.

[16]Stephen Ellingson, *The Megachurch and the Mainline: Remaking Religious Tradition in the Twenty-
First Century* (Chicago: University of Chicago Press, 2007), p. 178.

[17]Perry L. Glanzer, P. Jesse Rine and Phil Davignon, "Assessing the Denominational Identity of
American Evangelical Colleges and Universities, Part I: Denominational Patronage and Institutional
Policy," *Christian Higher Education* 12 (May–June 2013): 181-202.

[18]Sydney E. Mead, "Denominationalism: The Shape of Protestantism in America," *Church History* 23
(December 1954): 291-320.

if their nexus of stakeholders represents a unique problem. Organizational identity studies classify the coordination of individual member practices around the shared acknowledgment of institutional mission as a primary focus of solution-seeking inquiry.[19] Accomplishing synergy between individual member activity and organizational mission is a tenuous and delicate practice dependent on the organization's legitimating philosophy. Catholicism mediates the relationship between the subjective experience of individual identity and organizational identification doctrinally with clear dictates for faith practice, achieving in some measure the community Newman argued for. In Protestantism, the trend has long favored dispersion.

Mead specifically attributes the dispersive trend in American Protestantism to the Pietist movement, which, "cut off from the forms of a traditional church, has successfully loaned itself to whatever live movement seemed to give structure to current problems and their solutions."[20] The result: a lack of clarity regarding organizational purpose, since prior distinctions that set denominations apart are deemphasized for the practical work and effective results of church activity. Mead's analysis positions schools with pietistic theological heritage as fitting examples of the tension between organizational identity and members' organizational identification. In Pietism, suspicion persists toward confessional forms of orthodoxy, which are perceived as diminishing the subjective spiritual vitality of Christian life. Pietism advocates the cooperative practice of personal piety to mediate the diverse subjective experience of Christian identity and faith. Coherent organizational identity, from the beginning of the Pietist movement, relies on consistent pious practice as the basis for organizing a purposeful Christian community. Organizationally, this emphasis propels a lack of formally defining the principle(s) of coordinating corporate Christian piety, weakening the possibility of sustaining a coherent pietistic organizational identity. In Pietism, since identification is specifically related to the regenerative relationship that each believer shares with Christ, the practices of sharing Christ's word together with members of like heart and mind predicate communities with a visible pietistic organizational identity.

---

[19]Philip Jerold Aust, "Communicated Values as Indicators of Organizational Identity: A Method for Organizational Assessment and Its Application in a Case Study," *Communication Studies* 55 (Winter 2004): 515-24.

[20]Mead, "Denominationalism," p. 312.

PIETIST IDENTITY

Pietism, as a theological heritage, poses interesting challenges for formally sustaining an organizational identity. Colleges and universities with pietistic theological heritage contend with both economic pressure and denomination dissipation, with the potential to suffer greater effects. Pietism as a strain or movement in American Protestantism eludes clear distinction.[21] Attempting to define contemporary forms of Pietism as a commonly expressed theological heritage is beyond the limitations of our current discussion. Consequently, we will look at the origins of Pietism for possible distinctions and markers of Pietist organizational identity that may provide coordinates for current institutions.

Historically, Pietists have often been accused of anti-intellectualism, of being opposed to systematic thought as a guide for Christian life and practice. Faculty colleagues of early Pietist scholars Philipp Jakob Spener and August Hermann Francke faulted them for over-concern with students' piety.[22] Both were specifically criticized for their organization of *conventicles*, small reading groups formed to induce greater Christian piety, for fear they would compromise church orthodoxy and promote division. This perception of Pietism works in stark contrast to the actual contribution Pietist colleges and universities have made to higher education and the practice of Christianity in North America. In many places where Pietist immigrants settled, institutions of higher learning have been a feature of this organizing. Schools begun by Pietists are by no means few, and they continue to be a significant part of the American liberal arts scene.[23] The dynamic between the myth of Pietist anti-intellectualism and the reality of pietistic educational efforts raises interesting questions about how Pietist practices have been judged to be at odds with the task of higher education and Christian organizing.

Contemporary Pietist scholars have diligently attempted to correct this false perception, arguing that the Pietist view of higher education fundamentally differs from faith-and-learning integrationist models typical of Christian liberal arts institutions. According to Kurt Peterson and R. J. Snell, pietistic education is "rooted in conversion and committed to the ongoing task of con-

---

[21]Michelle A. Clifton-Soderstrom, *Angels, Worms, and Bogeys: The Christian Ethic of Pietism* (Eugene, OR: Cascade, 2010), p. 3.

[22]Dale W. Brown, *Understanding Pietism,* rev. ed. (Nappanee, IN: Evangel, 1996), p. 13.

[23]See the list of colleges and universities with Pietist theological heritage on p. 22 above.

verting the student" and, much more than "the shaping of worldviews," emphasizes "the formation of the whole person."[24]

However, these claims do not form a set of unique assertions that differ from
those made by many other Christian liberal arts colleges and universities with
different theological heritages. Education for the whole person is a standard
label, not only in Christian educational literature but also understood secularly
as a pedagogical tactic with similar practical assumptions.[25] If indeed the pietistic motive does not divorce the student from reason and promotes learning
of a special type, what are the attributes sui generis of pietistic education?

This question must be addressed if pietistic institutions of higher education
intend to offer a distinct and important experience within the larger milieu of
evangelical Christian liberal arts colleges and universities. If actively answered,
pietistic institutions, as a result, will better articulate the unique character of a
pietistic educational experience and also strengthen the coherence of pietistic
organizational identity. Pietism's emphasis on subjective experience and its
focus on personal regeneration over institutional affiliation have challenged the
specificity of pietistic organizing. These attributes are sometimes considered
conditions of contemporary Pietism rather than its origins but are still generally traced back to the beginnings of the movement that suffered from sepa-
ratist and individualist tendencies.

Roger Olson argues that Pietism itself is "no longer a movement but an ethos
or spirit" that flows through contemporary communities in more or less pure
forms depending on group practice.[26] Pietism, as ethos, remains faithful to the
emphasis on personal regeneration and yet requires considerable sustenance
from a concertedly collective practice of Christian piety. Without these pal-
pable practices, the likelihood of an organization sustaining this ethos and
being able to positively and coherently identify as distinctly pietistic becomes

---

[24]Kurt W. Peterson and R. J. Snell, "Faith Forms the Intellectual Task: The Pietist Option in Christian
Higher Education," in *The Pietist Impulse in Christianity*, ed. Christian T. Collins Winn et al. (Eugene:
Pickwick, 2011), p. 217.

[25]See, for example, Lyle Yorks and Elizabeth Kasl, "Toward a Theory and Practice of Whole-Person
Learning: Reconceptualizing Experience and the Role of Affect," *Adult Education Quarterly* 52 (May
2002): 176-93; and Ivy Lamb, "Educating the Whole Person," *U.S. Airways Magazine* (November
2013): 68-77.

[26]Roger E. Olson, "Pietism: Myths and Realities," in *Pietist Impulse in Christianity*, p. 6. The coupling
of ethos and spirit here is indicative of current disagreement about whether Pietism can be defined
as an intangible spirit or as a series of identifiable and formal practices.

dubious. Organizational identity solidifies around symmetrical statements by members about specific objectives and practices coupled with external perceptions formed through observation by, and interaction with, external stakeholders. Pietism as ethos, in one way, actively resists an organization mandating collective goals or outcomes that inevitably work contrary to the nature of subjective spiritual experience. Organizations that wish to identity as Pietist not just in heritage but also practically should adopt a set of collective practices considered evidential of the pietistic ethos.

ORGANIZATIONAL REGENERATION: ADOPTING PIOUS PRACTICES

Philipp Jakob Spener's *Pia Desideria,* German Pietism's founding document, outlines a similar situation to the one currently bearing on educational institutions with pietistic heritage. A consideration of Spener's recommendations for the church of his time not only provides helpful analysis about the consequences of missional dispersion but also clarifies effects on organizational identity and organizational identification. The crux of Spener's claims focuses on the failure of piety in the Lutheran Church and the resulting consequence for organizational coherency and growth. Spener specifically identifies the church members' impiety for the lack of new Jewish conversions, because the differences between Christian and Jewish piety are indistinguishable.[27] I do not mean by this example to compare Christian conversion with boosting college enrollments. However, I do believe Spener's analysis and his recommendations for restoring practical piety to Christian community are illustrative of an organizational recasting having similar effects.

As Spener viewed the Lutheran church in Germany, he linked the lack of growth to a lack of piety. He writes, "This tragic situation, meanwhile, is the chief thing that prevents many well disposed individuals who are still in other and heterodox churches, especially Roman churches, and who are fairly well aware of this abomination, from uniting with us, as they would have done in former times."[28] He demonstrates an astute understanding of a compromised identity and begins by outlining the pious practices by which the church can redeem its distinctiveness. Spener also does not reserve his critique for church members. He argues for the role of the university in transforming the church,

---

[27]Philip Jacob Spener, *Pia Desideria,* trans. Theodore G. Tappert (Philadelphia: Fortress, 1964), p. 68.
[28]Ibid., p. 70.

asserting that "the professors could themselves accomplish a great deal here by their example (indeed, without them a real reform is hardly to be hoped for)."[29] Spener's focus on both the distinctiveness of the church and the parallel activity of the university teacher make his text appropriate for addressing the broader problem of schools' slackening ties to their theological heritage. Furthermore, his special attention to pious practice can be especially instructive for organizations wishing to achieve a more visible pietistic ethos.

Two practices that Spener recommends for his original purpose of encouraging Christian piety are worthy of note, the first specific to church organizing and the second related to the role of the university. In *Pia Desideria* Spener encourages church congregations to meet in small reading groups to more intimately consider their Christian identity. His reading groups, called *ecclesiolae in ecclesia* ("little churches in the church"), formed the basis of the Pietist church renewal movement. However, because Spener attends to the role of university teacher these recommendations could also be entertained as a means of bolstering organizational identity and fostering organizational identification in an educational institution.

Introducing distinctively "pious practices" could prompt uniquely informative interactions within an organization. Involving all faculty, students, staff and administration in these practices would multiply the beneficial encouragement and ensure that friendships are shared through different levels of normative organizational hierarchy. These groups would also encourage identification through shared fellowship. Spener assumed that these more intimate meetings would provide greater opportunity so that those "who have been blessed with gifts and knowledge would also speak and present their pious opinions on the proposed subject to the judgment of the rest, doing all this in such a way as to avoid disorder and strife."[30]

Second, Spener proposes a concerted effort by the faculty of the university to demonstrate for students pious engagement in Christian worship. Faculty should regard Christian piety of equal concern in their relationship with students, who "should have it impressed upon them that holy life is not of less consequence than diligence and study, indeed that study without piety is

---

[29]Ibid., p. 104.
[30]Ibid., p. 89.

worthless."[31] This concern for student piety should not only be demonstrated in the classroom but should be visibly practiced by faculty to demonstrate this truth in ordinary living. Spener's claims outline a general model for increasing organizational identification and thereby organizational identity and could be especially effectual for an institution of pietistic heritage with their linkage to this historical narrative. The continued existence of church groups with Pietist heritage provides sufficient evidence for their efficacy.

Spener's response to the critical failures of the church demonstrates his vision for the practical character of organizational recasting. He provides helpful criteria for organizational purpose and its correlation with organizational identity and organizational identification. Organizationally, these cooperative practices are often officially unrecognized and unremunerated, but when undertaken by an organization's members they play a key role in solidifying the organization's identity and supporting the organization's overall goals.

The fundamental principle is a concerted organizational encouragement of particular pious practices. These principles and others constitute what Spener recommends specifically as a "philosophy of sacred things."[32] The contemporary liberal arts institution of Pietist theological heritage could adopt a similar philosophy for its curriculum and a generative idea for remodeling organizational identity. Along with this philosophy, the recommended cooperative practices of *ecclesiolae in ecclesia* and visible faculty piety demonstrated *outside* the classroom provide the coordinates for a pietistic organizational regeneration.

Of course, this change cannot be implemented by policy because this approach would undermine the subjective character of the Pietist ethos. Instead, organizational members must willingly and earnestly engage in these activities, voluntarily and individually recognizing their importance.

Organizations enduring the strain of uncharitable economies could also heed these tenets of organizational regeneration. The present case intends specifically toward pietistic educational institutions, but the principle of mining organizational history and narrative for the practices of organizational recasting is transferable. Pietist organizations are especially poised to integrate these practices. In general, organizations that suffer from missional drift, member distrust and diminished cooperative behavior may address these

---

[31]Ibid., p. 104.
[32]Ibid., p. 107.

threats to organizational coherency by putting in place the original practices that gave life to its distinctive value proposition.

The current economic crisis in American higher education has rightfully focused conversation around the value of institutional distinction. Many educational institutions have responded to this question procedurally, offering accelerated degrees, numerical evidence of effectiveness and, upon graduation, employment guarantees. Schools still bearing the trace of their theological heritage could alternatively develop market distinction by regenerating their organizational identity. Organizational regeneration or recasting is best accomplished around collective practices that express communal ethos. Not only does the adoption of these practical attributes promote a distinctive student experience, but also it solidifies the strategic mission and identity of the institution internally for organizational members, and externally in stakeholders' perceptions.

In Christian liberal arts colleges with theological heritage, organizational identity previously emerged between faculty, administration, students and churches with common ethnic and religious narratives. Colleges of this kind were formed with the specific purpose of educating students with a particular theological heritage from a well-defined constituency. In many cases regional focus and ethnic heritage have been abandoned, along with strong denominational affiliations, and replaced by token events that gesture toward organizational history, which primarily fail as coordinating principles that buttress and clarify institutional mission.[33] This is no doubt aggravated by the decreased enthusiasm of an impermanent faculty disinterested in the ethnic and religious heritage of the institution.

Recalling narrative history to reinvigorate cooperative practice arrests identity dissolution and restores purposeful growth. How to achieve this organically always poses unique problems. In the particular case of colleges and universities with pietistic heritage the subjective character of the Pietist ethos further obscures the possibility of reestablishing organizing principles. Organizational identification may be replaced with distrust if managers mandate

---

[33]See Robert Reyes and Kimberly F. Case, "National Profile on Ethnic/Racial Diversity of Enrollment, Graduation Rates, Faculty, and Administrators Among the Council for Christian Colleges & Universities," January 2011, www.goshen.edu/intercultural/files/2010/11/CCCU-Diversity -Report-2011-1-25-11.pdf.

new mediating practices as a means of institutional refocus. The essential principle of personal piety, if compromised, could further weaken claims by an institution to be specifically pietistic in orientation. Considering these two problems, recommendations made to an institution considering this kind of organizational change must attend to the fact that these original principles of Pietism emerged from and within the specific set of practices that early Pietist thinkers considered essential for reform in the Christian church.

Conclusion

Cardinal Newman's Catholic pedigree might make some in the academy balk at the recommendation to situate theology or even pious practice as the mediating discipline in a university's organization. In fact, they may feel more comfortable with Jacques Ellul's claim that there is no permanent Christian ethic, and that to promote particular practices within a Christian organization, especially one with pietistic theological heritage, would stymie the spiritual vitality of the community.[34] However, the corrosive nature of market-based competitiveness among disciplines of study should be reckoned with for what it is, the death of Christian unity. This is the unity that Newman saw at the heart of the educational promise, a unity necessary for the establishment of a coherent identity, not only for the organization but also for its beneficiaries. This is the truth hidden in the simplicity of Spener's innovation. The collective practice of piety restores and regenerates, not only the organization and its identity but also the very lives of its members.

---

[34]Jacques Ellul, *The Presence of the Kingdom* (Colorado Springs, CO: Helmers & Howard, 1989), p. 13.

13

Curating the Usable Past
for a Vital Future

An Anabaptist Vision for Pietism

Kent T. K. Gerber

◆

O N DECEMBER 23, 1943, Goshen College professor Harold S. Bender de-livered his presidential address to the American Society for Church History, using the "heroic past" to confront the social and cultural changes pressuring his school, his church and the identity of the larger Mennonite community.[1] The speech, titled "The Anabaptist Vision," communicated three characteristics of the sixteenth-century Swiss Brethren that were essential to engage these current challenges: *discipleship*, modeled on following the life and teachings of Christ; *brotherhood of believers*, involving voluntary adult baptism and sepa-ration of church and state; and an *ethic of love and nonresistance*.[2] The speech shifted how historians viewed Anabaptists—from an inconsequential, radical sect of the Reformation to an important contributor to the life, thought and identity of Western Christianity distinct from the four major traditions of An-glicanism, Lutheranism, Calvinism and Roman Catholicism.[3] As a focus of research and conversation continuing into the twenty-first century, the success

---

[1]Albert N. Keim, "The Anabaptist Vision: The History of a New Paradigm," *Conrad Grebel Review* 12 (September 1994): 255.

[2]Harold Stauffer Bender, "The Anabaptist Vision," *Church History* 13 (March 1944): 3-24.

[3]F. Ernest Stoeffler, *The Rise of Evangelical Pietism* (Leiden: Brill, 1971), pp. 6-7.

of Bender's "vision" is celebrated as a "source of identity and renewal"[4] for the Mennonite community and institutions like Goshen.

Institutions influenced by Pietism can learn from Bender's model to develop a better understanding of their own heritage and apply its strengths while also recognizing that it has drawn criticism for its narrow definition of true Anabaptism and for focusing more on ethical than spiritual themes.[5] In the current climate of increased scrutiny and external pressures, an understanding of historical influences is an important strategy for all higher education institutions. The disruptive forces of financial constraint, increased calls for accountability, and technological development are pressuring leaders to decide which of their "institutional DNA," or core values, to change or retain in order to innovate for market changes while staying true to their mission.[6]

Staying rooted in their mission can be a challenge for evangelicals, who tend to neglect the insights of the past and privilege the immediate and popular over long-term strategies.[7] By exploring the Anabaptist model that Bender considered to be a "consistent evangelical Protestantism"[8] that involves experiential characteristics shared by evangelicals and Pietists—concern for biblical authority, ethics, the possibility of holy living, and expressions of peace and love—Pietists might focus on their own strengths to cast their own vision.[9] But they should then remember that the Anabaptist vision depended upon Bender and his Goshen College colleagues spending decades both curating artifacts and creating new ones through research and publication.

PIETISM DEFINED

Pietism is credited as a major contributing tradition to the mosaic of evan-

[4]John D. Roth, "Living Between the Times: 'The Anabaptist Vision and Mennonite Reality' Revisited," *Mennonite Quarterly Review* 69, no. 3 (July 1995): 323.

[5]Scholarship on the Anabaptist Vision is extensive. A good introduction is Brian Froese, "'The Anabaptist Vision': A Half-Century of Historical and Religious Debate in Twentieth-Century America," *Fides et Historia* 35 (June 2003): 105-17.

[6]On disruptive innovation applied to higher education, see Clayton M. Christensen and Henry J. Eyring, *The Innovative University: Changing the DNA of Higher Education from the Inside Out* (San Francisco: Jossey-Bass, 2011).

[7]Mark A. Noll, *Jesus Christ and the Life of the Mind* (Grand Rapids: Eerdmans, 2011), p. 152; and Noll, *The Scandal of the Evangelical Mind* (Grand Rapids: Eerdmans, 1994), pp. 55-56.

[8]Albert N. Keim, *Harold S. Bender, 1897–1962* (Scottdale: Herald Press, 1998), p. 325.

[9]Theron F. Schlabach, "Mennonites and Pietism in America, 1740–1880: Some Thoughts on the Friedmann Thesis," *Mennonite Quarterly Review* 57 (July 1983): 224; Michelle A. Clifton-Soderstrom, *Angels, Worms, and Bogeys: The Christian Ethic of Pietism* (Eugene, OR: Cascade, 2010), pp. 23-25.

gelical Protestantism.[10] However, this acknowledgment is often not well articulated or moves on to emphasize the negative or excessive aspects, particularly in North America.[11] The definition of Pietism itself is a subject of scholarly debate, and I use a twofold definition that treats Pietism as both a historical movement and a continuing ethos. The historical movement is centered seventeenth- and eighteenth-century Germany led by the writings and institutions founded by Philipp Jakob Spener and August Hermann Francke. Brethren historian Dale W. Brown and Evangelical Covenant ethicist Michelle Clifton-Soderstrom use this approach to establish the prototype Pietist characteristics. Treating Pietism as an ethos follows persistent characteristics beyond Germany throughout time and geography.[12] For example, F. Ernest Stoeffler defines four characteristics of "evangelical pietism":

1. A "personally meaningful relationship of the individual to God," often expressed as "experiential, inward, or personal" and having to do with "new birth" and "conversion."

2. A "religious idealism, often expressed with words like 'whole, perfect, or entire' including an optimistic view of the future and of humans ability to be more holy."

3. A "biblical emphasis" especially influenced by the practical and ethical orientation of Puritans and Anabaptists.

4. An "oppositional" impulse, inherited from a historical movement that arose in opposition to another dominant force.[13]

Norris Magnuson describes the historical movement of Pietism as "warmhearted personal faith, holy living, and lay Bible study, expressed in missionary

---

[10]For example, C. John Weborg, "Pietism: Theology in Service of Living Toward God," in *The Variety of American Evangelicalism*, ed. Donald W. Dayton and Robert K. Johnston (Knoxville: University of Tennessee Press, 1991), pp. 161-83.

[11]The misunderstanding or misuse of the term *Pietism*—associating it exclusively with characteristics like overly emotional, otherworldly, legalistic—is so prevalent in the English-speaking context that these negative connotations, or bogeys, must be addressed at the beginning of any work on the topic. The most pointed discussion of this is Dale W. Brown, "The Bogey of Pietism," *The Covenant Quarterly* 25 (February 1967): 12-18. More recent is Clifton-Soderstrom, *Angels, Worms, and Bogeys*, pp. 9-17.

[12]Donald F. Durnbaugh, "Pietism: A Millennial View from an American Perspective," *Pietismus Und Neuzeit* 28 (2002): 11-14.

[13]Stoeffler, *Rise of Evangelical Pietism*, pp. 13-25.

work and social philanthropy."[14] Transmitted through the Moravian, Wesleyan and other smaller revivals throughout Europe, Pietism in Magnuson's reading reached North America in the form of an ethos emphasizing experiential Christianity. Pietism made its way to Bethel via Swedish immigrants who were influenced by a blend of pietistic reaction to the Lutheran state church, Methodist revival and Baptist missions.[15] Adolf Olson's seminal 1952 *Centenary History* of the Baptist General Conference, through its extensive documentation and articulation of the influence of Pietism on the Swedish Baptists in Sweden and North America, served as the foundation for his son Virgil (a church history professor and later dean of Bethel College), Bethel president Carl H. Lundquist (1954–1982), history and political science professor G. W. Carlson and others who have emphasized the influence of Pietism on Bethel.[16] The clear articulation of this pietistic heritage, though always affirmed, receded in the movement toward a broader evangelical identity during the presidency of George K. Brushaber (1982–2008).[17] A resurgence of interest and efforts to better communicate and understand the Pietist influence began during the 125th anniversary of Bethel's founding, with the publication of a commemorative booklet that stated, "Bethel has developed from a school for dissenting Swedish Baptist immigrants to an educational environment for today's broader evangelical world. As one develops a more broadly defined evangelical mission, it is useful to explore Bethel's historic pietist tradition and ways in which it can be effectively articulated."[18]

CURATION AND INSTITUTIONAL IDENTITY

One way in which Pietist heritage can be effectively articulated is through the curation of observable artifacts. Artifacts are the first and most observable of

---

[14]Norris A. Magnuson and William G. Travis, *American Evangelicalism: An Annotated Bibliography* (West Cornwall, CT: Locust Hill, 1990), p. xiv.

[15]The transfer of Pietism from Germany to Sweden is covered most extensively in Nicholas Hope, *German and Scandinavian Protestantism, 1700-1918* (Oxford: Clarendon, 1995), pp. 143-59, 211-37. For an account focusing on the Swedish Baptist experience, see Norris A. Magnuson, *Missionsskolan: A History of an Immigrant School: Bethel Theological Seminary, 1871–1981* (St. Paul, MN: Bethel Theological Seminary, 1982), pp. 1-19.

[16]Adolf Olson, *A Centenary History, As Related to the Baptist General Conference of America* (Chicago: Baptist Conference Press, 1952), pp. 5-42.

[17]Paul L. H. Olson, "A University and Its Denomination: The Ties That Bind in the 21st Century" (EdD diss., University of Pennsylvania, 2005), pp. 85-89.

[18]G. William Carlson and Diana L. Magnuson, *Persevere, Läsare, and Clarion: Celebrating Bethel's 125th Anniversary* (St. Paul, MN: Bethel College and Seminary, 1997), p. 2.

the three levels of hierarchy used to examine aspects of culture in organizations, followed by increasingly internalized and less observable levels—values, and assumptions/beliefs.[19] Items involving personal connections in the informal communication networks of evangelicals and Pietist groups, such as correspondence, books, periodicals and hymnals, serve as useful artifacts that communicate identity and transmit values, assumptions and beliefs.[20] Seeking artifacts that have characteristics of Pietism, as defined by Stoeffler and Magnuson in the previous section, can build on the story initiated by Adolf Olson of how a Pietist ethos shaped Bethel's community and culture. As stewards of these artifacts, scholars, librarians and archivists carry the responsibility to curate these items so that new connections and understandings can be made in teaching, learning, research and discussion of institutional identity.

Curators exercise care or guardianship over culturally significant items of the sort that one would find in a library, archive or museum. The founder of the Halle Institutions, August Hermann Francke, was a curator himself. He had a room known as the Cabinet of Artifacts and Curiosities that contained cultural and natural items from around the world that his students could handle, in order to encourage them to "move from curiosity to wonder."[21] In the context of a twenty-first-century university like Bethel, curation refers to a life cycle of activity involving artifacts that are intentionally sought, selected, organized, interpreted or displayed to make them accessible (physically, digitally, intellectually) and preserved in a way that adds value, makes use of the digital options available and "moves people to wonder" at the way Pietism has influenced the character and culture of the school.[22]

CURATING THE ANABAPTIST VISION: COLLECT, COMMUNICATE, SUSTAIN AND EXTEND

The story of the Anabaptist vision demonstrates all the functions of curating artifacts in a three-part strategy: *collecting* (seeking, selecting, organizing),

---

[19]George D. Kuh and Elizabeth J. Whitt, *The Invisible Tapestry: Culture in American Colleges and Universities* (College Station, TX: Association for the Study of Higher Education, 1988), p. 16.
[20]Mark A. Noll, *American Evangelical Christianity: An Introduction* (Malden, MA: Blackwell, 2001), pp. 15-17.
[21]Clifton-Soderstrom, *Angels, Worms, and Bogeys*, p. 26.
[22]Christine L. Borgman, *Scholarship in the Digital Age: Information, Infrastructure, and the Internet* (Cambridge, MA: MIT Press, 2007), pp. 68-69, 227-36.

communicating (interpreting, displaying for access), and *sustaining and extending* (displaying for access, preservation).

In the collecting stage of the Anabaptist vision, Bender and his Anabaptist scholar colleague Ernst Correll sought, selected and organized the primary sources that served as the foundation of the Mennonite Historical Library.[23] Bender was inspired by the efforts of the European librarians, archivists and scholars who curated the artifacts of the sixteenth-century Anabaptists. His efforts to gather the body of works produced by Mennonite immigrants to America culminated in his 1929 bibliography, *Two Centuries of American Mennonite Literature*.[24] Robert Friedmann, the Austrian-born Jewish-Christian scholar who greatly influenced Bender's perceptions of Mennonites and Pietism, shared in the work of cataloging or organizing the artifacts for later use.[25]

In the second or communicating stage of Bender's work he interpreted the sources he had been curating for two decades in order to articulate an identity that was successfully applied to the challenges of the present. His interpretation of the artifacts, in the form of the 1943 "Anabaptist Vision" speech, introduced these ideas not only to the ecumenical group of church historians in the room but to the whole Mennonite community.[26] Access to his interpretation re-energized the community in the face of the uncertainty of World War II and cultural forces infringing on already-eroding boundaries of Mennonite identity.

In the third or sustain-and-extend stage, Bender preserved and continued to display the artifacts of the Anabaptist vision through institutions such as the Mennonite Historical Library and Mennonite Historical Society, and publications such the *Mennonite Quarterly Review* and the scholarly monograph series Studies in Anabaptist and Mennonite History. Without a vehicle to publish the research and conversations widely, and the institutions to preserve the artifacts and maintain access to them for future use, these conversations may have remained only within their immediate context. Bender and other scholars would not have been able to make a distinctive impact without this threefold strategy involving all the functions of curation.

---

[23]Keim, "Anabaptist Vision," pp. 242-43.
[24]Harold S. Bender, *Two Centuries of American Mennonite Literature: A Bibliography of Mennonitica Americana, 1727-1928* (Goshen, IN: Mennonite Historical Society, 1929).
[25]Keim, "Anabaptist Vision," p. 247.
[26]Bender's address was also published in *Mennonite Quarterly Review* 18 (April 1944): 67-88.

To this day, the Anabaptist vision can be credited for the current interest in Anabaptists from outside the tradition. For example, the Anabaptist Network, centered in England and Ireland, makes clear the impact of Bender in the capsule history provided on its website:

> For the next four centuries the Anabaptist movement would be ignored or re-garded (on the basis of such hostile accounts) as subversive, heretical and or of only marginal significance in the history of the church. *Not until the middle of the 20th century did Mennonite historians succeed in presenting the Anabaptist tradition through its own writings* rather than those of its enemies—and a very different and much more attractive picture emerged.[27]

In a time when denominational affinity is decreasing, Woodland Hills Church, an evangelical megachurch in St. Paul, Minnesota, is currently ex-ploring formal affiliation with Mennonite and Brethren groups. Strikingly, that process includes a congregation-wide discussion of a book on the usable past of Anabaptists.[28] This is a clear example of the power of curation.

One additional aspect of curation that is ripe with opportunity is digital curation, which involves all of the above functions but includes the added ca-pabilities that digital files, software and the Internet provide.[29] Digital pub-lishing and digital collections provide an opportunity that was unavailable to Bender and can create spaces where disparate physical items can be rejoined through digital formats and new forms of collaboration.[30] For example, the third characteristic of the Bender's "Vision," the ethic of love and nonresistance, provided a common theme for three Christian higher education institutions within the state of Indiana—Goshen College, Earlham College and Manchester College—to create the Plowshares Digital Archive, containing a shared col-lection of Peace Studies artifacts.[31]

---

[27]"What Happened to the Anabaptists?" *The Anabaptist Network* (February 29, 2008), www.anabap tistnetwork.com/node/7. Italics added.

[28]Kelli Yoder, "Seeking a Tribe, Megachurch Weighs Its Anabaptist Options," *Mennonite World Review* (February 4, 2013), www.mennoworld.org/archived/2013/2/4/seeking-tribe-megachurch-weighs -its-anabaptist-opt/.

[29]Tyler Walters and Katherine Skinner, *New Roles for New Times: Digital Curation for Preservation* (Washington, D.C.: Association of Research Libraries, 2011), pp. 15-18.

[30]Borgman, *Scholarship in the Digital Age*, pp. 168-77.

[31]Anne Meyer Byler and Amy Bryant, "Plowshares Collaborative Digitized Archives for Peace Stud-ies," *Microform & Imaging Review* 37 (Summer 2008): 111-20.

A Curation Proposal for a Pietist Vision

The power of the Anabaptist vision lay in Bender's ability to tell a compelling story of the legacy of the past in the midst of uncertainty. With evangelicalism in a time of flux and some questioning its usefulness as a category altogether, a similar effort to cast a Pietist vision could provide a useful alternative, or at least a fresh perspective, for evangelicals and their churches and other institutions.[32] In addition, curation of Pietist artifacts may feed the ongoing revival of Pietism studies, which promises to enhance scholars' understanding of

> the transatlantic dimension of American religion, underscore the importance of non-English speaking religious communities, provide a stronger contextualization of the early evangelical awakenings in America, further the study of the social and cultural aspects of religious history, and geographically diversify narratives of American religious history by reorienting them away from their preoccupation with New England.[33]

The curation of Pietist artifacts has great value for many individual disciplines and encourages interdisciplinary collaboration.

At the same time, there is still work to be done in the history of Pietism in North America. For example, in a 2002 survey of the field Brethren scholar Donald Durnbaugh's section on bodies formed from Scandinavian American Pietism included the Evangelical Covenant Church and Evangelical Free Church but neglected to mention the Baptist General Conference, which is the third branch of that family.[34] The following section will explore earlier curation of Bethel's pietistic artifacts and how continuing efforts at collecting, communicating, sustaining and extending can help fill this scholarly void and move people to wonder at the possibility of a Pietist vision.

Collecting a Pietist vision. As early as 1892, twenty-one years after John Alexis Edgren founded the seminary that would become Bethel, a Historical Committee was established for the purpose of collecting material on the Swedish Baptist experience. However, the initiative did not produce results

---

[32]Donald W. Dayton, "Some Doubts About the Usefulness of the Category 'Evangelical,'" in *Variety of American Evangelicalism*, pp. 245-72.

[33]Jonathan Strom, "Introduction: Pietism in Two Worlds," in *Pietism in Germany and North America 1680–1820*, ed. Strom, Hartmut Lehmann and James Van Horn Melton (Burlington, VT: Ashgate, 2009), p. 4.

[34]Durnbaugh, "Pietism: A Millenial View from an American Perspective," p. 27.

until scholars Carl G. Lagergren and Emanuel Schmidt revitalized it. In 1900 Lagergren, the dean of the seminary and an author in his own right, was visiting a church in Village Creek, Iowa, when he found valuable annual conference reports stuffed in a container for cloth and sewing material. They would have been thrown out had he not asked the pastor whether he could investigate![35] Without intentional efforts like Lagergren's, future histories of the Baptist General Conference and its educational institution, Bethel University, would have been impossible.[36] Collection efforts continued through the twentieth century and into the twenty-first thanks to the efforts of people such as John Eric Klingberg, Adolf Olson, Norris Magnuson and current BGC/Bethel archivist Diana Magnuson. In 2013, for example, the archives added the papers of Virgil Olson.

For our purposes, three individuals—Emanuel Schmidt, Norris Magnuson and Carl Lundquist—are particularly notable because they added to Bethel's holdings literary collections that can answer some interesting questions related to the pietistic ethos described above by Ernest Stoeffler and Norris Magnuson. "Books are the mirror of the spirit," wrote Mennonite scholar Robert Friedmann, "and the story of books is the story of the spirit which they reflect."[37] So what would a Swedish American Pietist have read, and what do these works tell us about the pietistic spirit?

Emanuel Schmidt, former president of Adelphia College in Seattle, bought his personal library from theology professor and hymn writer C. G. Skarstedt of Lund University, Sweden, and brought it to the Bethel Seminary Library when he arrived in 1919. It includes now-rare editions representing literature that would have been familiar to a well-read Swedish Pietist, including devotionals, hymnals and theological works. Interestingly, Schmidt's collection includes not only works by Martin Luther and Philipp Jakob Spener but those of the Radical Pietist biblical scholar Johann Albrecht Bengel (1687–1752).[38]

Long-serving seminary librarian Norris Magnuson collected the personal library of the Swedish American Baptist pastor John Eric Klingberg, who

---

[35]Olson, *Centenary History*, pp. 442-44.

[36]Ibid., p. xii.

[37]Robert Friedmann, *Mennonite Piety Through the Centuries: Its Genius and Its Literature* (Goshen, IN: Mennonite Historical Society, 1949), p. 91.

[38]Carlson and Magnuson, *Persevere, Läsare, and Clarion*, p. 27.

founded an orphanage in Connecticut in conscious imitation of August Hermann Francke's similar efforts two centuries before in Halle.[39] Klingberg's books were collected and placed in that home as a source of devotional reading for himself and the children who stayed in his care. The collection consists primarily of Puritan authors who had inspired Klingberg in his devotion and social efforts, including some that represent the close relationship between Puritans and Pietists: for example, John Bunyan, Richard Baxter and John Dod.[40] In addition to these commentaries, Klingberg's collection includes more than a hundred different editions of Bunyan's work *Pilgrim's Progress,* providing a unique opportunity to study and compare what is considered a "major achievement of the pietistic tradition" and a classic of English and devotional literature, second only to the Bible for some.

A third collection of literature comes from the personal library of Carl Lundquist. Displayed in the Bethel Seminary Library Flame Room, it shows the ecumenical, pietistic nature of his spiritual tastes. Pietist classics such as *True Christianity*, by Johann Arndt, and *Pia Desideria*, by Spener, stand alongside spiritual, devotional and mystical writings by Catholic, Methodist, Lutheran and other Christian spiritual writers. While few of the books are likely rare or unique, their arrangement together communicates the ecumenical nature of the Pietist tradition. It recreates the conditions of seventeenth- and early eighteenth-century Europe, where the growing need for devotional literature broadened the scope for sources of inspiration. Lundquist joined men who "appealed to a spiritual tradition common to Catholic and Protestant."[41] The same room also has the Bible collection one would expect at an institution rooted in a biblicist movement like Pietism, and a hymnal collection, speaking

---

[39]"The thought," wrote Klingberg, "that I should perhaps be allowed to trust in God as had these men [Francke and his colleagues] who had become such mighty laborers in God's vineyard, gave my heart new strength"; quoted in G. William Carlson, "John Eric Klingberg: Experiencing the Blessing of God," *The Baptist Pietist Clarion* (May 2008), p. 6.

[40]Stoeffler, *Rise of Evangelical Pietism*, pp. 49-108. For more on the connections between Pietism and Puritanism, see Tom Schwanda, "The Puritan and Pietist Tradition," in *Reading the Christian Spiritual Classics: A Guide for Evangelicals,* ed. Jamin Goggin and Kyle Strobel (Downers Grove, IL: IVP Academic, 2013), pp. 273-99; and Donald G. Bloesch, *The Evangelical Renaissance* (Grand Rapids: Eerdmans, 1973), pp. 101-22.

[41]W. Reginald Ward, *The Protestant Evangelical Awakening* (Cambridge: Cambridge University Press, 1992), pp. 48-49. Ward continues, "The men who ushered in new ways of christianizing their world, Spener and Francke, Baxter and Watts, Dodderidge and Wesley all appeared as middle men of one kind or another. Someone needed to mediate between the world of ecclesiastical precision, and the world of spiritual nutriment" (ibid., p. 49).

to what some scholars consider Pietism's most enduring legacy for its experience-oriented contribution to Protestant worship.[42]

In addition to his deep commitment to spiritual formation, Lundquist exemplified the irenic spirit underlying Spener's fourth proposal of reform in *Pia Desideria*, "We must beware how we conduct ourselves in religious controversies," which invited edifying dialogue amid controversy by focusing on a core of essential beliefs, and respectful, loving discussion in all situations.[43] To that end, Lundquist stood by Bethel's invitation to Martin Luther King Jr. to speak in chapel despite criticism from theological conservatives:

> The people who are being brought to Bethel for the various lectures are being invited for some special contribution that they can make in a particular field and not because we subscribe to the totality of their viewpoints in any area, including their religious beliefs. . . . Dr. King has been invited because he is today one of the foremost leaders in promoting non-violent programs for racial equality. This is a concern for every Christian . . . cooperation "with all other groups of God's people wherever no compromise of principle or doctrine is involved." I think this is one of the distinctives of the Baptist General Conference and can be one of its greatest contributions to these troublesome times in the evangelical world.[44]

This document came to light as Bethel Library staff and archivist Diana Magnuson researched why King was ultimately unable to visit Bethel, research that was made available through Bethel's Digital Library and presented in a library event—excellent examples of how curation can help an institution understand the implications of its Pietist heritage.[45]

Communicating a Pietist vision. The "Anabaptist Vision" was written to communicate to an ecumenical audience the positive legacy of the Anabaptists and to confront negative associations. For Pietists a similar effort began in the

---

[42]On Pietist hymnody, see G. Thomas Halbrooks, *Pietism* (Nashville, TN: Broadman, 1981), pp. 397-414; and Alice T. Ott, "Singing to the Lord a New Song: Hymnody and Liturgy in George Rapp's Harmony Society, 1805-1847," in *The Pietist Impulse in Christianity*, ed. Christian T. Collins Winn et al. (Eugene, OR: Pickwick, 2011), pp. 234-36.

[43]Philip Jacob Spener, *Pia Desideria*, trans. Theodore G. Tappert (Philadelphia: Fortress, 1964), p. 97.

[44]Carl H. Lundquist, minutes of 1960-1961 Convocation and Commencement Committee, Bethel University Digital Library, http://cdm16120.contentdm.oclc.org/cdm/ref/collection/beunhisco/id/1073.

[45]The story of King's invitation and nonappearance is told in Diana Magnuson and Kent Gerber, "Martin Luther King Invited to Address Bethel Convocation: Reaping the Legacy of President Carl Lundquist's Correspondence with Dr. Martin Luther King, Jr.," *The Baptist Pietist Clarion* (June 2011), pp. 6-11.

late 1960s and 1970s with the extensive work by Stoeffler, plus Dale Brown's accessible *Understanding Pietism*.[46] At Bethel, Virgil Olson, Carl Lundquist, Norris Magnuson and G. W. Carlson have all built on Adolf Olson's foundation, communicating the influence of Pietism on the institution.

Virgil Olson played a particularly important and transitional role, bridging the generation of Conference Baptists who were born and lived in Sweden with those who were born in the United States. His translation of Gunnar Westin's *The Free Church Through the Ages* (1958) brought that Swedish church historian's work to an English-speaking audience.[47] And articles in journals such as *Baptist History and Heritage* and *Bethel Seminary Quarterly* helped communicate what Olson saw as Pietist values central to the distinctive identity of the BGC: reaction against formalism; revivalism, with an emphasis on new birth; lay involvement; and the irenic spirit.[48]

As Bethel president at that time, Carl Lundquist submitted annual reports to Bethel's denomination that communicated a Pietist identity and educational philosophy. They are now getting wider exposure through the publications of Bethel history professor Chris Gehrz, who argues that Lundquist was "reinterpreting, in light of contemporary concerns, what [he] found valuable about a tradition that, for many of [his] readers and listeners, was unknown, forgotten, or irrelevant."[49]

Trained as a historian of nineteenth-century evangelical participation in social work, seminary librarian Norris Magnuson helped to frame Bethel's heritage and ethos in the context of evangelical historiography, contributing articles on BGC founders Anders Wiberg, Gustav Palmquist and F. O. Nilsson to the *Dictionary of Evangelical Biography*. In an annotated bibliography on evangelicalism in the United States, he addressed the relationship between evangelicals and Pietists: "While not all evangelicals are pietists, virtually all pietists are evangelicals."[50]

---

[46]Dale W. Brown, *Understanding Pietism* (Grand Rapids: Eerdmans, 1978).

[47]Gunnar Westin, *The Free Church Through the Ages*, trans. Virgil A. Olson (Nashville, TN: Broadman, 1958).

[48]Virgil A. Olson, "Neither Jew nor Greek: A Study of an Ethnic Baptist Group, the Swedish Baptists, 1850-1950," *Baptist History and Heritage* 25 (January 1990): 32-42; and Olson, "The Baptist General Conference and Its Pietistic Heritage," *Bethel Seminary Quarterly* 4 (May 1956): 54-66. He also spoke at Bethel, even in retirement; see Olson, "Influential Factors in the History of Bethel College," a 1988 faculty retreat address published in *Bethel Faculty Journal* (Fall 1988): 1-14.

[49]Christopher Gehrz, "Recovering a Pietist Understanding of Christian Higher Education: Carl H. Lundquist and Karl A. Olsson," *Christian Scholar's Review* 40 (Winter 2011): 145.

[50]Magnuson and Travis, *American Evangelicalism*, p. xiv.

G. W. Carlson and Diana Magnuson's 125th anniversary exhibit publication, *Persevere, Läsare, and Clarion,* rekindled an interest in Bethel's Pietist heritage. With BGC pastor Ron Saari, Carlson founded the newsletter *The Baptist Pietist Clarion* in 2002 to resist an effort within the denomination to impose a "strict creedal" approach in the midst of a debate over open theism.[51] "One of the missing pieces of the current theological debate," wrote Carlson in the newsletter's first issue, "is the failure of many to appreciate and value the pietistic heritage which has played a major role in the heritage of the Baptist General Conference. . . . The pietist principle for theological inquiry was 'in essentials unity, in non-essentials liberty, in all things charity.'"[52]

Sustaining and extending a Pietist vision. How will such efforts be sustained and extended, and what role could curators at a Pietist university play in that process? Can there be Pietist equivalents of the institutions centered at Goshen College: the Mennonite Historical Society, Mennonite Historical Library and *Mennonite Quarterly Review*?

The first sustained effort in the United States for Pietism studies was organized by Ernest Stoeffler at Temple University in 1971. Both Elizabethtown College and Messiah College host centers dedicated in part to Pietism studies, and in the past ten years alone conferences have been held at Emory University (in 2004 and 2006) and Bethel University (in 2009 and 2012).

But the advent of the digital age suggests even more promising possibilities for the purposes of sustaining and extending a Pietist vision. New, informal networks over which scholars of Pietism can communicate (e.g., via the Twitter account of the Pietism Studies Group and the scholarly hub called H-Pietism[53]) are emerging in a way that was not possible even ten years ago. These informal efforts could be built upon to have a regular publishing platform for these conversations, and the existing ones could be sustained and extended. Before

---

[51]Current and back issues of *The Baptist Pietist Clarion* may be found at the History Center: Archives of the Baptist General Conference and Bethel University, or online, at the Baptist Pietist Clarion, or in the Bethel University Digital Library. On the debate over open theism, see G. William Carlson and Diana Magnuson, "Bethel College and Seminary on the Move," in *Five Decades of Growth and Change: The Baptist General Conference and Bethel College and Seminary, 1952-2002,* ed. James and Carole Spickelmier (St. Paul, MN: The History Center, 2010), pp. 49-50.

[52]G. William Carlson, "What Is Pietism? 'In Essentials Unity, in Non-Essentials Diversity, in Everything Charity,'" *The Baptist Pietist Clarion* (March 2002), p. 2.

[53]The Pietism Studies Group can be found at http://twitter.com/pietismstudies; H-Pietism is at www.h-net.org/~pietism.

digital publishing matured, establishing a journal dedicated to Pietism studies would have been cost prohibitive, but that is no longer the case with software tools such as Open Journal Systems and bepress Digital Commons.[54]

Bethel has already established a foundation of digital artifacts in its digital library, with selections of its books, publications, personal papers and photographs that are publicly available. These resources make these artifacts more available for teaching and research into Bethel's historical identity; additional curation provides a great opportunity for further understanding and research.

However, given the dispersal of Pietism across ethnic, denominational and other lines, it is likely that a Pietist vision would be most effectively curated by a consortium of institutions. One way to approach these kinds of efforts in a new way is to focus on a region. Three pietistic, historically Scandinavian American denominations and their educational institutions—Converge Worldwide (Baptist General Conference) and Bethel University; the Evangelical Covenant Church and North Park University; and the Evangelical Free Church and Trinity International University—are located around the urban centers of Chicago and Minneapolis/St. Paul and could work more closely on shared projects. In 1960 David Moberg, a prominent evangelical sociologist then working at Bethel College, proposed a collaboration among those groups (plus the North American Baptist Conference) based on their shared history, doctrine and polity.[55] While it is not clear whether anything resulted from this at that time, some recent developments in this vein include Chris Gehrz's work on North Park president Karl Olsson and a 2012 issue of *The Covenant Quarterly* on Pietism guest-edited by Gehrz and his Bethel colleague Christian Collins Winn, which included a roundtable discussion of Pietism providing a usable past for contemporary denominations such as the Covenant Church, Converge Worldwide and two Lutheran denominations also historically rooted in northern European immigration.[56]

---

[54]For Open Journal Systems see http://pkp.sfu.ca/ojs; for Digital Commons see http://digitalcommons.bepress.com. *The Covenant Quarterly* (out of North Park Theological Seminary) occasionally publishes research on Pietism, and such articles do appear in other journals for theology, church history and other fields. There is, however, no journal dedicated to Pietism studies.

[55]David O. Moberg, "A Suggestion for Long Range Planning," *Bethel College Faculty Journal* 1 (March 1960): 10-11.

[56]Gehrz, "Recovering a Pietist Understanding of Christian Higher Education," pp. 139-54; "Roundtable: Pietism, Contemporary Churches, and a 'Usable Past,'" *The Covenant Quarterly* 70 (August/November 2012): 48-65.

In addition, that roundtable also featured Brethren in Christ historian Devin Manzullo-Thomas, now the director of the Sider Institute for Anabaptist, Pietist and Wesleyan Studies at Messiah College.[57] Indeed, Pennsylvania is also a potential regional center, with Pietist-oriented publishing and research centers already well established at Messiah, Elizabethtown College and Moravian Theological Seminary.[58] The regional model makes use of the historical and social influences of shared immigration conditions, because many of these groups came in the nineteenth century and settled in Midwest states, such as Kansas and Minnesota, and the West, particularly California.

Combining such efforts with the aid of new technologies could cultivate vibrant conversations that both highlight the contributions of Pietism to evangelical identity and model its irenic spirit of ecumenical cooperation. Just as the Plowshares Digital Archive builds on the foundation of the Anabaptist Vision to bring institutions around a shared theme and shared artifacts, the collaborative curation of artifacts could provide more opportunities for Pietist institutions to tell their stories and seek a vital future together. This is an extraordinary time to seize these opportunities because even though technology is a force of fragmentation, it also has the ability to powerfully aid curation when there is a central organizing interest. Distributed artifacts, influenced by Pietism, could be digitized and curated in ways that more people could access and use them. Gathered together, these collections could be a fruitful resource for Pietist studies and aid efforts to connect, collaborate and publish with other institutions. A broader, richer Pietist vision can, in the words of Carl Lundquist, "take the best of the past and . . . make it a gift to the future."[59]

---

[57]Devin C. Manzullo-Thomas, "Pietism as a 'Usable Past' in the Brethren in Christ Church," *The Covenant Quarterly* 70 (August/November 2012): 60-65.

[58]For a complete list of research centers, archives, publications, blogs and other resources for scholars of Pietism, see www.h-net.org/~pietism/resources.html.

[59]Carl H. Lundquist, "Pietism: The Roots of a Heart and Mind Commitment," in *Give First Priority to Jesus Christ: Key Values for Chrstian Living Taken from the Life and Ministry of Carl H. Lundquist*, ed. James and Carole Spickelmier (St. Paul, MN: The History Center, 2010), p. 155.

14

Neoliberal Challenges to the Pietist Vision of Christian Higher Education

Samuel Zalanga

◆

STRINGENTLY OPPOSED TO state intervention in the form of publicly subsidized social services such as higher education and public assistance to the
poor, middle and working classes, the late Margaret Thatcher was among the
foremost articulators of the moral and ethical implications of neoliberalism.[1]
"Economics are the method," asserted Thatcher, "but the object is to change the
soul."[2] What this means is that neoliberalism is not just about public policies
to achieve the efficient allocation of scarce resources through the strict application of market criteria. Rather, the main target is the transformation of the
human soul, with a view to creating a new person who fits the new social and
economic order that is envisioned.[3] So neoliberalism can hardly avoid tension

---

[1]*Neoliberalism* is used here to describe the kind of economic and public policy concerns that became
triumphant in the 1980s after (1) what in the 1970s seemed to be the collapse and irrelevance of
Keynesian economic and public policies in the developed countries of the Western world and
(2) the dismal collapse of Soviet communism, even as China embraced free market capitalism.
Advocates of neoliberalism see it as a constellation of policy instruments that would best lead to the
creation of the best social, economic and political environment for the generation of wealth and
economic prosperity in society.

[2]Quoted in Catherine Kingfisher and Jeff Maskovsky, "The Limits of Neoliberalism," *Critique of Anthropology* 28 (June 2008): 119.

[3]Rob Van Horn and Philip Mirowski, "The Rise of the Chicago School of Economics and the Birth of
Neoliberalism," in *The Road from Mont Pèlerin: The Making of the Neoliberal Thought Collective*, ed.
Philip Mirowski and Dieter Plehwe (Cambridge, MA: Harvard University Press, 2009), pp. 139-78.

with Christian higher education in the Pietist tradition, which is committed to molding a whole and holy person as part of a Christian community that thinks globally while acting locally.

Neoliberalism is characterized as market fundamentalism because as an approach to public policy decisions and organizational leadership it has a "single-minded focus on economic priorities."[4] Because the main priority of neoliberalism is the efficient allocation and use of scarce resources, this commitment becomes the organizing principle and the value orientation through which human beings are viewed, evaluated and valued, and decisions about who gets what, when, how and where are made. While the application of market fundamentalism may mean pain and suffering to many people, proponents of the idea believe that the idea that one cannot make an omelet without breaking an egg applies here.

The moral vision of market fundamentalism is one of atomistic individualism, as Thatcher observed: "There is no such thing as society. There are individual men and women, and there are families."[5] Thatcher is not wrong in calling on people to be socially responsible and not totally dependent on the government. No freedom is viable without a sense of responsibility. But in doing so she elevates the role of the individual and diminishes the role of the state and the institutional structures of a society that shape a human being. Consequently, she was committed to dismantling the welfare state through the privatization of as many public services as possible, insisting that people should raise themselves by their bootstraps.

Thus this chapter is inspired by my desire to explore the role that Christian higher education plays in transforming the individual and society in a world that has become dominated by neoliberalism. My main focus is on Pietism, its role in Christian higher education and the challenges it faces because of the emergence of market society in the contemporary United States. In the market society of today, we face the phenomenon of the increased "colonization" of more spheres of human life, endeavors, enterprise and relations by deep market

---

[4]Neoliberalism is best defined as *market fundamentalism* because of its "rather single-minded focus on economic priorities" to the detriment of other equally important social and human concerns; David N. Balaam and Michael Veseth, *Introduction to International Political Economy*, 3rd ed. (Upper Saddle River, NJ: Prentice Hall, 2005), pp. 58-67.

[5]Quoted in Simon Clarke, "The Neoliberal Theory of Society," in *Neoliberalism: A Critical Reader*, ed. Alfredo Saad-Filho and Deborah Johnston (London: Pluto Press, 2005), p. 51.

rationality that is the organizing principle and the normative worldview in such a society. This colonization of human endeavors by the market has serious consequences and implications for higher education in general but particularly for Christian higher education in the Pietist tradition.

The expansion of market rationality is in many respects functionally equivalent to a secular "evangelical project" that is as deeply and equally committed to transforming human beings and society as evangelical Christianity is.[6] Christianity ultimately promises a new Jerusalem to human beings at the eschaton, while the market promises "the age of high mass consumption" as the ultimate goal of economic development.[7] The challenge here is that the vision of the market as we know it today and the vision of Christianity are not necessarily coterminous. Yet they often end up in collusion because often the terms for survival for Christian organizations and believers in a market society are primarily dictated by the market with no regard for Christian priorities or sensibilities. The tension between the two is necessitated by the fact that Christians and Christian organizations have to live out their faith and commitment in a market society that operates on a different logic. They are often compelled to adapt to the dictates of the market in order to survive and flourish, although there is variation in how different Christian traditions and organizations pursue this.[8] Rather than delve into a detailed discussion of key policy components of neoliberalism, this chapter will focus on three moral, ethical and social consequences of neoliberalism and the implications for Christian higher education in the Pietist tradition.[9]

THREE MORAL, ETHICAL AND SOCIAL CONSEQUENCES OF NEOLIBERALISM

At the center of the Christian vision of human beings and their society is a moral and ethical calling that is accompanied by certain social, cultural and

---

[6]Robert H. Nelson, "The Theological Meaning of Economics," *The Christian Century* (August 1993): 11-18; Harvey Cox, "The Market as God: Living with the New Dispensation," *The Atlantic Monthly* (March 1999): 18.

[7]As envisioned in W. W. Rostow, *Stages of Economic Growth: A Non-Communist Manifesto* (Cambridge: Cambridge University Press, 1991).

[8]Brian Steenland and Philip Goff, *The New Evangelical Social Engagement* (New York: Oxford University Press, 2014), pp. 1-27.

[9]For such an analysis see, for example, Dani Rodrik, "Understanding Economic Policy Reform," *Journal of Economic Literature* 34 (March 1996): 9-41.

institutional expectations. In this section, I want to draw the reader's attention to three areas of profound tension, if not conflict, between the moral and ethical implications of neoliberalism vis-à-vis Christianity.

First, under neoliberalism, one sees a systematic and real shift from the biblical concept of human dignity to a functional conception of what it means to be human.[10] Orthodox Christian teaching roots one's dignity as a human in the person being created in the image of God. But under neoliberalism, while in theory people still maintain their God-given status and dignity as human beings, in reality and practice, their dignity and status in a neoliberal economy is contingent upon achieving certain statuses: their human capital, their effective purchasing power as consumers, their entrepreneurial status or capacity, and whether they produce any commodity that is crucial to the functioning of the economic system. Without any one of these statuses in the affirmative, a person is irrelevant in terms of the calculus and function of the economy and society, except as nuisances and liabilities to the system. Indeed, such persons can veritably be described as surplus people. Because the market always produces winners and losers, without charity or compassion, many persons who are systematically categorized as surplus people in a neoliberal economy and society can easily perish without upsetting the system. What this means, of course, is that under neoliberalism, there is a gradation of citizenship to the extent that one's value or status as a citizen/human being and what one can enjoy as a citizen/human being is contingent on a person's valuation in the neoliberal marketplace.

While the Pietist vision of Christian higher education tries to shape a whole and holy person created in the image of God, under neoliberalism human dignity is made fragile and diminished in reality if not validated by the market. Human beings who represent the epitome of neoliberal human personality are self-calculating and always committed to pursuing their selfish interests in an enlightened manner in the marketplace; they are entrepreneurial, innovative and audacious. They also see themselves as human capital, have independent measure of utility as individuals and are not inspired in their behavior by any

---

[10]Kevin J. Vanhoozer, ed., *Dictionary for Theological Interpretation of the Bible* (Grand Rapids: Baker Academic, 2005), pp. 310-13. This reference discusses the doctrine of the human being in theological interpretation of the Bible; Craig M. Gay, *With Justice and Liberty for Whom? The Recent Evangelical Debate over Capitalism* (Grand Rapids: Eerdmans, 1991), pp. 143-52.

divine moral order, only those principles that have emerged spontaneously through the process of commutative exchange in the marketplace. They only pursue actions that further their own self-interest as they define it.[11]

Second, under neoliberalism, many decisions are made that degrade or undermine human dignity for the ultimate goal of achieving market efficiency in the allocation of scarce resources and increasing economic and organizational competitiveness.[12] The consequences of such decisions under normal circumstances are reasons for great lamentation and regret because of the pain and suffering they impose on others.[13] But in practice the market society encourages people to faithfully absorb such decisions that are otherwise dehumanizing in decent human relationships. In this respect, neoliberalism is engaged in the reconstruction of human beings and disciplining them to become socially abnormal.

When workers are encouraged, for the ultimate goal of increasing efficiency and economic competitiveness, to tolerate the violation of certain moral and ethical principles that would normally be abhorred in a Pietist community, it amounts to what Søren Kierkegaard calls "the teleological suspension of the ethical."[14] Pat Buchanan lamented this consequence of neoliberal capitalism when he noted,

> Unbridled capitalism is an awesome force that creates new factories, wealth and opportunities that go first to society's risk takers and holders of capital. But unbridled capitalism is also an awesome destructive force. It makes men and women obsolete as rapidly as it does the products they produce and the plants that employ them. And the people made obsolete and insecure are workers, employees.[15]

Third, what responsibilities do corporations have to society given the huge amount of power they have accumulated in today's economy? Milton Fried-

---

[11]Charles McDaniel, *God & Money: The Moral Challenge of Capitalism* (New York: Rowman & Littlefield, 2005), pp. 105-142; Paula England, "The Separative Self: Androcentric Bias in Neoclassical Assumptions," in Marianne A. Ferber and Julie A. Nelson, eds., *Beyond Economic Man: Feminist Theory and Economics* (Chicago: University of Chicago Press, 1993), pp. 37-53.

[12]Thomas S. Moore, *The Disposable Work Force: Worker Displacement and Employment Instability in America* (Piscataway, NJ: Aldine Transaction Publishers, 1996), pp. 15-32.

[13]Robert H. Nelson, *Economics as Religion: From Samuelson to Chicago and Beyond* (University Park: Pennsylvania State University Press, 2001), pp. 52-88.

[14]Søren Kierkegaard, *Fear and Trembling*, trans. Alastair Hannay (New York: Penguin, 1985), pp. 83-95.

[15]Patrick Buchanan, "Schism Beyond Repair on the Right?" *Washington Times*, March 25, 1998.

man's answer to that question brings into relief the moral and ethical dimensions of neoliberalism:

> But the doctrine of "social responsibility" taken seriously would extend the scope of the political mechanism to every human activity. It does not differ in philosophy from the most explicitly collectivist doctrine. It differs only by professing to believe that collectivist ends can be attained without collectivist means. That is why, in my book "Capitalism and Freedom," I have called it a "fundamentally subversive doctrine" in a free society, and have said that in such a society, "there is one and only one social responsibility of business—to use its resources and engage in activities designed to increase its profits so long as it stays within the rules of the game, which is to say, engages in open and free competition without deception or fraud."[16]

What Friedman is promoting is the privatization of social responsibility. He assumes that the legal system and customs of a society are inherently fair and just, so operating within their limits necessarily brings about justice. This is a kind of society whose concept of justice is mechanical and procedural, otherwise nothing substantive is guaranteed. From a sociological point of view, Friedman and people like him are not completely wrong in conceptualizing law in society the way he has, but they are naive in ignoring how the social structure, the relative distribution of power, and the variation in ethical commitment in every human society affect the process and content of law making. This in turn results in a situation in which laws, even when framed in neutral language, tend to allow well-organized social groups and rich and powerful people to have a disproportionate influence on the system. They are able to make it reflect their interests in a pluralistic society.[17]

Throughout the history of the Pietist movement, starting with the Moravians, social responsibility has never been considered merely a private matter. In spite of the internal debates within the community, the great majority of Moravians were highly inspired by their faith to initiate projects of social transformation.[18]

---

[16]Milton Friedman, "The Social Responsibility of Business Is to Increase Its Profits," *The New York Times Magazine*, September 13, 1970.

[17]Steven Vago, *Law and Society* (Boston: Prentice Hall, 2012), pp. 159-88; John Defore, "Inequality for All," *Washington Post*, September 26, 2013.

[18]While I will focus on the Moravians, similar concern for social transformation can be seen in Halle and Württemberg Pietism. See Michelle A. Clifton-Soderstrom, *Angels, Worms, and Bogeys: The Christian Ethic of Pietism* (Eugene, OR: Cascade, 2010), pp. 71-89; and Frank D. Macchia, *Spirituality and Social Liberation: The Message of the Blumhardts in the Light of Wuerttemberg Pietism* (Metuchen, NJ: Scarecrow Press, 1993), pp. 1-3.

Thus an ethic of privatized social responsibility as envisioned by neoliberals will be inconsistent with a true Pietist vision of Christian higher education.

THE IMPACT OF NEOLIBERAL ECONOMIC POLICIES ON HIGHER EDUCATION

How and how much neoliberal economic policies affect higher education in the United States can be critically examined by analyzing the state of higher education in the decades after World War II.[19] In the immediate postwar period many minorities and women did not have access equal to that of white men from influential European ethnic groups. Yet by and large higher education was comparatively cheap in the two decades after 1945, when public opinion was open to state intervention in order to provide affordable social services and restructure society.[20] Higher education was highly subsidized by state and federal governments as a social service, an integral part of national development strategy. Youth were highly concentrated across American universities, and many of them participated actively in social movements that challenged the prevalent establishment values of the United States and the social classes that benefited from them. Many members of the American ruling elite blamed this rebellion on the liberal education youth had received in universities. Consequently the elite developed a long-term strategy to counter such a threat once and for all, exemplified by the Lewis Powell Memorandum, which interpreted students' social movements on campus as an attack on the American free enterprise system.[21]

The Powell Memorandum called on corporate America to play a more critical role in shaping American politics, law and education. There was consequently an effort to increase the involvement of corporate America in curbing what was perceived as liberal social movements on American university campuses. This was executed through sponsoring politicians at the state and federal level who would use their official power to defund or drastically reduce higher

---

[19]Michael Mumper, "The Future of College Access: The Declining Role of Public Higher Education in Promoting Equal Opportunity," in *The Annals of the American Academy of Political and Social Science: Higher Education in the Twenty-First Century,* ed. Paul Rich and David Merchant (Thousand Oaks, CA: Sage, 2003), pp. 97-117.

[20]Ira Katznelson, *When Affirmative Action Was White: An Untold History of Racial Inequality in Twentieth-Century America* (New York: Norton, 2006), pp. 113-41.

[21]Hendrick Smith, *Who Stole the American Dream?* (New York: Random House, 2012), pp. 3-8.

education funding, so that students would have to pay more (i.e., quasi-privatization). Soon after universities were pressured to shift from emphasizing liberal arts education to vocational education. What this shift suggests is the instrumentalization of education. The assumption is that a total focus on vocational education is less likely to adequately expose students to critical literature that will compel them to examine themselves, their nation, and its institutions, history and culture. Not only did this corporate initiative exert pressure on universities to shift from liberal arts to vocational education, but there was also an attack on humanities and social science disciplines because they were perceived as promoting antiestablishment discourses. Consequently, courses in these disciplines were either cut or defunded.[22]

Neoliberalism also affected higher education by exerting pressure on colleges and universities to develop new mechanisms for cutting costs in order to manage institutions more efficiently. One result is the increased trend toward the deprofessionalization of teaching in higher education by increasing the employment of adjunct faculty instead of full-time faculty. Adjuncts now represent 70 percent of all faculty members in American colleges and universities.[23] Their pay is low, and their positions are very insecure.[24] Many live not far above poverty, which affects their mental and physical stability given that often they have to teach in more than one institution.[25] Added to this, their impact on students is constrained by the fact that they are not allowed or expected to play any role in curriculum design or academic advising. This also results in the full-time faculty in many private colleges and universities being saddled with teaching more courses, which in turn limits their ability to mentor students to the degree that is highly desired by many students who need close attention and supervision. From an economic point of view, a heavy teaching load is a mechanism for colleges and universities to cut costs and maximize labor productivity by extracting more from faculty.

The emphasis on economic efficiency highlighted above is a precursor to

---

[22]Christopher Newfield, *Unmaking the Public University: The Forty-Year Assault on the Middle Class* (Cambridge, MA: Harvard University Press, 2008), pp. 142-58.

[23]Stacey Patton, "The Ph.D. Now Comes with Food Stamps," *Chronicle of Higher Education,* May 6, 2012.

[24]Alan Finder, "Decline of the Tenure Track Raises Concerns," *New York Times,* November 20, 2007.

[25]Between 2007 and 2010, the number of those with doctoral degrees who received food stamp assistance increased from 9,776 to 33,655; Patton, "The Ph.D. Now Comes with Food Stamps."

what can be perceived as a total adoption of corporate-style management in higher education institutions, especially private colleges and universities. As was the case with the health care industry, in which the emergence of health care management organizations increased the privatization of services, similarly the increased use of educational management organizations in higher education increased the ratio of administrators to faculty, shifting the proportion of budgetary expenses for administration higher compared to teaching or academics. The reallocation of funds from faculty development to administration, executive salaries and perquisites means that there is less focus on faculty development and teaching.[26] In addition, there is an increased use of legal and marketing firms for consultancy, further adding to noninstructional expenses for many private colleges and universities.

In this context, the official gimmick is efficiency and the rational allocation of scarce resources. But in practice, it is more a shift of resources from academic concerns to corporate-style concerns—one of which is higher pay for executives, presumably in order to attract the best talent.[27]

With the increased penetration of this approach to college and university business administration, there is a slowly but progressively increasing displacement of the value and mission of the university from its traditional and ideal form to one that is corporate driven.[28] This helps explain the shifting emphasis on vocational training, so as to produce alumni with greater potential to procure jobs in lucrative professions. This shift generates revenue for the institution in the future. Administrators are also forced to adopt primarily market criteria to evaluate progress in all spheres of an institution because financial survival has become decisive in the competitiveness of the institution in the higher education market. The increased struggle to survive also means that many colleges and universities resort to the adoption of private-sector revenue generation strategies such as outsourcing, off-campus and extra-mural classes as part of survival strategies in the marketplace. Furthermore, as colleges and universities become more corporate in style, there often emerges a conflict of interest between the objective professional roles

[26]Newfield, *Unmaking the Public University*, pp. 173-94.
[27]A. H. Halsey et al., eds., *Education: Culture, Economy, and Society* (New York: Oxford University Press, 2003), pp. 19-31.
[28]Newfield, *Unmaking the Public University*, pp. 51-67.

of many faculty members and their roles in corporate outfits whose mission and values tend to conflict with the institutional mission and values of the university or college.[29]

One major consequence of all this corporate orientation in higher education is a trend toward an increase in the cost of education, making it less accessible and even prohibitive for many students. At the same time, faculty salaries in many private colleges and universities have either remained below or just at inflation level.[30]

The cumulative effect of all the policy decisions highlighted above has brought about qualitative transformation in higher education in the form of deteriorating learning environments for many students. The widening inequality in American society has had a decisive impact on the quality of K-12 education, with many students from disadvantaged backgrounds coming to college with inadequate preparation.[31] With higher numbers of inadequately prepared students in college, many faculty are compelled to "dumb down" course material as a coping mechanism for keeping students enrolled. For many of the students there is an emergence of the "diploma disease," owing to the overemphasis on acquiring the credential by just trying to conform to academic rituals, with no deep commitment to learning, conversion and the transformation of consciousness.[32]

WHAT NEOLIBERALISM MEANS FOR THE PIETIST VISION FOR CHRISTIAN HIGHER EDUCATION

In conclusion, I would like to highlight some principles that I believe to be central to the Pietist vision of Christian higher education but that have come under serious threat by the increased penetration of market rationality and the pursuit of competitiveness as described above.

First, the Pietist vision of Christian higher education promotes a hermeneutic of suspicion toward the existing social order by exposing the unfairness

---

[29]Ibid., pp. 195-207.

[30]Sam Dillon, "At Public Universities, Warning of Privatization," *New York Times*, October 16, 2005.

[31]Jacqueline Murray Brux, *Economic Issues & Policy*, 4th ed. (Mason, OH: Thomson Higher Education, 2008), pp. 87-107.

[32]Ronald Philip Dore, *The Diploma Disease: Education, Qualification, and Development* (Berkeley: University of California Press, 1976).

in the system and maintaining a commitment to social transformation.[33] Today there is a need for a bold commitment to the struggle for justice, which is different from and beyond fairness and charity. Unfortunately contemporary universities and colleges in the Pietist tradition cannot faithfully do so because they would be perceived as anti-American, socialist and anticapitalist. Such charges would drain away institutional social capital and financial support, and draw negative publicity, which would be a distraction. At best institutions can appeal for charity and compassion but not rigorously and openly critique the injustice in the contemporary social order.

Related to the preceding observation, the Pietist vision of higher education as a matter of principle is committed to providing equal access to education.[34] For example, August Hermann Francke initiated processes that provided education across different social classes in Halle, empowering both men and women to get out of poverty. Pietists in colonial America likewise provided equal educational access to men and women at a time when the social structure was not just rigidly patriarchal but also racist. Today neoliberalism has solidified and rigidified inequality in access to education based on socioeconomic status and race. Many universities with Pietist heritage are struggling financially while receiving little financial support from their denominations.[35] Notwithstanding the good intentions of leaders in universities and colleges with Pietist heritage, there is little they can do about this kind of inequality, especially when it is considered part of the normal functioning of contemporary American society.[36] To complicate things further, most such universities and colleges arise from denominations populated by people who traditionally provide greater support for politicians more committed to the privatization of higher education or to making higher education reform market driven.[37]

Second, conversion and spiritual regeneration, leading to the transfor-

---

[33]Dalphy I. Fagerstrom, "Thoughts on the Pietist Heritage and the College," address to Bethel College Faculty, March 21, 1956, Carl H. Lundquist Papers, box 31, The History Center: Archives of the Baptist General Conference and Bethel University.

[34]Clifton-Soderstrom, *Angels, Worms, and Bogeys*, pp. 71-89.

[35]Chris Gehrz, "An Open Letter to American Churches: The Crisis of Christian Higher Education," *The Pietist Schoolman* (October 15, 2013), http://pietistschoolman.com/2013/10/15/an-open-letter -to-american-churches-the-crisis-of-christian-higher-education/.

[36]Milton Friedman, *Free to Choose: A Personal Statement* (New York: Mariner Books, 1990), pp. 128-49.

[37]William Martin, *With God on Our Side: The Rise of the Religious Right in America* (New York: Broadway Books, 1996), pp. 299-328.

mation of consciousness, is a key principle of the Pietist vision of higher education. Conversion transforms a person's consciousness, which in turn transforms the church, and the transformation of the church leads to societal transformation. The spheres of people's lives affected by such transformation include worldview, sense of self, perception of others, and capacity and willingness to contribute to building a community. When such transformation takes place, Pietists believe that people interpret their experiences in a new manner. In brief, a person's will, desire and emotions are reordered and reoriented for a new purpose.

A major implication that follows from the Pietist idea of conversion and its impact on the transformation of human consciousness in relation to Christian higher education is that there is a prioritization of personal encounter and relationship in the educational process in order to transform others. In this respect, Pietists would not be totally against the use of advanced technology as an aid for educational instruction, but they would be reluctant to promote the benefits of technological instruction over and above the transformation of human consciousness that comes from personal encounters and relationships. The question one needs to ask is whether the kinds and quality of relationships and personal encounters realized through modern technology (e.g., online education) are equal in effect with the types realized through the personal encounters and human relationships that are prototypically envisioned by Pietism. Lamentably, at the present moment, market reforms and corporate-style administration are increasingly diminishing this vision.

Finally, the Pietist approach to higher education emphasizes holistic understanding of the human person because it is committed to developing and transforming the whole person. This necessitates an understanding of people who must then be treated in a holistic way rather than piecemeal. The latter manner of perception results in a caricature of people that is then used to inform policy.

For Pietists, community is central to changing the individual, and so the conditions for nurturing faith are in the community, not the atomized individual alone wrestling with his or her faith.[38] Because the transformation of the whole person is instigated and inspired by God's love through the Christian

---

[38]Kurt W. Peterson and R. J. Snell, "'Faith Forms the Intellectual Task': The Pietist Option in Christian Higher Education," in *The Pietist Impulse in Christianity*, ed. Christian T. Collins Winn et al. (Eugene, OR: Pickwick, 2011), pp. 228-30.

community, the entire subjective consciousness of the person is transformed. When such transformation takes place, it leads to a commitment to all areas that represent the common good of a society.

In summary, to apply the insights from the holistic understanding of the human being in the Pietist tradition of Christian higher education will entail huge investments of time and resources because of the emphasis on personal relationships and encounters. However, such an investment is difficult to realize in a society that is increasingly sacralizing the value of privacy and individualism while also emphasizing cost-cutting measures as the most effective survival strategy in a ferociously competitive higher education market. Concerns and questions must be raised about the extent to which a narrow commitment to efficiency, necessitated by the imperatives of the contemporary marketplace and governed by neoliberalism, can undermine some of the ennobling ethos of Pietism when this commitment is applied to Christian higher education today.

CONCLUSION

Then I saw a new heaven and a new earth; for the first heaven and the
first earth had passed away, and the sea was no more. And I saw the
holy city, the new Jerusalem, coming down out of heaven from
God, prepared as a bride adorned for her husband.
And I heard a loud voice from the throne saying,

"See, the home of God is among mortals.
He will dwell with them;
they will be his peoples,
and God himself will be with them;
he will wipe every tear from their eyes.
Death will be no more;
mourning and crying and pain will be no more,
for the first things have passed away."
And the one who was seated on the throne said,
"See, I am making all things new."

REVELATION 21:1-5

"Their Mission Is Innovation"

The Pietist University in the Twenty-First Century

Christopher Gehrz

◆

C AN CHRISTIAN COLLEGES AND UNIVERSITIES in the twenty-first century find a "usable past" in seventeenth- and eighteenth-century Germany, nineteenth-century Sweden, and twentieth-century Minnesota? I hope that the preceding chapters have convinced our readers that there is something distinctive about an approach to Christian higher education rooted in the movement and ethos known as Pietism. But this far into the twenty-first century, they might well feel like we've been covering ground that has long since shifted beneath us.

How we teach and mentor students, prepare them for service to others, conduct research, navigate the challenges of life together and reach out to neighboring communities can scarcely escape the influence of economic, political, demographic and technological forces that seem to be restructuring higher education as we know it. Universities, claim Clayton Christensen and Henry Eyring, "are both at great risk of competitive disruption and potentially poised for an innovation-fueled renaissance." They warn that "to play its indispensable function in the new competitive environment, the typical university must change more quickly and more fundamentally than it has been doing."[1]

---

[1]Clayton M. Christensen and Henry J. Eyring, *The Innovative University: Changing the DNA of Higher Education from the Inside Out* (San Francisco: Jossey-Bass, 2011), pp. xxii-xxiii.

How to change? Christensen and Eyring urge colleges and universities to better understand the "DNA" of their own institutions as they seek to be innovative. Doing so, they argue, would help such institutions resist the temptation recklessly—and expensively—to emulate inappropriate models.[2] From that perspective, this is precisely the right moment to seek a "usable past." No one doubts that a small, tuition-dependent university like Bethel must sharpen its sense of distinctiveness in order to stand out in a too-crowded marketplace. But as Youngme Moon, one of Christensen's colleagues at Harvard Business School, has observed, organizations seeking differentiation tend to imitate their competitors, producing a "myth of competitive separation" (or "heterogeneous homogeneity") rather than offering something genuinely unique.[3] If we were to combine these insights, we would likely end up back at Richard Hughes's argument that Christian colleges have no choice but to draw on usable pasts. Instead of the panicked imitation of trendsetters or the awestruck emulation of secular elites, Christian colleges and universities must differentiate themselves by understanding the religious traditions that provide their DNA.

At the same time, Christensen and Eyring decry how, "in the spirit of honoring tradition, universities hang on to past practices to the point of imperiling their futures."[4] So how do we reconcile the usable past with a changeable future? How do we know when to change and when to stay the same? As a conclusion to this book and a prompt to continuing conversation, let me suggest how Pietism may help those who value Christian higher education to both embrace change and rethink innovation.

EMBRACING CHANGE (TO AN EXTENT)

First, if Pietism is as much *ethos* as *movement*, then we should not lock our image of Pietist higher education too rigidly within any particular frame. Bethel University today, after all, looks quite different from the eighteenth-century University of Halle (start with the fact that some 60 percent of Bethel's

---

[2] For example, they argue that too many schools try to "climb the Carnegie ladder" by emulating elite research universities such as Harvard; Christensen and Eyring, *Innovative University*, pp. 20-30.

[3] Youngme Moon, *Different: Escaping the Competitive Herd* (New York: Crown Business, 2010), p. 13. (Thanks to Jay Barnes for recommending this book.) Echoing Christensen and Eyring's argument about emulation, Moon particularly warns against mistaking bigger for better: "If the story of augmentation has a parable, it's that it's possible to improve yourself all the way to mediocrity"; ibid., pp. 113-14.

[4] Christensen and Eyring, *Innovative University*, p. xxii.

student population is female, versus zero percent for its early modern precursor), yet we might plausibly describe both as Pietist universities. John Alexis Edgren's tiny Swedish Baptist seminary in Chicago and the master's level university that descended from it are just as different but just as similar. In fact, given Pietism's innate suspicion of institutionalized forms of Christianity, Pietists would likely regard with suspicion any Christian college or university that has remained relatively static over any prolonged period of time.

But if avoiding innovation suggests that an institution would rather preserve than renew itself, carelessly embracing innovation can present the same problem. It's possible, for example, that the changes required for a school like Bethel to survive a restructuring of colleges and universities will prove inimical to what we've described as a Pietist vision of Christian higher education. I hasten to add that there are limits to which any Christian institution of higher learning ought to absorb the values of market-driven competition. Christian colleges and universities, unlike other institutions in a market economy, do not exist for their own sake but to further the mission of God in this world. Better we shut our doors, liquidate our assets and redistribute them to other outposts of the kingdom than survive at the cost of compromising our mission.[5]

At a number of levels, then, decision makers will need to discern carefully whether or not an innovation, whatever its economic benefits, serves the mission of their institution. Most of the choices will not be black and white. To adapt a favorite example of Christensen, Eyring and other "disruptive innovators": Could a Pietist university exist purely online, without any face-to-face instruction or residential experience? The Pietist tradition provides resources for those on both sides of that debate.

At its best, online education promises to make higher education more accessible to more of the population, by reducing costs that keep college out of the reach of lower-income students. That goal would warm the heart of August Hermann Francke, whose educational innovations in Halle were made available

---

[5]According to Virgil Olson's son, Dan, when his father was dean of Bethel College in the early 1970s, the institution faced the possibility of bankruptcy. "Doesn't that bother you?" he asked his father. Virgil replied, "Well sure it bothers me. I've worked hard and committed many years of my life to Bethel.... [But] you have to remember that Bethel isn't going to last forever. It's just a human organization. Someday it will end. But ultimately I don't work for Bethel. I do what I do because I want to contribute to God's Kingdom. Bethel is my way of doing that. Bethel may fail, but God's Kingdom is forever." Dan Olson, "Tribute to My Father," *The Baptist Pietist Clarion* (May 2011): 18.

to all socioeconomic classes.[6] The global potential of a model of education not bound to a particular place evokes the transnational reach of the Halle and Herrnhut Pietists who pioneered Protestant missions.[7] And advocates of online education might also appeal to Pietists' historic eagerness to take advantage of the changing media of their day.[8] In nineteenth-century Sweden, for example, pietistic evangelicals were simply called "readers" (*läsare*), connected as they were by common use of the Bibles, devotionals, tracts and newspapers churned out by increasingly efficient printing presses.

But if what takes place in a Pietist college is more transformation of persons than acquisition of information, can such change take place within a model trumpeting its ability to let students learn on their own terms, in their own time, in comfort and convenience? Evangelical Covenant educator Karl Olsson thought it necessary that at least some educational experiences would "end in a mood of fear and trembling; no student ever matures who has not felt the earth shaking beneath his feet." Profoundly uncomfortable and inconvenient, such world-changing transformation had to be mediated by a relationship between the student and a teacher who "will see his student as a person and will be a steady, firm, but gentle midwife of the soul."[9] Olsson's contemporary Carl Lundquist likewise concluded that "in the end the impact of one life upon another is probably greater than the impact of an idea or a method of teaching or a favorable physical setting."[10] Does online (or any "distance") education permit "the impact of one life upon another"? Can we form whole and holy persons apart from an embodied community that centers on the shared experience of an incarnate Christ?

---

[6]Douglas H. Shantz, *An Introduction to German Pietism: Protestant Renewal at the Dawn of Modern Europe* (Baltimore: Johns Hopkins University Press, 2013), pp. 117-34.

[7]A concise introduction to this topic can be found in Richard V. Pierard, "German Pietism as a Major Factor in the Beginnings of Modern Protestant Missions," in *The Pietist Impulse in Christianity*, ed. Christian T. Collins Winn et al. (Eugene, OR: Pickwick, 2011), pp. 285-95.

[8]Shantz notes the astonishing proliferation of Bible translations and commentaries printed by German Pietists: "Thanks largely to the work of the Pietists, the eighteenth century is rightly considered 'the century of the Bible.'" Shantz, *Introduction to German Pietism*, p. 205.

[9]Karl A. Olsson, "The Meaning of Comprehensive Education," address to the faculty of North Park College, Sept. 7, 1961, Karl A. Olsson Papers, series 6/1/2/1/32a, box 19, Covenant Archives, Chicago.

[10]Carl H. Lundquist, "1958-1959 Presidential Report," *1959 Annual—Baptist General Conference* (Chicago: BGC, 1959), p. 144. For an extended analysis of the similarities and differences between these two Swedish American Pietists, see Christopher Gehrz, "Recovering a Pietist Understanding of Christian Higher Education: Carl H. Lundquist and Karl A. Olsson," *Christian Scholar's Review* 40 (Winter 2011): 139-54.

Perhaps, but in evaluating online education or any other potentially "disruptive" innovation, Pietist educators ought to bear one principle in mind: Their mission does not depend on innovations; their mission *is* innovation.

RETHINKING INNOVATION: NEW PERSON, NEW CHURCH, NEW WORLD

The Oxford English Dictionary is helpful here: its first definition of *innovate* is "to change . . . into something new . . . to renew." If nothing else, German Pietism sought renewal, and the same desire for new life runs through the ethos we've observed in the history of Bethel and the Swedish revivals out of which it grew. In his biography of Philipp Jakob Spener, K. James Stein organizes that Pietist patriarch's theology around three themes: "The New Person," "The New Church" and "The New World."[11] We might adapt these three *News* to help us decide whether any particular innovation serves the larger innovation that is the mission of the Pietist college or university.[12]

First, does it help bring about *the new person*? In line with the classic Pietist emphasis on the new birth and the new life, we should ask whether an innovation helps produce a conversion and regeneration of the whole person, not only providing head knowledge but also changing the heart.

My own opinion is that this test should lead Pietist schools to resist fiercely one particular change: deemphasizing the liberal arts in favor of professional and STEM (science, technology, engineering and mathematics) training. There are many reasons to defend a model of education that is well rounded, integrative and—because it's not especially instrumental—easy to undervalue. But one is particularly relevant for pietistic Christians like Carl Lundquist who are suspicious of nominal, cultural or purely formal Christianity: the liberal arts are *liberating* arts, freeing us from "the chains of ignorance, provincialism, bigotry and narrowness" to choose to follow Christ, and to become our "unique and creative best for the glory of God."[13] Not just "the training of cooks and bakers, engineers and physicists, teachers and preachers," said Karl Olsson (not even "the zest and the joy of intellectual and aesthetic adventure" for their own sake), the Christian liberal arts college in the Pietist tradition "is primarily interested in pointing

---

[11]K. James Stein, *Philipp Jakob Spener: Pietist Patriarch* (Chicago: Covenant Press, 1986), pp. 183-255.

[12]I'll treat them separately, but Spener would surely remind us that none of the *News* is sufficient without the others, even if some innovations may conduce more to one than the others.

[13]Lundquist, "1979 Presidential Report," *1979 Annual—Baptist General Conference* (Evanston, IL: BGC, 1979), p. 96.

beyond itself and beyond all created things to the Source of life and truth, who by giving Himself to us sustains within us the hunger for salvation."[14]

Second, does the innovation help the college bring about *the new church*? Even as he lamented the "wretched conditions" prevailing in them, Spener still had hope for the renewal of German state churches after the Thirty Years' War. He offered several practical proposals meant to bring about "better times for the church," but the chief means by which Pietists sought ecclesial renewal was through the establishment of *ecclesiolae in ecclesia*—"little churches within the Church."[15] Just as conventicles in Frankfurt, Leipzig, Dresden and other early modern German cities sought to revive churches from which they were distinct but not separate, we might think of the Pietist college as an *ecclesiola*, more intimate and more specialized than the *ecclesia* to which it is connected but vital to the renewal of the larger body. During his tenure at Bethel, Lundquist emphasized that the church needed to support autonomous "renewal groups" that could act as "experimenting agenc[ies]" on behalf of the larger body of Christ.[16]

This has at least two implications for the Pietist university. First, professors and students must retain the freedom to ask questions and seek answers. Free Methodist theologian Howard Snyder hypothesizes that, as a Christian renewal movement, German Pietism owed much to "the atmosphere of intellectual inquiry and of greater personal and academic freedom in university settings."[17] Of course, readers who are Christian college trustees or donors, or pastors or members of sponsoring churches, may now fear that we've hit on another, more troubling meaning for "innovation." A generation before Pietists criticized "dead orthodoxy" in German state churches, heresy-hunting Puritans in England's parliament imprisoned William Laud, the archbishop of Canterbury, for "bringing Innovations into the Church."[18]

---

[14]Olsson, "The Meaning of Comprehensive Education" (1961).

[15]See Harry Yeide Jr., *Studies in Classical Pietism: The Flowering of the* Ecclesiola (New York: Peter Lang, 1997).

[16]But also that a college like Bethel needed to support its own "experimenting agencies." This line of thought comes from his 1976 sabbatical report, in which he suggested (to no effect, as it turned out) that Bethel build its own spiritual retreat center, with retreats built into college and seminary curricula; Carl H. Lundquist, "Enduring Values of the Renewal Movement," November 12, 1976, Bethel Seminary Library.

[17]Howard Albert Snyder, "Pietism, Moravianism, and Methodism as Renewal Movements: A Comparative and Thematic Study" (PhD diss., University of Notre Dame, 1983), p. 156.

[18]From an account of Laud's trial in John Browne, *A Discovery of the Notorious Proceedings of William Laud in Bringing Innovations into the Church, etc.* (London: Henry Walker, 1641).

All Christian colleges and universities struggle to balance their commitments to academic freedom and orthodox witness. Pietists, with their characteristic theological eclecticism and playfulness, might struggle more than most. But Carl Lundquist's answer to the problem exemplifies how the Pietist school may serve, faithfully and creatively, as an *ecclesiola* within the larger *ecclesia*. Writing on the importance of free inquiry for professors and students in his 1961 annual report to the Baptist General Conference, Lundquist concluded,

> Our hope at Bethel is to find the golden mean where there exists sturdy confidence in the spiritual and intellectual integrity of the school even when it raises disturbing questions, engages in rigid self evaluation, expresses dissatisfaction with the status quo and seeks less popular but more consistently Christian solutions to the problems that vex mankind.

For the sake of the *ecclesia*, the college-as-*ecclesiola* must have sufficient autonomy to question, evaluate and even agitate; the alternative, Lundquist wrote, was for the school to accept a "dull mediocrity" and fail to give leadership. There is hardly hope for "better times" for a renewed church if there's no one free to draw attention to the "wretched conditions" that exist.

But equally the college must remember that it serves the church. "If a school moves so far out ahead of its people so that no one follows," warned Lundquist, "it no longer is giving leadership." Striking this balance is difficult, and Lundquist, if forced to choose, preferred meeting "the expectations of the majority" to "pursuing an academic ideal to which our people hesitate to subscribe."[19] Perhaps he erred to one side of the golden mean, but in any case, Pietist scholars must take seriously their role in renewing the church. At the very least, they should join historian Tracy McKenzie in recovering a "dual calling" to academe and church, in part by resisting "the pervasive assumption that *the only scholarship that matters is the scholarship for other scholars.*"[20]

Finally, does the innovation help bring about *the new world*? Brethren historian Dale Brown complained that

> there is probably nothing in which historians have been more unfair to Pietism

---

[19]Carl H. Lundquist, "1960-1961 Presidential Report," *1961 Annual—Baptist General Conference* (Chicago: BGC, 1961), p. 137.

[20]See Robert Tracy McKenzie, "The Vocation of the Christian Historian: Re-envisioning Our Calling, Reconnecting with the Church," *Fides et Historia* 45 (Winter/Spring 2013): 1-13. The quotation (italics original) is on p. 8.

than in defining the mission of the church to society. A frequent stereotype of Pietistic Christianity portrays it as almost exclusively preoccupied with inward devotion and private moral scruples. On the contrary, the Pietist milieu resulted in a desire to transform the living conditions of the poor and oppressed, reform the prison system, abolish slavery, break down rigid class distinctions, establish a more democratic polity, initiate educational reforms, establish philanthropic institutions, increase missionary activity, obtain religious liberty, and propose programs for social justice.[21]

Earlier chapters have explored how Pietists think about mission, service and social transformation within the context of higher education. So here I'll limit myself to one general observation about how Pietist educators might understand their role in preparing people to be, in Roger Olson's phrase, "created cocreators of a new creation with God through the Holy Spirit."[22]

Rather than "Christ the transformer of culture" or other Niebuhrian categories, Dale Brown encouraged Pietists to follow the model of "Christ the servant of culture."[23] Elsewhere I've summarized this model as Brown suggesting that "Christ-centered devotion be accompanied by a Christ-like activism—in the world *to serve it*, not of the world, ruling it, or detached from it."[24] For Carl Lundquist, it meant that Bethel College was preparing "a task force for the evangelical penetration of society." He didn't mean that Bethel graduates should aspire to the power, status or wealth of elites but that they should seek "vocations which will involve significant human relationships in order that their influence for Christ may have maximum impact. Consequently, they go from Bethel into teaching, Christian ministries, medicine, social work, and business, in that order, and then into a great variety of other walks of life."[25] Moved by "a pained awareness" of illiteracy, hunger, illness and every other kind of human indignity and suffering, Lundquist wished Bethel graduates to enter professions out of a desire to serve others and proclaim the gospel of Jesus Christ.[26]

---

[21]Dale W. Brown, *Understanding Pietism*, rev. ed. (Nappanee, IN: Evangel, 1996), pp. 86-87.

[22]Quoted from p. 105 above.

[23]H. Richard Niebuhr, *Christ and Culture* (New York: Harper, 1951).

[24]Christopher Gehrz, "Missional Pietists: Lessons from Dale W. Brown and Carl H. Lundquist," *The Covenant Quarterly* 70 (August/November 2012): 41. Italics original.

[25]Carl H. Lundquist, "1967 Annual Report," *1967 Annual—Baptist General Conference* (Chicago: BGC, 1967), p. 109.

[26]Lundquist, "1968-69 Annual Report," *1969 Annual—Baptist General Conference* (Chicago: BGC, 1969), p. 123.

Modest as these individual vocations may seem, they contribute to the completion of an unimaginably grand mission. "See, I am making all things new" (Rev 21:5) heralds the most disruptive innovation in history, as God brings into being not just a new heaven but a new earth. For his good reasons, God chooses to accomplish that renewal of the world through renewed persons gathered together as a renewed church. May Pietist colleges and universities—finding new life in their usable pasts—continue to take up their share of that mission, in hope and with joy.

List of Contributors

Phyllis E. Alsdurf (PhD, University of Minnesota) is professor of English at Bethel University, where she directs the Johnson Center for Journalism and Communication.

Christian T. Collins Winn (PhD, Drew University) is professor of historical and systematic theology at Bethel University. He is author of *"Jesus Is Victor!": The Significance of the Blumhardts for the Theology of Karl Barth* and coeditor of *The Pietist Impulse in Christianity* (both Wipf & Stock).

Janel M. Curry (PhD, University of Minnesota) is provost of Gordon College. She served as both a dean and a geography professor at Calvin College prior to going to Gordon. A graduate of Bethel, she has more than forty publications and has been awarded two Fulbright Fellowships.

Dale G. Durie (DMin, Gordon-Conwell Theological Seminary) teaches missional ministry courses as part of the Biblical and Theological Studies Department at Bethel University. He is a licensed pastor and served various congregations prior to joining the Bethel faculty.

Christopher Gehrz (PhD, Yale University) is professor of history at Bethel University, where he also coordinates the Christianity and Western Culture program. Coeditor of *The Pietist Impulse in Christianity* (Wipf & Stock) and author of articles on Pietism and Christian higher education, he also blogs regularly at *The Pietist Schoolman* (pietistschoolman.com).

Kent T. K. Gerber (MLIS, Syracuse University) curates Bethel University's cultural and scholarly heritage as digital library manager of the Bethel University Libraries. His specialties and research interests include digital libraries, digital curation and scholarly communication.

Marion H. Larson (PhD, University of Minnesota) is professor of English at Bethel University, where she teaches courses in writing, literature and humanities. Her research and writing interests are interfaith engagement, faculty development and hospitality in the classroom.

Katherine J. Nevins (PhD, University of Minnesota) is professor of psychology at Bethel University. In her thirty-five years at Bethel she has served as faculty development coordinator, acting associate dean for faculty, department chair, and acting director of the Honors Program. Yet her first love has always been teaching and mentoring students.

Nancy L. Olen (EdD, University of St. Thomas) is professor of nursing emerita at Bethel University, and recently retired from serving as faith community nurse at Salem Covenant Church in New Brighton, Minnesota. She enjoys using nursing as a ministry to bless members of God's family in and outside the church.

Roger E. Olson (PhD, Rice University) is Foy Valentine Professor of Christian Theology and Ethics at Baylor University's Truett Seminary. He taught theology at Bethel for fifteen years and is the author of several acclaimed books, including *The Journey of Modern Theology* (IVP Academic).

Jenell Paris (PhD, American University) is professor of anthropology at Messiah College. Previously she taught at Bethel University, where she earned her under-graduate degree. Her most recent book is *The End of Sexual Identity* (Inter-Varsity Press).

Richard W. Peterson (PhD, Michigan State University) is University Professor of Physics Emeritus at Bethel University and a past president of the American Association of Physics Teachers.

Sara L. H. Shady (PhD, University of South Carolina) is associate professor of philosophy and Honors Program director at Bethel University, where she teaches courses in philosophy and Western civilization. Her academic work ranges in topic, including interfaith engagement and pedagogy, inclusion and democracy, gender studies and existentialism.

Raymond J. VanArragon (PhD, University of Notre Dame) is professor of philosophy at Bethel University. He is the coeditor of *Evidence and Religious Belief* (Oxford University Press).

Joel S. Ward (PhD, Duquesne University) is assistant professor of Communication Studies at Geneva College, having previously taught at Bethel University. His research focuses on the role of communication in the relationship between authority and personality.

David C. Williams (PhD, University of Utah) is professor of philosophy at Azusa Pacific University, specializing in ancient Greek thought. A graduate of Bethel and former professor there, he now lives just outside Yosemite National Park and is the chair of academics at Azusa's High Sierra Semester.

Samuel Zalanga (PhD, University of Minnesota) is professor of sociology at Bethel University, where he teaches courses on social responsibility, social theory and religion in society. He is the author of *Post-Colonial States and Economic Development: Ruling Coalitions and Economic Changes in Nigeria and Malaysia* (forthcoming, Carolina Academic Press).

NAME INDEX

Subject Index

Finding the Textbook You Need

The IVP Academic Textbook Selector
is an online tool for instantly finding the IVP books
suitable for over 250 courses across 24 disciplines.

ivpacademic.com